Understanding Disputes:
The Politics of Argument

Edited by Pat Caplan

EXPLORATIONS IN ANTHROPOLOGY
A University College London Series

Series Editors: Barbara Bender, John Gledhill and Bruce Kapferer

Joan Bestard-Camps, *What's in a Relative? Household and Family in Formentera*

Henk Driessen, *On the Spanish-Moroccan Frontier: A Study in Ritual, Power and Ethnicity*

Alfred Gell, *The Anthropology of Time: Cultural Construction of Temporal Maps and Images*

Tim Ingold, David Riches and James Woodburn (eds), *Hunters and Gatherers*
  Volume 1. *History, Evolution and Social Change*
  Volume 2. *Property, Power and Ideology*

Bruce Kapferer, *A Celebration of Demons* (2nd edn)

Guy Lanoue, *Brothers: The Politics of Violence among the Sekani of Northern British Columbia*

Jadran Mimica, *Intimations of Infinity: The Mythopoeia of the Iqwaye Counting System and Number*

Barry Morris, *Domesticating Resistance: The Dhan-Gadi Aborigines and the Australian State*

Thomas C. Patterson, *The Inca Empire: The Formation and Disintegration of a Pre-Capitalist State*

Max and Eleanor Rimoldi, *Hahalis and the Labour of Love: A Social Movement on Buka Island*

Pnina Werbner, *The Migration Process: Capital, Gifts and Offerings among Pakistanis in Britain*

Joel S. Kahn, *Constituting the Minangkabau: Peasants, Culture, and Modernity in Colonial Indonesia*

Gisli Polsson, *Beyond Boundaries: Understanding, Translation and Anthropological Discourse*

Stephen Nugent, *Amazonian Caboclo Society*

Barbara Bender, *Landscape: Politics and Perspectives*

Christopher Tilley (ed.), *Interactive Archaeology*

Ernest S. Burch, Jr. and Linda J. Ellanna, *Key Issues in Hunter-Gatherer Research*

Daniel Miller, *Modernity – An Ethnographic Approach: Dualism and Mass Consumption in Trinidad*

Robert Pool, *Dialogue and the Interpretation of Illness: Conversations in a Cameroon Village*

Cécile Barraud, Daniel de Coppet, André Itéanu and Raymond Jamous, *Of Relations and the Dead: Four Societies Viewed from the Angel of their Exchanges*

Christopher Tilley, *A Phenomenology of Landscape: Places, Paths and Monuments*

Victoria Goddard, Josep Llobera and Cris Shore, *The Anthropology of Europe: Identity of Europe: Identity and Boundaries in Conflict*

Understanding Disputes:
The Politics of Argument

Edited by
Pat Caplan

BERG
Oxford Providence, USA

First published in 1995 by
Berg Publishers
150 Cowley Road, Oxford, OX4 1JJ, UK
221 Waterman Street, Providence, RI 02906, USA

© Pat Caplan 1995

All rights reserved.
No part of this publication may be reproduced in any form or by any means without the written permission of Berg Publishers Limited.

Library of Congress Cataloging-in-Publication Data
A catalogue record for this book is available from the Library of Congress.

British Library Cataloguing in Publication Data
A catalogue record for this book is available from the British Library.

ISBN 0 85496 924 1 (Cloth)
      0 85496 925 X (Paper)

Printed in the United Kingdom by WBC Book Manufacturers, Bridgend, Mid-Glamorgan.

Contents

Preface: A Dedication to P. H. Gulliver Pat Caplan and Marilyn Silverman		vii
Acknowledgements		xvii
Note on Contributors		xix
1	Introduction: Anthropology and the Study of Disputes *Pat Caplan*	1
2	Imperfect Communications *Sally Falk Moore*	11
3	Civilization and its Negotiations *Laura Nader*	39
4	The Contentiousness of Disputes *Elizabeth Colson*	65
5	Gentlemanly Values: Contesting Corruption Accusations in the Cities of London and Lagos in the mid-1950s *Christina Johnson*	83
6	The 'Inhabitants' vs. the 'Sovereign': A Historical Ethnography of the Making of the 'Middle Class' in an Irish Corporate Borough, 1840–1 *Marilyn Silverman*	111
7	The Milieu of Disputation: Managing Quarrels in East Nepal *Lionel Caplan*	137
8	Disputing Human Passion: The Negotiation of the Meaning of Love among the Giriama of Kenya *David Parkin*	161
9	'Youth-Development': Conflict and Negotiations in an Urban Irish Youth Club *Stephen Gaetz*	181
10	'Law' and 'Custom': Marital Disputes on Northern Mafia Island, Tanzania *Pat Caplan*	203
11	Courts of Death among the Alur of Uganda *Aidan Southall*	223
Index		241

Phil Gulliver, 1994.

Preface

A Dedication to P. H. Gulliver

This collection of essays has been brought together in honour of Philip Gulliver, to whom the volume is dedicated. Gulliver studied at London University, gaining his doctorate at the LSE in 1952 while he was holding an assistant lectureship there. His earliest research (1948–51) was amongst Turkana nomads in Kenya and Jie agro-pastoralists in Uganda, resulting in his first major monograph, *The Family Herds* (1955a). This was also the beginning of a long period in his career that focused on East Africa.

Upon completion of his doctorate Gulliver was, for six years, Research Sociologist to the Government of Tanganyika. His first research in that period was among the Ngoni and Ndendeuli of southern Tanganyika, on labour migration, history and political change, economic development and law. However, his main scholarly work which emerged from this research (*Neighbours and Networks: the Idiom of Kinship in Social Action among the Ndendeuli*) was not published until 1971, largely because the then current models in anthropology were of little use in making sense of a society without corporate groups. In the 1960s, whilst re-examining the data he had collected a decade earlier, Gulliver had to discover some new ways of conceptualizing and describing social relations in action. This he did by using network analysis and the concept of action-set.

The next period of fieldwork (1954–5) was spent among the Nyakyusa, and focused on labour migration and problems of land scarcity and social change. It resulted in *Land Tenure and Social Change among the Nyakyusa* (1958). This was followed by a spell amongst migrant and settled plantation workers in north-eastern Tanganyika, after which Gulliver worked amongst the Arusha from 1956–8, a period of fieldwork which led to one of his most important books, *Social Control in an African Society* (1963).

At the end of his contract with the Government of Tanganyika in 1958, Gulliver spent several years in the United States, teaching first at Harvard and then at Boston Universities. In 1962, he returned to Britain and joined the fledgling anthropology department at the School of Oriental and African Studies, University of London. He remained there as Lecturer, then Reader (1965) and Professor (1967) until 1971, apart from a brief visit to teach again in North America at the Universities of Minnesota and Washington.

During his time at SOAS, Philip Gulliver was able to re-visit some of his research areas in East Africa. He also published a good deal, including (apart from numerous articles) *Social Control in an African Society* (1963), *The Family Estate in Africa* (with Robert Gray) (1964), *Tradition and Transition in East Africa* (1969) and *Neighbours and Networks* (1971). This was also a productive period in terms of supervision of a number of postgraduates who went on to become academic anthropologists: Janet Fitton Bujra, Caroline Ifeka-Moller, David Parkin, Lionel Caplan, Pat Bailey Caplan, Walter Johnson, Jan de Wolf and many others. Several of his students from that period are represented in this volume, along with a number of his colleagues.

A major theme which runs through much of Gulliver's writing from his 'African' period concerns social control, dispute-management and the anthropology of law. As well as two monographs which he published around those themes (1963, 1971), he also wrote some important chapters and articles (1961, 1969, 1973). He published too on labour migration, kinship, age-set systems and other topics, but his interest increasingly centred on dispute-management and negotiations. In looking at Gulliver's work in terms mainly of his contributions to legal anthropology, we can see that he has always been concerned with ethnographic understandings – with 'concrete manifestations' (1971: 13). He has seen these as propelling conceptual and theoretical advance because, in his view, the final purpose of ethnography is to arrive at generalizations: 'Monographic single-mindedness (concern for the particular) has undoubtedly advanced anthropological studies. ... [However] there might well have been greater progress ... had anthropologists been more ready to voice, and their colleagues more prepared sympathetically to attend to, attempts at generalised observations' (Gulliver 1965b: 103).

This concern to tie the particular to the general as a central purpose for anthropology has been rooted in a second theme which has typified Gulliver's work: his belief in the indissoluble link between field research and theory, ethnography and anthropology: 'The firmly rooted tradition of personal field research and of theoretical development in the context of monographic accounts of social systems and cultures must surely be maintained as the foundation of anthropological studies' (Gulliver 1965b: 103).

In pursuing this ideal, a third general theme can be discovered in Gulliver's work, namely his involvement with the key conceptual and empirical dualities which have long informed the discipline and its practitioners: social relations and material interests, change and history, small-scale and wider context. In his earliest book, Gulliver saw the first duality as central to his general approach (1955a). In that same year and from a different ethnographic context, he also put forward a plea for historical understandings: 'Concerning the Ngoni ... a knowledge of their history is, I believe, essential to an understanding of the people and their social system because ... today, they remain closely connected with that early evolution' (Gulliver 1955b: 17). Nevertheless, a decade later, when he reviewed the state of African ethnography, Gulliver still found it necessary to criticize a still-dominant synchronic approach and to reiterate the importance of history and change:

> It is clear that anthropological research, theory and methods can (and must) expand to embrace the factor of change. Its exclusion as a convenient working device is now quite outmoded. Concomitant with this requirement is the need for anthropologists to take steps to build up as full a historical record as possible of the evolution of African societies and cultures (Gulliver 1965b: 102).

Complementing his concern with social relations and materiality, history and change has been his clear focus on the micro-level: 'Anthropologists' specialisation in dealing with micro-structures and sub-systems and with the details of interpersonal small-group relationships can continue to produce information and lead to understanding in a way no other discipline can, (Gulliver 1965b: 101). However, for Gulliver, the micro-focus of anthropology had to be connected to, and located within, broader contexts. In commenting on the historico-ethnographic research methods which he more recently used in fieldwork in an Irish town and its hinterland, he noted: 'In any case, in whatever way a sociogeographical unit ... is defined, social relations and social interaction have significantly and constantly extended well beyond any boundaries which could be delineated' (Gulliver 1989: 334).

In the early 1970s, Gulliver decided that it was time to move on and to return to North America. In 1971 he became Professor of Anthropology at the University of Calgary, Alberta, subsequently moving to York University, Ontario. Although continuing his primary interest in dispute-management, he shifted to the collection of comparative materials on the processes of industrial negotiations in Western societies. This led to one of his best-known works, *Disputes and Negotiations: a Cross-Cultural Perspective* (1979). In the same period, he edited a symposium, *Cross-Examinations* (1978), in honour of Max Gluckman, whose work on the anthropology of law he much admired.

Following this, Gulliver decided that he wanted to undertake further field research and to pursue his research interests in a Western society and to develop the kind of historical perspective that had been difficult in some of the East African societies he had previously studied, which lacked any depth of written records. Accordingly, and in co-operation with York University anthropologist Marilyn Silverman, he began to carry out ethnographic and archival research in the Republic of Ireland, focusing on a small town and its hinterland in County Kilkenny. Together they have engaged in field and archival research in Ireland totalling 24 months to date, and have accumulated something like 40,000 pages of materials. In addition to a number of articles, Gulliver and Silverman have published a social history of their locale (*In the Valley of the Nore: a Social History of Thomastown, County Kilkenny, 1840–1983* [1986]), edited a collection of essays in historical anthropology utilizing Irish case studies (*Approaching the Past* [1992]), and completed another book entitled *Merchants and Shopkeepers: An Historical Anthropology of an Irish Market Town 1200–1986* (in press).

Philip Gulliver retired officially in 1992, although he continues to do some teaching. He is Distinguished Research Professor Emeritus at York University, and continues to carry out research and to publish.

Overall, then, Gulliver's work has displayed his firm commitment to the ethnographic analysis of material relations and social change in small-scale locales contextualized in wider arenas and, increasingly, in historical understandings underpinned by theory. Nested in these broad themes, however, has been a lifelong commitment to the practical doing of anthropology and to the notion that each new piece of research makes a further contribution to the discipline.

Preface: A Dedication to P. H. Gulliver

[T]here is great value in trying out methods and concepts, asking new kinds of questions and pushing some old questions a little further, examining new problems, and testing hypotheses, in relation to particular and limited ethnographic data. It is also useful to contribute new ethnographic data, for the plaint that we already have more raw data than we can use is palpably false (Gulliver 1971: 1).

It is in the spirit of this viewpoint that we dedicate this volume to him.

Pat Caplan and Marilyn Silverman

Philip Gulliver: Selected Bibliography

Books, Monographs

Merchants and Shopkeepers: An Historical Anthropology of an Irish Market Town, 1200–1983 [with M. Silverman]. Submitted for publication

1992 *Approaching the Past: Historical Anthropology through Irish Case Studies* [with M. Silverman]. New York: Columbia Univ. Press

1986 *In the Valley of the Nore: A Social History of Thomastown Co. Kilkenny 1840–1983*. Dublin: Geography Publications [with Marilyn Silverman]

1979 *Disputes and Negotiations: A Cross-cultural Perspective*. New York: Academic Press

1978 *Cross-examinations: Essays in Memory of Max Gluckman* [ed., with Introduction], Leiden: E. J. Brill

1971 *Neighbours and Networks: The Idiom of Kinship among the Ndendeuli*. Berkeley and London: Univ. of California Press

1969 *Tradition and Transition in East Africa: Studies in the Tribal Factor in the Modern Era*. London: Routledge and Kegan Paul; Berkeley: Univ. of California Press

1964 *The Family Estate in Africa* [ed. with R. F. Gray], London: Routledge & Kegan Paul; Boston: Boston Univ. Press

1963 *Social Control in an African Society*. London: Routledge and Kegan Paul; Boston: Boston Univ. Press
1972. Second impression

1958 *Land Tenure and Social Change among the Nyakyusa*. Kampala: East African Institute of Social Research [E. A. Studies, No.11]

1955 *Labour Migration in a Rural Economy*. Kampala: East African Institute of Social Research (E.A. Studies, No.6) (1955c)

1955 *The Family Herds: A Study of Two Pastoral Tribes in East Africa*. London: Routledge and Kegan Paul (1955a)
    1966   Second impression with new Introduction and bibliography
    1973   Third impression
    1974   New edition. New York: Greenwood Press

1953 *The Central Nilo-Hamites* (with Pamela Gulliver), London: International African Institute (Ethnographic Survey of Africa)

1951 *A Preliminary Survey of the Turkana*, Comm., School of African Studies, No.26, University of Cape Town. 1965 Reprint

Chapters and Articles

1992 'Historical Anthropology and the Ethnographic Tradition: A Personal, Historical and Intellectual Account' (with M. Silverman), *in* Marilyn Silverman and P. H. Gulliver (eds), *Approaching the Past: Historical Anthropology through Irish Case Studies*. New York: Columbia University Press

1992 'Shopkeepers and Farmers in South Kilkenny, 1840–1981', *in* Marilyn Silverman and P. H. Gulliver (eds), *Approaching the Past: Historical Anthropology through Irish Case Studies*. New York: Columbia University Press

1990 'Social Life and Local Meaning: 'Thomastown', County Kilkenny' (with M. Silverman), *in* W. Nolan and K. Whelan (eds), *County Kilkenny: History and Society*. Dublin: Geography Publications

1989 'Doing Anthropology in Rural Ireland', *in* C. Curtin and T. Wilson (eds), *Ireland from Below*. Galway: Galway University Press

1986 'Arbitration and Mediation', in *The Social Science Encyclopedia*. London: Routledge

1986 'An Applied Anthropologist in East Africa', *in* R. Grillo (ed.), *Social Anthropology and Development Policy*. London: Academic Press

1978 'Networks and Factions', *in* M. Silverman and R. Salisbury (eds), *A House Divided? Anthropological Studies of Factionalism*. St John's: Memorial University (Institute of Social and Economic Research), pp. 37–65

1978 'Process and Decision', *in* P. Gulliver (ed.), *Cross-examinations: Essays in Memory of Max Gluckman*. Leiden: E. J. Brill, pp. 27–52

1977 'On Mediators', *in* T. Hamnett (ed.), *Law and Social Anthropology* (A.S.A.14). London: Academic Press, pp. 15–52

1975 'An Arusha Land Dispute', in M. Karp (ed.), *African Perspectives*. Boston: African Studies Program, Boston Univ.

1975	'Nomadic Movement, Causes and Consequences', *in* T. Monod (ed.), *African Pastoralism*. London: Oxford Univ. Press, pp. 369–86
1972	'The Turkana Of Northwest Kenya', *in* A. Molnos (ed.), *Cultural Source Materials for Population Planning in East Africa*. Nairobi: East African Publishing House
1970	'Peoples of East Africa', *in* W. T. W. Morgan, *Natural Resources of East Africa*. London: Oxford Univ. Press
1969	'The Commitment to Tradition: the Arusha and the Masai', *in* P. Gulliver (ed.), *Tradition and Transition in East Africa*. London: Routledge & Kegan Paul; Berkeley: Univ. of California Press, pp. 223–42
1969	'Introduction: Case Studies in Non-Western Societies', *in* L. Nader, *Law in Culture and Society*. Chicago: Aldine Press, pp. 11–23
1969	'Dispute Settlement without Courts', ibid., pp. 24–63
1969	'Preface' to S. Charsley, *Princes of Nyakyusa*. Nairobi: East African Publishing House
1969	'Nomadism, its Social and Natural Environment', *in* P. Rigby (ed.), *Society and Social Change*. Kampala: East African Institute of Social Research (Nkanga 4), pp. 30–41
1968	'The Turkana: The Jie', *in* Y. Cohen (ed.), *Man in Adaptation*. Chicago: Aldine Press, pp. 323–61
1967	'Age Differentiation', *International Encyclopedia of the Social Sciences*.
1965	'Anthropology', *in* R. Lystad (ed.), *The African World: A Survey of Social Research*. New York: Praeger, pp. 57–106
1965	'The Jie of Uganda', *in* J. Gibbs (ed.), *Peoples of Africa*. New York: Holt, Rinehart & Winston, pp. 157–96
1964	'The Arusha Family', *in* P. Gulliver and R. F. Gray (eds), *The Family Estate in Africa*. London: Routledge & Kegan Paul, pp. 197–229
1963	'The Evolution of Arusha Trade', *in* P. Bohannan and G. Dalton (eds), *Markets in Africa*. Evanston, I11.: Northwestern Univ. Press, pp. 431–56 1965. Reprint in paperback edition of selections from that book.

Articles in Journals

1993	'Hucksters and Petty Retailers in Thomastown, 1880–1945', *Old Kilkenny Review* 4, No. 8, 1094–1100
1988	'Anthropological Contributions to the Study of Negotiations', *Negotiation Journal* 4, 247–66
1985	'Anthropology in Ireland', *Focus* (Summer)
1984	'Fieldwork', *R.A.I.N.*, No. 62
1980	Review Article: 'The Economics of Pastoralism', *International J. of African History* 12, 753–6
1975	'Political History of the Songea Ngoni Chiefdom', *Bulletin of the School of Oriental and African Studies* 37, 82–97
1974	'Negotiations and Mediation', Berkeley: Univ. of California Law and Society Program
1973	'Dispute Settlement by Negotiations: Towards a General Model', *Law and Society Review* 7, 667–91
1966	'The Development of Labour Migration in Africa', *Kroniek van Afrika* 6.
1964	'Political Parties and Tribes in Kenya', *Race Relations Bulletin*.
1963	'Kenya: Independence and the Tribes', *New Society*
1961	'Land Shortages, Social Change and Social Conflict', *Journal of Conflict Resolution* 5, 16–26
1961	'Structural Dichotomy and Jural Processes among the Arusha', *Africa* 31, 19–35
1960	'The Population of the Arusha Chiefdom: A High Density Area in East Africa', *Rhodes-Livingstone Journal* 28, 1–21
1960	'Incentives in Labour Migration', *Human Organization* 19, 150–64 (reprinted in P. Van Den Berghe, *Social Problems of Change and Conflict in Africa*, 1965)
1959	'A Tribal Map of Tanganyika', *Tanganyika Notes and Records* 52 & 54, 61–74
1958	'The Turkana Age Organisation', *American Anthropologist* 60, 900–22
1957	'Nyakyusa Labour Migration', *Rhodes-Livingstone Journal*
1957	'A History of the Relations between the Arusha and the Masai', *Conference Papers of the East African Institute of Social Research*.
1955	'A History of the Songea Ngoni', *Tanganyika Notes and Records* 49, 16–30 (1955b)

1954	'The Population of Karamoja', *Uganda Journal* 17, 179–85
1954	'Jie Agriculture', *Uganda Journal* 18, 65–70
1953	'The Age Organisation of the Jie', *Journal of the Royal Anthropological Institute* 83, 147–68
1953	'Jie Marriage', *African Affairs* 52 (*reprinted in* S. Ottenberg (ed.), *Cultures and Societies of Africa*, 1961)
1952	'The Karamajong Cluster', *Africa* 22, 1–22
1952	'Bell-oxen and Ox-names among the Jie', *Uganda Journal* 16
1952	'Nomad Anthropologist', *Corona* 129–32
1951	'The Name Lango as a term for the Nilo-Hamites', *Uganda Journal* 16

Acknowledgements

The editor acknowledges gratefully the co-operation of the authors of the chapters in this volume, who submitted with grace to editing suggestions. Marilyn Silverman suggested the theme for the volume and gave other advice. Jenny Gault, Marilyn Stead and Karen Catling helped in communicating with contributors and other ways. Staff at the Computer Centre, Goldsmiths College, managed to convert to a single format whatever disc was put in front of them. Predrag Zivkovic and Susan Greenwood dealt with the subsequent re-formatting, as well as entering corrections. My thanks to them all, and most particularly to Lionel Caplan, who in addition to giving much-needed encouragement throughout this project, also took on the onerous task of seeing the book through its final stages while I was away in Tanzania.

Notes on Contributors

Lionel Caplan was born in Montreal, Canada where he attended McGill University. He later studied anthropology at the University of London and was appointed to a Lectureship in 1965, a Readership in 1975, and in 1987 to the title of Professor of South Asian Anthropology at the School of Oriental and African Studies. He has maintained an ongoing research interest in Nepal since he first did fieldwork in the country in 1964–65.

Elizabeth Colson, Professor Emeritus, University of California, Berkeley has carried out research among native Americans of California, Washington and Arizona; in Darwin, Australia; and over many years, from 1946 to present, in the southern province of Zambia among Plateau and Gwembe Tonga. She is sole or joint author of 12 books arising from this research.

Steve Gaetz conducted research on the provision of youth services in Cork, Ireland, in 1987–88. He has written numerous articles on the subject and has a book forthcoming. He was a graduate student of Philip Gulliver from 1984–90. His present research focuses on the provision of health services to street youth. He is currently working as Health Promoter at Shout Clinic, a street youth serving agency in Toronto, Canada.

Christina Johnson is an independent researcher and anthropologist. Awarded a William Hayter Scholarship she carried out her PhD fieldwork in eastern Nigeria under the benign supervision of Philip Gulliver, then at the School of Oriental and African Studies, London. In the last twenty years Christina Johnson has worked in several regions of the world, more often than not investigating issues of power and conflict over scarce resources. She is currently directing a long-term research project, funded in part by the ODA (UK), on changing land tenure systems and dispute resolving strategies in communities abutting national parks in Nigeria's wet and dry forests.

Sally Falk Moore is Professor of Anthropology at Harvard University, where she served as Dean of the Graduate School from 1985 to 1989. She also regularly teaches 'Anthropological Approaches to law' at Harvard law School. She is a fellow of the American Academy of Arts and Sciences and is a past president of the American Ethnological Society and the Society for Political and Legal Anthropology.

Laura Nader is Professor of Anthropology at the University of California at Berkeley where she has taught since 1960. Her current work enlarges on her Mexico fieldwork by examining Controlling Processes in the context of law, science and business.

David Parkin is Professor of African Anthropology at the School of Oriental and African Studies, London and a Fellow of the British Academy. He has carried out fieldwork in Kenya, Uganda and Zanzibar among such peoples as the Giriama, Digo, Luo and certain Swahili-speakers on topics covering religion, including Islam. indigenous uses of space and environment, local medicines, cross-cultural semantics and informal politics.

Marilyn Silverman received a PhD from McGill University in 1973. An Associate Professor of Anthropology at York University, Toronto, she has done field research in Guyana, Ecuador and Ireland. Her foci are political anthropology and political economy, agrarian systems and historical anthropology.

Aidan Southall is Emeritus Professor of Anthropology, University of Wisconsin-Madison: Sometime Dean of the Faculty of Social Sciences, Makere University, Uganda, Professor of Social Anthropology and Sociology, Chair of the East African Institute of Social Research. Field research: Kenya Luo 1946, 1947; Alur three years between 1947 and 1992; Kisenyi, Kampala 1952–54; Padhola 1955; status of women in Northern Nigeria 1960; Madagascar (Ambositra, Paliarivo) 1966–7, 1973.

Chapter 1

Introduction: Anthropology and the Study of Disputes

Pat Caplan

In the latter half of this century, the study of dispute settlement has been relegated to a sub-discipline known as the anthropology of law, an area which has all too often tended to be marginalized (Gulliver 1978: xvi; Snyder 1992 [1981]: 3). This is somewhat strange, given that the study of disputes leads us straight to key issues in anthropology – norms and ideology, power, rhetoric and oratory, personhood and agency, morality, meaning and interpretation – and enables us not only to see social relations in action but also to understand cultural systems. The study of disputes also raises questions about the role of anthropologists, and some work in this area has involved advocacy anthropology, a highly participant form of observation (cf. Bell 1984–5).

This volume has been written in honour of one of the most significant contributors to the study of disputes, P. H. Gulliver (see Preface). The ten contributors are all either former students or colleagues of Gulliver. Some, such as Nader, Moore and Colson, are among the discipline's foremost experts and have published widely in this area. Yet whether they classify themselves as anthropologists of dispute processes or not, virtually every contributor, like anthropologists elsewhere, will at some stage have made use of information on disputes collected during the course of fieldwork. In their articles here they seek to bring the study of disputes back into the centre of anthropology, a move which has also been seen as necessary by a number of recent commentators. Comaroff and Roberts (1981), for example, argue that 'instead of isolating dispute processes or rule systems for separate study, anthropologists should study disputes and invocations of rules for what they reveal about systemic processes' (p. 2) and conclude that 'the dispute process may provide an essential key to the disclosure of the socio-cultural order at large' (p. 249). More recently, in their introduction to an edited collection, Starr and Collier suggest that the volume is about 'conceptualizing the anthropology ... of law not as a discipline "apart from" social anthropology, but as a theory-building "part of" social anthropology' (1989: 5). To this end, they argue that legal orders have to be treated as 'codes, discourses and languages in which people pursue their varying and often antagonistic interests' (ibid.: 9).

So what are disputes about? On one level, they are about material goods – rights to land and other forms of property, for example. In this volume, Lionel Caplan writes of land disputes in Eastern Nepal between indigenous Limbus and more recent arrivals, high-caste Hindus who have deprived them of many of their land rights. Laura Nader utilizes a broader canvas, considering international river disputes and the effect that recourse to different forums – courts or negotiating teams – may have upon the outcome.

Disputes are also about the right to make decisions. Thus Steve Gaetz's article concerns on-going disputes at an Irish youth club between the youth workers and the young members about how the club should be run. Marilyn Silverman, also writing about Ireland but from a historical viewpoint, describes a series of struggles which took place in a small town there in the nineteenth century about who should control the town's corporation.

Disputes are, of course, about social relations. In this volume, a number of contributors consider quarrels between men and women, particularly marital partners. David Parkin's article begins with the dramatic story of a suicide committed by a woman as a result of accusations of adultery. Lionel Caplan considers the way in which problems caused by the break-up of young marriages by Limbus are not only tolerated but also sorted out by elders – a significant contrast to the way marital relations are conducted by their high-caste neighbours. Pat Caplan's article discusses a number of marital disputes, some of which are resolved and appear to end in reconciliation, while others lead to divorce, and even continue to be prosecuted after divorce in quarrels over shares of property. In considering these happenings, we learn a great deal about gender relations in each society.

Disputes can, of course, be interpreted on many levels. The ostensible reason for quarrelling may be land or sexual jealousy, but, as Parkin points out in his article, deeper reasons may be the need to work out what he terms 'existential predicaments'. He asks what is the meaning of love in a particular society? And does its meaning differ depending on, for example, age or sex? Southall too shows that the disputes that are aired in the Second Funerals among the Alur of Uganda are essentially about understanding death and the reasons why it strikes, as well as being about concepts of morality and ethics.

As Gulliver so ably demonstrated in his work, disputes are ways of grouping people together, even if only momentarily, even as they are also an obvious mechanism for keeping people apart. Silverman's article shows how a dispute in an Irish town in the middle of the nineteenth century brought together a fairly disparate collection of people who in the process effectively turned themselves into a middle class.

But other articles in this volume consider the way in which disputes may highlight important differences between the parties. Gaetz's article shows how problematic it may be for people of different class backgrounds to work together. Youth workers and youth club members have very different views of the way to go about things, and thus the running of the youth club is punctuated by an on-going series of struggles between them. Johnson's analysis of a Tribunal set up by the British in still-colonial Nigeria in the 1950s shows that it was used as a way of pointing out that senior Nigerian politicians had not fully absorbed the 'gentlemanly values' of their masters, thereby implying that they were not yet ready for self-government. Lionel Caplan's study of two kinds of dispute in Eastern Nepal – land struggles and marital quarrels – highlights the differences in culture and therefore ways of coping with them between the indigenous Limbus and the high-caste Hindus.

How Do People Pursue Disputes?

Until recently, there was a good deal of emphasis in the study of disputes on mechanisms for their resolution. The work of Schapera (1938) and Gluckman (1955, 1965) on courts, for example, focused on social organization and bureaucratic procedures, with the work of judges being highlighted. Other work, notably by Gulliver, Colson, Turner, Bailey and Nader, shifted the emphasis to social processes, and looked at the parties in the dispute. Gulliver's distinction between negotiation and adjudication (1979) has been widely utilized, and indeed, is referred to by most of the contributors to this volume. His work on dispute settlement without courts among the Ndendeuli of Tanzania (Gulliver 1971) is viewed as seminal. But people do not only have recourse to forums of various kinds – courts, moots, etc. – they utilize other means to prosecute their quarrels, as a number of contributors suggest here. These may include violence (Parkin, Moore and P. Caplan), self-help (Gaetz), ridicule (P. Caplan), public humiliation (Johnson), and witchcraft (Southall).

Yet the truth is, as Gulliver has admitted (ibid.), that disputes are often not resolved at all. In this volume, Elizabeth Colson criticizes much anthropological work on dispute settlement for its expectation that disputes are resolved and lead to harmony. She cites Nader's assertion that this premise is a Western construct derived from Christianity, for example Turner's notion of *communitas* (1969), and that there has been too little consideration by anthropologists of law as being about justice – a point which Nader also takes up in this volume. Colson notes from her own fieldwork among the Gwembe Tonga in Zambia that when people appeal to the law they appeal for remedies for ills, not recipes for harmony. She concludes that 'Negotiation and adjudication can settle particular claims because moots and courts have means to persuade contenders to accept a verdict ... They have much less success in convincing contenders that they are in the wrong, and they do little or nothing to heal ruptured social relationships or abate anger and contempt' (pp. 79–80).

Indeed, as Moore states in her commentary on the work of Gulliver and Habermas, few anthropologists have dealt with disputes in terms of the feelings they arouse. Parkin's essay is an attempt to look at this issue, recognizing that passion, jealousy, despair and other powerful emotions can lead to violence and death. Indeed, recognition of the role played by emotions renders it unlikely that we should expect disputes always to be settled and resolved.

How Do We Understand Disputes?

The strength of much anthropological work on disputes has been at the micro-level; indeed, as Colson points out here, classic

Introduction: Anthropology and the Study of Disputes

anthropological studies have been in small-scale societies with multiplex relations. Furthermore, most of them have taken place in non-Western societies, particularly in Africa. Some are critical of the tendency of many anthropologists to ignore wider processes – the impact of the state, including the colonial state, for example. This issue is addressed in this volume with two studies which move beyond the micro-level. Nader's work on river disputes involves consideration of power relations between nations, such as Bangladesh and India on the Ganges, France and Spain on Lake Lanoux, Israel and Jordan on the Jordan river and, particularly, the states through which the Danube river runs. Here Nader is following her own dictum of the need for anthropologists to 'study up' as she considers the culture of international negotiators, and the way in which powerful nations are able to use the 'alternative dispute resolution' (ADR) movement on an international scale as a hegemonic tool.

Nader's work here, unlike that of most anthropologists, does consider the role of law and processes of disputing in the West, noting particularly the way in which the US ADR movement borrowed heavily from anthropological ideas concerning mediation and negotiation in order to stem the popular movements for 'rights'. Johnson's article also considers a Western case – that of the 1956 Bank Rate Tribunal in London. She notes that the British in the 1950s, faced with allegations of corruption, appeared less likely to use the courts than quasi-judicial tribunals. The other Tribunal which she considers, the Foster-Sutton Tribunal set up to investigate corruption in pre-independence Nigeria, bore striking parallels to that on the Bank Rate, both in its procedures and in the allegations that it was set up to investigate. The difference lay in the accused – in the former case, British aristocrats highly placed in the City and government, in the latter, Nigerian politicians. Both appear to have utilized networks of kinship, affinity and patronage in their dealings, but the tribunals came to very different conclusions regarding the probity of the accused. Johnson shows that understanding of the tribunals comes not only from close reading of the texts of their proceedings, but also from placing them in their historical and politico-economic contexts. Gaetz's article, too, benefits from analysing the struggles between the youth club workers and members against a wider background of state policies in relation to unemployed youth in Ireland, as well as of differing class cultures.

In this regard, then, such work fits in very well with the admonitions of a number of recent anthropologists writing on law and disputes, including Gulliver, that it is essential to contextualize them as widely as possible, including historically. Starr and Collier's introduction to their 1989 volume concludes by suggesting that an integrative framework for bringing legal anthropology and the study of disputes into the mainstream of the discipline is world history. A number of articles in this book take a similar line. Lionel Caplan shows how land disputes between the Limbus and high-caste Hindus in Eastern Nepal can only be understood against a background of political transformations and struggles over a period of several centuries. Elizabeth Colson's work on the Plateau Tonga has now extended over more than forty years, and she is thus in a position to note both changes and continuities in the dispute process. Her article in this volume reveals that the incidence and seriousness of disputes has increased with growing economic pressures. The matters which people quarrel about are very similar, but the procedures have changed from a dependence upon kin-based moots to the use of courts, i.e. from negotiation to arbitration. Aidan Southall too has been working for a similar period among the Alur of Uganda. In his case study of a funeral which took place in 1972, he notes that the events alluded to took place over a period of more than forty years prior to the death of the people concerned. Marilyn Silverman utilizes archival material to reconstruct the course of a series of disputes in the nineteenth century which give important insights into the formation of a class.

But there is another way of understanding disputes than contextualizing them historically, and that is in terms of interpretation. This may appear to be considering a more recent set of debates in anthropology, but in fact it does go back a long way in the anthropology of law, to the so-called Bohannan–Gluckman debate of the 1960s. Paul Bohannan (1969) took issue with Gluckman's utilization of Western legal concepts to analyse African law and dispute settlement. He even argued that it was preferable to utilize local terms, rather than try to find English equivalents. Such a view resonates with that of Starr and Collier, that the 'command mode' of law (one imposed from above) makes it difficult to analyse the way in which subordinated people invoke wider legal orders to achieve their ends. They suggest that it is preferable to treat legal orders as codes, discourses and languages in which people pursue their varying and often antagonistic interests (1989: 9). Here then, law is viewed as a contested metaphor which only exists as it is invoked by human agency.

Several articles in this collection consider issues of interpretation and contestation of meaning. Parkin discusses concepts of love among the Giriama of Kenya, comparing them with Western views. In the latter case, he notes a distinction, indeed often a tension, between passion and compassion, and a debate about whether the two kinds of love can be fused or must always be antagonistic. Parkin draws parallels with Giriama views of love, noting that elders preach the fusion of the two, while women and young men recognize an inherent tension.

Johnson's article looks at the concept of 'the honest man' and the necessity of drawing a distinction between the public and private spheres: under a powerfully hegemonic ideology of 'gentlemanly values', men engaged on state duties must subordinate their private pecuniary interests to the greater national good, and not use their public position to private advantage. To be accused of failing to maintain such a distinction is tantamount to being called corrupt. Her article examines two tribunals in the mid-1950s. One was set up to investigate allegations that Dr Azikiwe, premier of the Eastern Region of Nigeria, had used public funds to prop up his ailing private bank. The other was to find out whether senior men in City of London firms had used their privileged position as directors of the Bank of England to leak to their companies the information that the bank rate was about to be raised to unprecedented heights. Johnson's interpretation of the Tribunals' Proceedings is that, on one level, they are about notions of truth and honesty. Yet when put into a wider political, economic and historical context, including that of the colonial relations between the two states, we find reasons why the two Tribunals' findings regarding the probity of the accused were so different.

Sally Falk Moore's article also considers the issue of intepretation. She compares two models of communication – that of Jurgend Habermas, writing about what he terms 'the ideal speech situation' and that of Philip Gulliver, writing about negotiations. The former uses grand theory, the latter ethnography. Gulliver's focus on realism can be used as a small but very sharp pin to prick Habermas's balloon of grand theory. As Moore points out, poststructuralist deconstruction and postmodernism make it more difficult today than formerly to be literal in the interpretation of the meanings and effects of legal ideas: 'The complexity of consciousness and intention, the intricate problems of determination and choice, individual and collective, are entwined in difficult questions of causality.' (p. 26.)

Moore's article raises again, this time in regard to disputes, the issue of the status of ethnography and the way anthropologists use it. Obviously, we should be asking here the same questions as elsewhere – Who is speaking? On what authority? Indeed, it might be suggested that it is precisely in the realm of disputes and the negotiations surrounding them that such questions are most necessarily posed.

The centrality of ethnography to the discipline of anthropology is a theme which has continued to be reiterated. Ethnography cannot ignore disputes, because they are part of the fabric of everyday life in all societies. Gulliver's work has always shown concern with ethnographic understandings, and a similar approach informs the articles in this volume. Most adopt an ethnographic approach, usually at the micro-level, in seeking to understand how disputes arise, and how they are subsequently handled. The two exceptions in this collection are those of Nader and Moore, yet they strengthen, rather than invalidate, the argument. The former utilizes the methods of anthropology, including ethnography, to understand the reasons for the shift from adjudication to negotiation in international disputes. Her article suggests that some of the methods of the micro-level study can be applied at the macro-level – i.e. the culture of negotiators can be studied in its own right; yet at the same time she cautions against the uncritical lifting of ethnographic examples to bolster spurious arguments about the applicability of negotiation where adjudication would be more appropriate and yield greater justice. Moore's article, in its comparisons of the theories and models of Habermas and Gulliver, reveals both the power of ethnography and its limitations. She notes that the work of Gulliver has contributed strong ethnographic texts for a momentous shift of anthropology away from the description of social and cultural systems to actor-oriented approaches. Gulliver also challenged the determination of norms, arguing that power and social context had to be part of the equation. Power and norms, she notes, are in play concurrently.

Indeed, one of the problems with much of postmodernist anthropology is its neglect of power, an issue which arises in virtually all the articles in this book: power of elders over juniors (Parkin), men over women (L. Caplan, P. Caplan, Parkin), large states over small (Nader), colonizer over colonized (Johnson), middle over working class (Gaetz). And yet, in each of these instances, power and its exercise is not uncontested, even where norms and ideology accord power to a particular category. Wives in Nepal run away (L. Caplan), among the Giriama they commit adultery (Parkin), on Mafia Island they sue their husbands for maintenance (P. Caplan); young men in an Irish youth club use self-help to carry their own point; weaker states use the International Court of Justice to seek their rights (Nader); colonized Nigerians seek to adopt and turn to their own advantage the gentlemanly norms of their colonizers (Johnson). And in the process of the ensuing disputes, norms are challenged and even changed.

If anthropologists are truly to represent the societies they study, part at least of the agenda must be set by the subjects themselves. No anthropologist conducting fieldwork can fail to come across quarrels, disagreements and conflicts. The argument of this volume is that we should seek to analyse such issues as fully as possible, since they provide, often in highly concentrated form, crucial keys to ethnographic understanding.

References

Bell, Diane (1984–5). 'Aboriginal Women and Land: Learning from the Northern Territory Experience', *Anthropological Forum* 5, 3: 353–63

Bohannan, Paul (1969). 'Ethnography and Comparison in Legal Anthropology', in *Law in Culture and Society*, ed. L. Nader. Chicago: Aldine

Comaroff, John and Roberts, Simon L. (1981). *Rules and Processes: The Cultural Logic of Dispute in an African Context*. Chicago: Chicago University Press

Gluckman, Max (1955). *The Judicial Process among the Barotse*. Manchester: Manchester University Press

Gluckman, Max (1965). *The Ideas in Barotse Jurisprudence*. New Haven: Yale University Press

Gulliver, Philip H. (1971). *Neighbours and Networks: The Idiom of Kinship in Social Action among the Ndendeuli of Tanzania*. Berkeley: University of California Press

Gulliver, Philip H. (1978). *Cross-examinations: Essays in Honour of Max Gluckman*. Leiden: E. J. Brill

Gulliver, Philip H. (1979). *Disputes and Negotiations: A Cross-cultural Perspective*, Studies in Law and Social Control. Academic Press: New York and London

Schapera, Isaac (1938). *A Handbook of Tswana Law and Custom*. London: Oxford University Press

Snyder, Francis G. (1992 [1981]). 'Anthropology, Dispute Processes and Law: A Critical Introduction', in *Law and Anthropology*, ed. P. Sack and J. Aleck. Aldershot: Dartmouth Publishing Co.

Starr, June and Collier, Jane. F. (1989). *History and Power in the Study of Law: New Directions in Legal Anthropology*. Cornell University Press: Ithaca and London

Turner, Victor (1969). *The Ritual Process: Structure and Anti-structure*. Chicago: Aldine; London: Routledge and Kegan Paul

Chapter 2

Imperfect Communications

Sally Falk Moore

Two models

When Philip Gulliver describes disputes and negotiations in rural Africa, he provides succinct accounts, selective distillations of what must often have been long interchanges. Those compressed narratives nevertheless have a remarkable immediacy (1969, 1971, 1979). They stand as classic examples of a selective, matter-of-fact style of ethnographic summary composed during a much less self-conscious period of anthropological writing. His abbreviated mode is quite different from recent textual analyses of disputes based on word-by-word tape-recorded data, where the preoccupation is with language (Brenneis 1988). Gulliver's pre-taping summaries, if less detailed, are numerous, and form a substantial basis for a very different kind of generalization.

The book which I shall take up here reaches beyond the description of the affairs of a particular people to undertake a comparative project (1979). Gulliver's topic is the structure of negotiations in very different kinds of societies. He focuses on situations in which the disputants are tied to each other in 'persisting' relationships (ibid.: 17). Rural African disputes are compared with labour negotiations in industrialized countries. His conclusion is that the structure of the bargaining process in both types of setting has much in common, despite great differences of context.

Thus Gulliver's 1979 work, *Disputes and Negotiations*, concludes with the construction of a model. The model represents a type of negotiation process, its stages and its themes. Gulliver argued that this abstraction was not culture-specific. It was a framework that would hold cross-culturally, a processual definition that could be as true for rural Africa as for industrial North America. Characteristically, this model was distilled from many actual instances in both places, not built out of *a priori* theoretical frameworks. But even this empirically grounded argument was presented with a prudence characteristic of Gulliver's cautious adventures in theorizing. Gulliver goes to some lengths to list the kinds of cases and problems he had *not* taken into account in reaching his cumulative conclusions, and proposes a number of specific topics for further research that he felt his study had not explored deeply enough (1979: 266–75).

Gulliver's factual detail and his technique of constructing his models largely out of empirical data can be productively contrasted with the deductive models Jurgen Habermas uses in his discussions of law, particularly those offered in his *Communication and the Evolution of Society* (1979) and his *Theory of Communicative Action* (1984, 1989). In all three works Habermas outlines his ideas on the evolution of law and society, and lays out the components of 'communicative action' and 'the ideal speech situation', to encapsulate what he sees as the fundamental connections between open debate, social and moral progress, and human freedom. I propose to juxtapose the Gulliver and Habermas approaches in this paper in order to pose some questions about the unworldliness of Habermas's ideal models and to examine the limits of Gulliver's inductive ones.

Both men speculate on the relative places of power and normative principle as these figure in the dynamics of debate and in the character of the outcomes. But they have very different views of the possibilities and how to think about them. Gulliver interprets disputants as acting out of interest, and using whatever resources are available to press their own causes forward. Principle is, in his eyes, just such a resource (1979: 193). Habermas takes a very different position. He treats debate as a potential path toward agreement about what is factually true and what is morally right. In outlining the 'ideal speech situation' he postulates that ideally discussions o: these matters should be carried out in a state of openness, with sincere good will on both sides and without a trace of coercion or any intention to mislead. For him, norms are not to be used simply as self-serving arguing points. 'Undistorted' communication is, in his conception, the royal route toward real consensus, interpersonal and political.

Habermas argues that in the course of the evolution of society substantial advances have been made in this direction both in law and in science. There is an underlying optimism in Habermas's conception of human striving in his tale of evolutionary progress. For him, self-interest need not make the world go around. With respect to the moral content of law, Habermas, curiously enough, seems in agreement with Clifford Geertz (1983). Geertz has argued that fact and law are the equivalent of truth and rightness, but to my way of thinking, there is a sleight of hand (sleight of word?) in this easy shift from one pair of terms to the other. Conceptions of morality, individual and collective, are thus made into the legal centre of gravity. This redefinition of the legal as essentially preoccupied with moral problems only fits a part of those ideas and activities which in our society are known as law. To ignore the rest, from taxes to jurisdictional boundaries, from the enablement to incorporate to the work of administrative agencies, is to redefine a very complex and variegated institutional domain with a long history to suit the convenience of a special-purpose argument.

Habermas's 'ideal speech situation' occupies an intellectual space that is intentionally 'unworldly'; but not so his evolutionary account, which purports to be grounded in human history. For him history is marked by an increasing emancipation from constraints on freedom of thought and from restrictions on the possibility of rational discourse, and law is one of the indicators of this development. Behaviours governed by a slavish adherence to norms, norms either dictated by mystical systems of belief or imposed by powerful élites, are irrational and unemancipated. He also deems such ways of thinking and behaving to be typical of past societies, to be the very essence of the premodern in his evolutionary scheme. While Habermas makes reference to actual instances, historical and contemporary, these are sparsely scattered through his writings. His purpose is plainly to construct models, not to assemble data.

The Ideal Speech Situation

The 'ideal speech situation' has considerable shock value for any anthropologist studying disputes. The interest of an ethnographer is, of course, in actual occurrences, in actual discussions and disputations. Habermas starts at the other end, with a completely theoretically constructed and totally abstracted imaginary, perfect interaction.

The pre-conditions are clearly spelled out. The participants must share the goal of reaching mutual understanding. They must also have an equal and open chance of entering the discussion, and there must be no external or internal constraints preventing participants from freely assessing evidence and argument. The ideal outcome is an agreement about truth and rightness achieved through rational discussion.

Habermas contends that four validity claims are always implied: that the statements made are (1) comprehensible, (2) true, and (3) normatively justified, i.e., that what is claimed is right, and (4) that the speaker is not being deceptive or coercive. As he himself says 'If full agreement, embracing all four of these components, were a normal state of linguistic communication, it would not be necessary to analyze the process of understanding from the dynamic perspective of bringing about an agreement' (1979: 3). 'The typical states are in the gray areas in between: on the one hand, incomprehension, concealed and open discord; and on the other hand, pre-existing or achieved consensus' (loc. cit.). He then goes on to discuss in detail what he calls 'consensual speech action', leaving aside both discourse and strategic action.

This ideal speech situation has political implications for Habermas, since he conceives of political legitimacy as founded on similar principles. For him, democratization does not mean a specific organizational form, but rather a process by which free agreement is reached through a process of 'discursive will formation' (1979: 186).

'It is characteristic of the development of modern states that they change over from the sacred foundation of legitimation to foundation on a common will, communicatively shaped and discursively clarified in the political public sphere' (Habermas 1989: 81). Thus in Habermas's thought the paradigm of undistorted communication in the dyad, the smallest unit of social interaction, is theoretically linked with the question of the legitimacy of political institutions and decisions in the largest formal political unit of modern times, the state. Consensus that exists because of a pervasive tradition, or that is achieved through the use of power, is not a rational consensus in Habermas's terms. Only through open discussion and argumentation can rational consensus be achieved. Emancipation from unquestioned traditions and emancipation from coercion, from any form of power and domination that is unchecked by moral considerations and democratic challenge, are the valorized aims embedded in Habermas's social theory.

The rarity or perhaps even the impossibility of the totally undistorted ideal speech situation either in dyadic interactions or in collective political circumstances seems obvious. Habermas anticipates just this objection and cuts us off at the pass. He says, 'The utopian sketch of an ideal communication community could be misleading if it were taken to be the introduction to a philosophy of history; this would be to misunderstand the limited methodological status that can sensibly be attributed to it. The construction of an unlimited and undistorted discourse can serve at most as a foil for setting off more glaringly the rather ambiguous developmental tendencies in modern societies' (1989: 107).

That position seems eminently reasonable. The ideal speech situation and the ideal speech communication community can then go into a tool-kit of paradigms of perfect systems to be used to understand the imperfect world. In that sense it belongs in the company of the perfect market and other such constructs. In those contrary terms the ideal speech situation and the ideal speech communication community might conceivably have some utility for anthropologists. One would have to explain in any particular case why they do not exist.

Gulliver's Model of Negotiations

Given the contrast of perspective, what is Gulliver's model of negotiations? Since he argues that negotiations over very different disputed matters in very different kinds of society nevertheless have a similar normal trajectory, he proposes an outine of the common sequence. He argues that a double course is followed. It is both developmental (i.e. it proceeds in a regular direction toward settlement) and cyclical (there is an alternation of displays of antagonism and of willingness to reach some level of mutual co-ordination). Gulliver's summary of the standard 'double' negotiating sequence is as follows (1979: 183):

Phase	Dominant Disposition
1. Search for arena	From antagonism to co-ordination
2. Agenda formulation	From antagonism to co-ordination
3. Exploration of the range of the dispute	Antagonism persists (possibly increases)
4. Narrowing differences	From co-ordination to antagonism
5. Preliminaries to final bargaining	From co-ordination to antagonism to co-ordination
6. Final bargaining	From antagonism to co-ordination
7. Ritual confirmation	Co-ordination remains

As Gulliver freely acknowledges, a generalized model that covers all possible situational variations is difficult if not impossible to assemble (1979: 180–207). There are further risks: that a model that could fit all ethnographic cases would be so reductionist as to be uninformative. He is not arguing that his model fits all cases. He has excluded many. Lawyers will be struck by the resemblances between Gulliver's summary outline of the structure of negotiations in 'persisting' relationships and conventional descriptions of the joining of issues in civil litigation.

Of course the model, being compressed, omits a great deal that can be found in Gulliver's extended text. There he makes much of treating negotiation as a process of exchanging information, yet this theme does not appear as such in the outline. The fact that the hostile/co-operative messages exchanged necessarily constitute a reflexive commentary on the progress of the negotiation itself is not developed. But surely, every hint that co-ordination might be in the offing communicates that the protagonists are disposed to continue to deal with each other. More importantly, such a stance implies that an option not to continue exists in the background.

Since Gulliver chose to analyse disputes arising in situations in which both sides were mutually dependent, his choice greatly increased the likelihood that the protagonists were strongly motivated to go on with discussions until reaching some kind of settlement. The interdependencies common in 'small-scale' society are evident in the Arusha and Ndendeuli material Gulliver harvested in his East African fieldwork. And for industrial society, since he relies principally on published records of labour–management negotiations, he has also chosen to look at a domain of interdependence. This was obviously quite intentional (1979: 66). Thus Gulliver's outline of the stages of the negotiating process *presumes* that a settlement will be reached in the end. It is surely tilted in that direction by the kind of case he chose to examine. The model is exclusively concerned with the exchange of messages during episodes of negotiation that terminate in an agreement. In short, the type of case Gulliver chose to look at is not only characterized by the interdependence of the protagonists, it is characterized by progressing to the point of settlement.

But, in fact, in many situations, negotiations break down. While breakdown is almost certainly less prominent in the types of cases to which Gulliver has given attention than it is in others, the spectre of a total breakdown of communication and its costs hangs over many such discussions, and is a sub-text of the bargaining. The possibility of failure is mentioned a number of times in Gulliver's text, but it is not taken account of in the model nor made much of in the analysis (1979: 54, 78, 127, 129, 168, 173, 215).

One has the sense in reading both Habermas and Gulliver that for both men the process of debate and negotiation is treated as an intellectual problem, rather at arm's length, not as what may be a highly charged confrontation. Yet the emotions stirred by a threat by one party to leave the negotiating table can be incendiary. To have the whole process blow up after an intense effort to fine-sift the issues point by point can be enraging for those ready to continue. To come to the table at all may be a considerable concession and may carry personal and political risks for the negotiators. In those circumstances the problem of keeping the protagonists talking constructively is no trivial matter. Exclusive attention to a process that is bound to culminate in agreement omits this riskier dimension. It omits the secondary consequences that anger can have. When Gulliver mentions phases of hostility and animosity that appear in the bargaining process, he seems to be talking about controlled strategic displays rather than about the possibility of uncontrolled emotional explosions (on the importance of the strategic display of emotion, see Bailey 1983). Of course, strategic action is often involved. But when the stakes are high for the participants, strong feelings may also play their part, not just cool strategies.

The possibility of abrupt interruption, or even of the complete breaking off of negotiations, hangs over many such debates (see Moore 1985). Potential failure is surely as much an element of the process as potential success. A withdrawal of one of the parties from the negotiations may be threatened at any stage, and indeed in certain discussions the threat of withdrawal may constitute one of the major pressures on the other party to make concessions. To the extent that success is a postulated outcome, it could be argued that in that respect the Gulliver model appears to resemble that of Habermas. Both are focused on the route that will lead to agreement, and acknowledge, but are far less interested in, the potential for failure.

Gulliver's interest seems to have been in outlining a total process, from start to finish, a process conceived as beginning with the choice of an arena and ending at the moment when a settlement is reached. (The analogy to the closure found in a judicial decision hovers in the background.) However, the avoidance of an extended comparison of failures may well limit the understanding of successes, to say nothing of the strategies that propel them. Gulliver, then, was well aware of breakdown, but narrowed his focus, presumably to make his topic more manageable. (In a later publication he gives the possibility of failure a more central place (1988: 253)). Habermas's model omits failure for quite a different reason. Failure need not concern him, since he is constructing an ideal model and not representing ordinary situations.

Another major difference between the two models of conflict resolution is worth keeping in view. One model is part of a total philosophical scheme of morality and politics, while the other is a limited schematic representation of common features extracted from some empirical instances. The Gulliver model of negotiation is not only a much more modest enterprise, but a deliberately narrow one. He seems cheerfully allergic to totalizing theoretical schemes.

Thus the fact that the models of Habermas and Gulliver both terminate in agreement makes for an apparent, but false, similarity. There is another, not fully evident, difference as well. Gulliver's 'co-ordination' or 'agreement' is not really the same animal as Habermas's 'understanding'. Habermas is talking about a consensus. Gulliver is talking about making a deal.

Dogma, Domination and Debate: Habermas on the Evolution of Law

Habermas's ideas about social evolution distinguish and link stages of technical and organizational development and stages in the development of moral–practical consciousness. In his scheme of things, the law develops in tandem with the evolution of critical consciousness. Related to this is a specific conception of the difference between the 'mythical' and the 'modern' ways of understanding the world (1984: 43). He sees these as antithetical (ibid.: 44). Habermas tells us (relying on his own version of Lévi-Strauss and Godelier) that the savage mind confuses nature and culture, that analogical thought weaves all appearances into a single network of correspondences, and that none of the ideas involved are open to challenge, that all knowledge is processed in myth: 'The concept of the world is dogmatically invested with a specific content that is withdrawn from rational discussion and thus from criticism' (1984: 51). Mythical world-views are not open to revision. They present a pre-interpreted world. Thus the consensus they produce is not arrived at through the sort of debate presumed by the 'ideal speech situation' (ibid.: 53, 71).

One of the peculiarities of this understanding of the 'mythical world-view' is that it not only postulates an unquestioned cosmology, it seems to assume that cosmological doctrine has a specific prescribed answer for everything. Yet the enchanted worlds known to anthropologists often allow a variety of interpretations to be generated out of the same package of mystical ideas. (For a classic illustration see a cause of death case in Bohannan 1957: 196–203). Besides, some elements of a pre-interpreted world are found in all social settings. That is virtually part of the definition of culture. Surely there are 'self-evident' truths in any mode of thought, inextricably mixed in with more debatable matters (see for example Bourdieu 1977, 1984 on this issue). However, Habermas evidently intends his argument about total pre-interpretation to apply to the 'savage mind' only, and *un*like Lévi-Strauss attributes that mentality to only one kind of society. Habermas's evolution of rationality is a modern version of the rationalism of Edward Tylor, with some threads of Karl Marx, Max Weber, and Sigmund Freud woven in.

While first held back by the constraints imposed by mythical thought, legal evolution is also limited by various 'early' ways of thinking about responsibility. This includes oft-repeated ideas about the supposed disregard of 'early' law for moral intention, its 'strict liability', its focus on retaliation and/or restitution, and on collective instead of individual responsibility, and the supposed absence of general doctrines – i.e., all conflicts are supposedly resolved instance by instance, situationally rather than according to principles. From kin-based societies entrapped in mystical thinking Habermas moves step by step to societies organized around a state. 'Because judicial office is itself a source of legitimate power, political domination can first crystallize around this office' (1989: 177). Political domination also precludes emancipation. However, eventually judicial power cannot be sustained on the basis of status and comes to acquire its legitimacy from a legal order respected as valid (ibid.). Habermas, like his nineteenth-century evolutionist predecessors, characterizes law at present as having the opposite characteristics. Certainly these are the clichés about legal evolution, many of them very misleading. Habermas did not invent them. However, though this oft-repeated sequence has some relation to known practices, the inferences drawn about the significance of these practices for 'moral consciousness' are mistaken.[1]

How does society manage to evolve nonetheless? What is the dynamic that propels it forward? How are the dictates of myth and power overcome? Culture has a favoured place in Habermas's vision of these things. He postulates that personal identities are linked with world-views. Some of these ideas, internalized by individuals, ultimately serve as the source of the evolving character of society itself (1979: 121). 'Individually acquired learning abilities ... must be latently available in world views before they can be used in a socially significant way' (ibid.). He sees self-awareness and open argument about truth and rightness as essential emancipatory activities which enable individuals and societies first to loosen the hold of mythological world-views and later to dislodge the dictates of tradition in order to move forward on the social plane (1979: 156–7).

Progress from one level of social integration to another takes place because 'system problems' arise which represent evolutionary challenges. He says, 'Societies can learn evolutionarily by utilizing the cognitive potential contained in world views for reorganising action systems ... Thus for social evolution, learning processes in the domain of moral–practical consciousness function as pacemakers' (1979: 160). Thus world-views get a good press both as a resource for learning and as a means of preparing the way for social change.

Habermas postulates an original congruence between lifeworld and system in primitive, small-scale societies. But eventually, in the modern world, the systems of money and power become increasingly uncoupled from the social domain of personal interaction and moral values (1989: 303). Habermas contends that this has been true both empirically and analytically. He says firmly that 'the fundamental problem of social theory is how to connect in a satisfactory way the two conceptual strategies indicated by the notions of system and lifeworld (1989: 151). Treating lifeworld and system both as levels of society (small-scale/large-scale) and as analytic strategies (hermeneutic analysis/systems analysis) makes for various problems in the argument, since it allows Habermas to alternate among these perspectives without giving notice.

The lifeworld/system problem in its empirical form is an issue which is certainly much nearer to the practical concerns of anthropologists than academic puzzles about the evolution of morality. The double perspective problem has been widely commented on. So Marcus and Fischer, in *Anthropology as Cultural Critique*, have divided current forms of ethnographic experimentation into two types, the ethnography of experience and the political-economy ethnography. Like Habermas, they, too, advocate combining the two perspectives and enjoin us to notice manifestations of large-scale systems in local affairs (1986: 77). They also conflate method (hermeneutic approaches/systems approaches) with the definition of the object to be analysed (experience/ political economy). They ultimately propose, as anthropologists often have before, that double-perspective ethnography should be used as a means of mounting a reflexive critique of the anthropologist's own society. Leaving the last exhortation aside, I want to return to the methodological problem of combining perspectives on lifeworld and system within the framework of localized fieldwork.

Habermas argues that 'the types of legal regulation of social relations are good indicators of the boundaries between system and lifeworld' (1989: 309). In his interpretation organizations and a variety of other domains (principally money and power) are 'systems' dynamically disconnected from lifeworld contexts and moral values. His terminology describes the lifeworld as 'socially' integrated, that is, it is informed by communicative action, mutual understanding and moral values, while he calls 'formally organized' all social relations in the media-steered subsystems, so far as these relations are first generated by positive law' (ibid.).

This includes organizations, but goes beyond them to encompass all 'exchange and power relations constituted by private and public law' (ibid.). In these circumstances the lifeworld is fragmented, 'colonized' by the media-steered systems. Much of daily life is 'rationalized' and 'instrumentalized' (ibid.: 353–5).

With modernity comes a 'tendency toward juridification' (ibid.: 356). The 'changeover from social to system integration ... takes the form of juridification processes' (ibid.: 357). 'The law is combined with the media of power and money in such a way that it takes on the role of a steering medium itself' (ibid.: 365). Thus we understand that when he says 'modern compulsory law is uncoupled from ethical motives' he is making a complex argument that mixes a particular vision of present political–economic structures with a critique of the divisions in social science between hermeneutic and systems-analytic approaches (ibid.: 309). A subtext is surely the history of Germany in this century.

This is not an appropriate place for a lengthy discussion of the way historical and ethnographic evidence in comparative law could be used to construct a detailed critique of these schemata. What is worth noting is the prominence of the theme of conscious and intentional societal reform that Habermas postulates. It reminds one of Roberto Unger and his thesis that when a society's conception of itself and the realities it experiences cease to be congruent, social change takes place, and, of course, law reflects (and can engender) that change (1976). Does it help to anthropomorphize society in this way? What ground is there for postulating such a drive toward consistency? One might, instead, ask whether such conceptions of society are ever unanimously held, whether they are always coherent, conscious, and controllable, and connected to practice.

Habermas's evolutionary arguments are complex and often jumbled. (His communication is imperfect, to say the least.) But what one can certainly argue on a general plane is that his is a heavily over-intellectualized, over-rational, over-conscious, over-intentional, and unified vision of the ways in which different types of societies have been organized, have been known to change, and the place of law and moral ideas in that process. There are serious questions about how a society may be said to 'act', about the relation between individual psychology and social action, about what is cause and what effect, about the theory of a progressive increase in rationality over the course of human history, let alone about the way a huge variety of legal and law-like arrangements can be explained. But it is not uninteresting that Habermas conceives so much of this story in terms of a critical difference between imposed normative structures and openly debated, freely negotiated agreements about truth, morality and action.

Negotiation and the 'Rules versus Power' Debate in Legal Anthropology

Detachment from practical realities has never been Gulliver's style. Quite the opposite is the case. He has never hesitated to consider the logic of an actor's self-interest. Strategic action always loomed large in his analyses. Today that seems anything but an unusual way to proceed. But when it was initially broached, Gulliver's strategic perspective constituted a break with the more normative, system-oriented approach of some of his predecessors. Along with others moving in the same direction, Gulliver's work contributed strong ethnographic texts for a momentous shift of anthropology away from conceiving the ethnographic task as the description of self-reproducing social and cultural systems toward actor-oriented approaches. In their turn, actor-oriented approaches served to draw into focus all the new roles and new 'choices' with which Africans were confronted in the changing economy that surrounded them.

Written over a critical thirty-year period in African history, Philip Gulliver's major writings on Africa are a vivid illustration of the ideas that were then revising the ethnographic project. Begun in the last ten years of the colonial period and continued at full speed for nearly twenty years after independence, his books and articles epitomized the way social relations were being rethought. Gulliver's materials on dispute were a direct challenge to earlier paradigms.

In that period, legal anthropology in England was dominated by the commanding presence of Max Gluckman. Gluckman's first major work on law described a Lozi court and the cases it heard (1955; 2nd edn 1967). He looked for the 'rules' of the cases to understand their outcomes. He used the same method to distil from the cases what he saw as the principles of Lozi law. Connected with this normative preoccupation was Gluckman's deep interest in the conceptual parallels between legal ideas found in Africa and those in other systems. His second major book on Lozi law was a comparative look at the ideas in that body of thought (1965). Since Gluckman thought of himself as at least half a Marxist, and Marxism and structural functionalism had certain congruences, and since he was very keen to show that in every way Africans were as logical and intelligent as Europeans, his comparisons were a complex exercise in evolutionary typology and intellectual politics. Gluckman's double logic led him to try to define what differences in law were likely to be found associated with different types of political economy, and also to show that there were universal modes of reasoning found in all legal systems (Gluckman 1955, 1965, 1969). Social typologizing was a specialty of the cuisine of comparative structural functionalism, and was also the house speciality of a Marxist evolutionism.

Until Gulliver came along, the major challenge to Gluckman's perspective was that of Paul Bohannan. Bohannan attacked Gluckman's comparative and generalizing bent on the ground that there was a cultural particularity to the ideas deployed in dispute that did not lend itself to simple comparison (Bohannan 1969: 401–18). Bohannan insisted on the *uniqueness* of the clusters of concepts and values and contexts found in any culture. The technical point he pressed was the importance of using indigenous categories and indigenous terms in ethnographic descriptions and analysis. Bohannan argued that it often did violence to the meaning of legal ideas to translate them into English terms for comparative purposes. From his point of view it was that very linguistic practice that produced Gluckman's neat parallels. Bohannan thought they were illusory constructs. Bohannan had no knowledge of nor any particular interest in comparative law, so the 'cultural uniqueness' position suited his training, his data and his personal intellectual configuration.

Gulliver entered this debate by diverting it to another topic. He put negotiated settlements of dispute into the legal anthropology canon, arguing that they were as important as, if not more important than, adjudicated outcomes (1969: 24–68). He argued that all societies had some form of negotiation, but that only some had adjudication in addition. In putting his case he raised a fundamental question that challenged the 'legal norms' arguments of both men. Gulliver questioned whether norms were always determinative, arguing that the rules (or legal concepts) did not 'decide' negotiated settlements. He argued that in negotiated outcomes (as opposed to judicial decisions) the relative power, or capacity to mobilize social support, of the protagonists had much to do with producing a particular mutual compromise. He also argued that the particular social context at the time of confrontation played a part in the outcome (ibid.: 60). He was not making this argument in the abstract and conjecturally. He had plenty of ethnographic data on which to stand (1963). Thus he constructed a powerful argument about the nature of bargaining in small-scale settings that raised entirely different issues from those that had previously been on the table. He had opened another route. 'The settlement of an intracommunity dispute among the Ndendeuli ... is dependent not only on ideas of norms, rights, and expectations and on the respective bargaining strengths of both principals and their supporters, but also on considerations of its effects on other men's interests and the continuance of neighbourly cooperation and concord' (1969: 67).

Gulliver's was a much more instrumental interpretation of the invocation of norms and legal ideas than had been put forward by the others. This was not an entirely new issue in anthropology. Long before the Critical Legal Scholars made their appearance in the law schools of the United States, in fact in Bronislaw Malinowski's *Crime and Custom* ... (1951 [1926]), there had been a commentary on the instrumental and situational use of norms. But in the high periods of structural functionalism and cultural determinism, normativeness had returned to centre stage. In the 1950s and 1960s a bounty of new ethnographic material on dispute settlements in other societies presented a special opportunity to readdress the problem. Gluckman's was the first ethnographic work on an African court in action (1955). Gulliver's was surely some of the earliest substantial and detailed ethnographic evidence on out-of-court negotiations (1963, 1969). Eventually a spirited ASA conference on 'Rules versus Power' grew out of Gulliver's challenge to the normative position (see Hamnett 1977, in which the papers of that conference were published).

The inexplicit comparison that lay behind the discussion there was, of course, the fact that so much is made of the use of normative propositions in Western courts and Western law, as if rules decided everything. The 'Rules versus Power' debate eventually evolved into a less adversarial and more nuanced approach such as that in the detailed analysis of arguments used in dispute and litigation in Comaroff and Roberts's *Rules and Processes* (1981). (They, too, had participated in the ASA meeting. See also Gulliver 1979: 186–94). Nor have these themes disappeared from view today. The problems they raise go to the underlying conception of the anthropological purpose itself. Now that post-structuralist deconstruction and post-modernism have had their impact it is fortunately far more difficult than it used to be to get away with being literal about the meanings and effects of legal ideas and arguments. The complexity of consciousness and intention, the intricate problems of determination and choice, individual and collective, are entwined in difficult questions of causality. Addressing them has required a reassessment of the relation between conventionalized, authoritative, cultural categories and ideas (in anthropology in general as well as in law in particular) and the analysis of social action. The kind of instrumentalism Gulliver's work brought to the fore was an early contribution toward opening these questions in the domain of legal anthropology.

It was also very early on in the transformation of anthropology into its current time-conscious mode that Gulliver treated negotiation as a process that moved forward, as a sequence in micro-time. From the start he looked at the process as one that could change relationships, that did not necessarily restore the *status quo ante*. The management of conflict was not necessarily undertaken in the service of reaffirming a pre-existing equilibrium or normative nexus, nor necessarily a 'reproduction' of a past structure, the repair of a 'system'. Gulliver's case orientation resulted in an explicit focus not on the 'system' that defined the 'event' but on the way the 'event' revealed the contingencies in the supposed system. He was concerned with the effectiveness of relative political power in winning a dispute, and on the variable relevance of normative considerations. There were processual, micro-historical implications embedded in the ethnographic approach even though these were not explicitly the conscious theoretical focus of the argument. Gulliver was doing this very early in the game in certain parts of his work. He trusted what he observed in fieldwork, and he wrote about it factually and candidly. One finds this time-conscious attitude toward data in his writings on labour migration, on networks, on the uneven and not at all neat way age-sets actually shifted among the Arusha, and most notably in his treatment of disputes and negotiations. In that aspect of his writings, he contributed toward a theoretical move away from structural-functional models and toward processual analyses. In some other parts of his work he continued to pay his respects to some of the dominant orthodoxies of the time (see for example his overview of African Studies (1965) in Lystad's book.

Exclusions, Inclusions and Conclusions: Causes, Contexts, Content and Sequence

One of the prime examples Gulliver offers in *Disputes and Negotiations* was a quarrel on which he collected ethnographic material in 1957 during his fieldwork in what was then Tanganyika (see Note 2 for a summary of this case).[2] The dispute was between two close neighbours. It concerned a piece of land they both claimed, rights to water from an irrigation channel, mutual quarrels, insults and a serious mystically loaded curse. On an agreed day they negotiated a settlement through lineage spokesmen in the presence of other lineage members.

Given the set of circumstances described in the Arusha case, and the long common history of the two protagonists it is impossible to identify any particular element that definitively 'determined' the complex outcome. The agreement arrived at was one in which the land was divided, a settlement about future water rights was reached and both men agreed to participate in a ritual that would undo the curse. Gulliver reports all this in a straightforward way and organizes the sequence of topics of discussion under the rubrics outlined in his model. But one is nevertheless left with many troublesome questions which also pertain to the reportage of other public negotiations.

Did the negotiation have hidden levels as well as visible (or audible) ones? And if so, are any of Habermas's imaginary goings-on useful counterfoils? Do his excursions into the formal-logical realm of the ideal speech situation or into the construction of a fictive evolution of legal/moral consciousness underline the opposite features of an observed ethnographic scene? In the Arusha case, there were many specific bones of contention mentioned by the parties. Gulliver's asides (included in the description of the progress of the negotiation) add useful contextualizing comments. He indicates which of the contenders was the more popular and better connected. And he comments on the changing environmental, economic and social conditions that exacerbated their mutual conflict. For example, he refers to the increasing population and consequent land shortage, the growing importance of cash crops with implications of increasing economic differentiation, and the background fact of colonial government. It is clear why both protagonists had much concern about assuring the future of their grown sons. They also evidenced considerable anxiety over the supernaturally caused misfortunes that might ensue if they could not undo the wishes-to-harm already launched into the space of their relationship and did not take ritual measures to insure against future damage.

Are Habermas's categorical dichotomies of any use in understanding this instance and the dynamic that led to its conclusion? Or is it the other way around? Does the instance provide the basis for a critique of the categories? For example, when Habermas separates the mythical, preconventional world-view from the modern, post-conventional ways of understanding the world to construct his evolutionary ideas about law, he seems to assume the necessity of a total replacement of the one by the other (1989: 159–75). Yet it is evident in this case (as in a large anthropological literature) that many different ways of understanding the world can exist in a seamless combination, and, in fact, commonly do (Tambiah 1990). Habermas also strongly emphasizes the amenability of the 'lifeworld' to consensual social integration, and to moral considerations. But are face-to-face interactions in the lifeworld as we experience them actually marked in this way? As Stanley Fish comments, citing a *New Yorker* cartoon about fighting spouses, 'The fact of a face-to-face exchange ... is no assurance that communication will be certain or even relatively trouble-free' (1989: 42). One can see the mystical rituals agreed to in the Arusha case as a set of performative pledges about morality. However, the rituals are necessary not because moral behaviour is assured in the lifeworld of the Arusha, but precisely because it is not.

Gulliver's case took place in a lifeworld of close relationships. But we have no idea whether, in any Habermasian sense, a 'true' consensus on any point was produced by the negotiation. All we know is that after a lot of talk, some of it hostile, an agreement was reached about the future that ended the episode. Though the moment the case describes is a tiny microcosm of pre-independence Tanganyika, what took place inside that rural 'lifeworld' was clearly moved by a much larger political and economic environment. What Habermas would call 'systems' of power and money were in place, and not just outside the lifeworld but inside it. In the background of this case, yet very much in public consciousness, there were colonial 'Native Courts' which the participants in this out-of-court negotiation were strategically avoiding. There is also mention that cash cropping had been newly adopted by one of the disputants, and that this figured significantly in the preamble to the dispute. Thus the 'systems' of power and money were deep inside the lifeworld. In these circumstances is it possible to disengage a lifeworld moral system from the total mix? Is there any analytic purpose served by trying to do so? Strategy dominates the interaction in the Arusha case. The ideal speech situation and its form of abjuring strategic moves looks remarkably like something from never-never-land, and the lifeworld of ethnography does not neatly match the philosopher's model.

None of the specific circumstances in contention between the parties are central features of Gulliver's model-building in *Disputes and Negotiations*. His engagement is entirely with the internal sequence. The unfolding of the negotiation and the rhythmic way the interaction proceeded to the result are the features that preoccupy him. He notes the background historical facts and relates for his readers the gist of the content of the verbal exchanges, but neither history nor the contentious issues are at the centre of his own analytic inquiry. That he informs the reader of these matters is sound reporting, but it only emphasizes the strong selectivity of focus involved in the formal analysis Gulliver puts forward in this particular book (1979).

Several concerns that are not uncommon in fieldwork emerge from the apparent facts of this Arusha case. The possibility suggests itself that at least part of the interaction described may well have been the public product of other, private conversations. Many people were involved, not just the two original protagonists, but their representatives. Had there been conversations between the representatives and their clients before the public exchange? Had any understanding been reached about particular issues, non-negotiable or open to concession? Had there been private contacts between representatives of the two sides, or with intermediaries between them? Discussions among neighbours, kinsmen and age-mates must have taken place, local gossip being what it is in small communities. The setting of a date for the public meeting alone would have occasioned such contacts. There was a time-gap between the initial making-public of the quarrel and the ultimate negotiation that reached a settlement. What took place in that time? And what of the history of relations between the two men long before the specific incidents brought out in the negotiation? To ask such questions is to raise methodological issues about the analysis of public hearings and negotiations. What is the evidentiary standing of what is actually observable in a formal exchange? Is it the whole story? Is it really the site of all the important decisions? Indeed, in the Arusha sort of community, it very probably was not. If that is the case, then the formal progress of the public aspects of the negotiation are only the visible part of a larger complex of events.

In fact, often, the total reaching-agreement-process may not be observable. That is a commonplace technical constraint on fieldwork. It does not make the public part less interesting or less important. That may be all that is accessible. But that practical limitation somewhat changes the meaning of the public communications, changes the definition of the boundaries of the process, and raises questions about causality and comparability.

Today, the old norms versus power issue has little salience and provides no answers. It looks only more and more like the false opposition it always was (a point that, after all, was visible in Gulliver's writing more than twenty years ago). Surely power and norms can both be in play concurrently. For Habermas these two elements can both be pernicious. Power for him resonates as domination and coercion, the very opposite of the free and voluntary and the challengeable. And the tyranny of *unquestionable* norms and ideas can be just as seriously defective, inhibiting as they do the free and open opportunity to question what is right. So norms and power figure in Habermas's grand opera of social evolution as enemies. For Gulliver, power and unquestioned cultural constructs are normal parts of the social world.

Without accepting the whole guidebook of directions that indicates the route to emancipation in Habermas, are there elements of the argument that can stand by themselves and can be profitably put to use in anthropology? Thus the dichotomy between the debatable and the unquestionable can be enormously clarifying for the ethnographer (Moore and Myerhoff 1977: 3–24). The 'unquestionable' is a broadly inclusive category that often encompasses the sacred and mystical, but may also include a broad sweep of unchallengeable secular ideas, from political doctrines and practices to matters of taste and value (Bourdieu 1984; Steiner 1993). Thus any interchange and many a text can be profitably inspected to see which assertions and even which background assumptions are treated as unquestionable and which matters are open to interpretation and argument. That is, in fact, what a lot of ethnography is about.

But there is another, related preoccupation of Habermas that deserves more of a place in studies of disputing and negotiation, and that is whether, at the end of the day, the protagonists think the outcome is fair. At the time of the settlement? Subsequently? Do they blame anyone? This can bear on ideas of 'morality' and 'consciousness' but it also has pertinence to another dimension: the dimension of time.

Opinions about whether injustice was done are worth soliciting, the problem worth thinking about. However, the purpose is not primarily to try to discern the shape of some presumed local culture or morality, nor to find out how much user satisfaction there is about a particular forum or a particular mode of dispute-processing (though those facts are sometimes interesting). It is to discover what kind of residue is left behind by supposedly 'closed' episodes, to reconceive the 'closed' episode in an ongoing flow of time, and to think about the range of possibility of subsequent consequences.

In his first volume on the judicial process among the Lozi, Gluckman described at great length and with some panache what he considered to be a remarkable judicial decision(1955, 'The Case of The Headman's Fishdams'). The decision, Gluckman thought, engineered a cleverly designed compromise between the parties without undermining widely held norms and values. For Gluckman, the outcome epitomized the judicial use of a situation of conflict to restore social and normative equilibrium. Alas for the happy ending: when Gluckman returned to Loziland on a subsequent visit, he found out that one of the interested parties was in gaol because he had killed the other some years after the decision (see a new chapter in the second edition of *The Judicial Process*, 1967, p. 432). The happy compromise had come completely unstuck because the parties did not, in fact, find the solution acceptable. Surely, in 'persisting' relationships, if not in others, it matters whether all concerned are satisfied. Chronic eruptions of dispute in certain structural relationships are not hard to find, even if each separate episode is 'settled' (Moore 1986a).

In a processual anthropology, the period of ethnographic study is conceived as a moment in a longer history, whether or not an actual sequence can be observed. Future possibilities are always part of the ethnographic present for the actors involved. Inquiring into present reactions to 'settlements' (just or unjust?) is a reminder that the whole story is never in, that it always goes on. An episode may have a marked beginning, a middle and a clear end. The episode can be analysed as a separate unit. But it also belongs to a longer story; usually to several longer stories. Held open analytically are the still-to-be-experienced futures of the individual protagonists and the unended story of the larger social collectivity. These, as imagined in prospect, may well be a practical part of present strategies.

Obviously, the task of making visible a combination of short-term and long-term history (actual or imagined), of showing the connections (and disconnections) between small-scale observation and large-scale background in a world of continuous transition, is highly problematic. Ethnography does not lend itself easily to such totalizing. Habermas is free to open the grandest of questions and to answer them all out of the constructs of his own thought. He is not tied to ethnographic observations in a specific milieu. In his philosophical carpentry shop, he can construct his ideal models very much according to his own design.

Gulliver goes the opposite way. He is directly tied to a great deal of specific field material. He deals with the more intractable theoretical issues by locating them somewhere in the large ethnographic background. He focuses. In *Disputes and Negotiations*, when Gulliver wants to make a model, he extracts it from the structured repetitions found in a selected set of foregrounded circumstances. Allusion to the broader, more untidy context appears in each case; but it appears as a set of asides. It is by means of this kind of exclusion that Gulliver can get to work and construct his cross-cultural model of negotiation sequences. Thus Habermas uses a model to limit what he considers. Gulliver limits what he considers in order to construct a model. And the Arusha (and their many confrères-in-dispute around the world) can be seen to have settled for distorted and imperfect communication.

Notes

1. At least that is what the ethnographic evidence from non-literate, non-state systems suggests (see Moore 1978, 1986b). In such societies intention does matter. Even where collective liability lies between groups, individual responsibility is very much in evidence *within* groups. General principles are not lacking, but they have a very different place in the thought, discourse and practice of a society without writing than they do in literate societies with professional jurists and a highly elaborated and documented system of argument and legitimation (Goody 1977). That difference in the place of general legal principles cannot be assumed to indicate the sort of difference in moral consciousness that Habermas seems to be talking about. There is an evidentiary leap there.

The absence of the kind of rule-elaboration that is found in industrial society may have many causes, none of which need rest on some difference of 'moral consciousness'. Surely some of the difference is the consequence of the absence of professional specialists and the absence of writing, and some of it is the product of a difference in the types of situation in which conflicts are resolved. To the extent that disputes in small-scale societies involve long-term relationships that will continue, the resolution of any particular episode of conflict is imbedded in that ongoing collective history and involves many considerations unique to that relationship-history. Besides, to have a precedent-based system, or one that looks to regular 'reapplications' of rules to instances, it is necessary not only to have records, but to have a sufficient density of instances to invite standardization. Moreover, standardization in rule form is often the adjunct of administrative delegations of authority and these, in turn, are associated with centralized political formations (Anderson 1983). None of these circumstances spring from differences in moral consciousness, but all have to do with contexts of practice. Habermas seems unconcerned with these nuances.

2. *An Arusha Case: Moore's Summary of Gulliver's Summary*. One of the prime examples Gulliver offers in *Disputes and Negotiations* is a quarrel on which he collected ethnographic material in 1957 during his fieldwork in what was then Tanganyika. It will serve here both to show how Gulliver fitted specific data into his model of negotiation and at the same time to show how distant from the

anthropologist's problems of analysis are many of the various schemata of Habermas.

The two principal parties in the Arusha case were men in their fifties who were near neighbours, Lashiloi and Kinyani. Between their individual plots of land was a third plot that each claimed. That unoccupied plot had been lived on and used for many years by a man to whom the land had been 'loaned' under a type of heritable tenancy agreement very common in Africa. In such situations the 'tenant-occupier' regularly marks his non-owner status by giving small gifts of produce or beer to the lender or his descendants. In this case the occupant gave gifts to both his neighbours, to whom he was, in fact, affinally related.

When the 'tenant' died his wife and children left the neighbourhood to live elsewhere. Immediately after their departure each neighbour claimed the land. Land shortage was beginning to be felt in the area. Both neighbours had grown sons who would soon marry and would need plots of land on which to establish their independent households. Each neighbour of the dead tenant claimed that it had been *his* father who had been the original owner, and the original lender. The ordinary practice was that when loaned land was left vacant and unclaimed it then reverted to the heir of the original owner. But in this case it was not at all clear which, if either, of the two neighbours had the sole rightful claim. After the 'tenant' died the two quarrelled intermittently over the land and over a number of ancillary matters.

The quarrel was first brought to a head publicly by Lashiloi, on the occasion of a gathering of the age-group to which both men belonged. Lashiloi was more popular in this group, and must have thought it a forum that would favour him. The group offered to hear the case. However, Kinyani would not agree to having the age-group settle the matter, and wanted it to go to a 'moot' in which both men would be represented by spokesmen from their respective lineages in the presence of other lineage members who would support their cause. On the appointed day the two protagonists and their lineage representatives met and ultimately negotiated a settlement. Gulliver tells us that Lashiloi's lineage was larger and more concentrated in the area in which they lived than Kinyani's, which was dispersed and less socially powerful. The land dispute was discussed at the moot; but it appears that much more time was spent on a group of ancillary issues over which they had also quarrelled.

Imperfect Communications

Those ancillary matters were as follows: (1) In a heated discussion over the land claims of each, Kinyani cursed Lashiloi. (2) There was a quarrel over water from an irrigation channel. Water had normally been allowed to flow at agreed intervals from the irrigation channel on Kinyani's land into a channel that watered Lashiloi's land. Lashiloi needed this water particularly urgently, as he had just started to grow onions as a cash crop for the market and they required watering. Kinyani controlled the sluice gate, as it was on his land. When Kinyani failed to open the irrigation gate, Lashiloi's son trespassed on Kinyani's land and opened it himself, in the course of which he broke the gate. Kinyani caught him and beat him. (3) Lashiloi's goats occcasionally wandered on Kinyani's land. (4) Lashiloi had a small cash debt to Kinyani which he had not paid. (5) Kinyani insulted Lashiloi publicly.

Gulliver describes the emergence and sequence of public negotiations in terms of his model of developmental and cyclical stages as follows:

Phase I. Agreeing on the forum:
As arranged after Kinyani refused to have the age-group mediate the dispute, a group of Kinyani's patrilineal spokesmen and supporters (ten men) met with a similar set of patrilineal spokesmen and supporters of Lashiloi (12 men) to negotiate a settlement.

Phases II and III. Statements of grievances and claims:
At first there was an exchange of insults and statements of intransigent demands. Eventually both groups agreed that an enumeration of the issues that needed settlement should be agreed to by both sides. Gulliver lists some 16 claims variously made by the two men against each other, all nuances of the five principal disputed matters listed above. What ensued subsequently was that Kinyani's counsellor offered to withdraw certain claims if Lashiloi would also do so.

Phase IV. Limiting the subjects in controversy:
The discussion then focused on the elimination of the less important issues in a kind of mutual exchange. Thus Lashiloi withdrew claims related to the beating of his son and Kinyani admitted he should not have beaten him. Kinyani withdrew his claim regarding Lashiloi's debt to him and Lashiloi withdrew his allegations about Kinyani's slanderous insults. These matters were then

dropped from discussion. This was followed by *the resolution of two further issues of secondary importance*. Thus it was agreed that the two protagonists would exchange reciprocal gifts of beer to settle the questions surrounding the trespass of Lashiloi's goats on Kinyani's land and the damage to Lashiloi's onion crop because of the interruption of the water supply. There then followed *the resolution of two major issues*, the matter of *the land and the water*. Lashiloi's lineage counsellor proposed that the vacant lot should be divided in two. Lashiloi was to take the portion that was undeveloped but watered by the irrigation channel, Kinyani to take the portion on which there was a banana grove and a house. Both men agreed to this. Lashiloi then induced Kinyani to acknowledge publicly his, that is Lashiloi's, water rights, which he did.

Phases V, VI and VII followed. That is to say, the remaining matters were addressed.

Final Steps Toward Closure:
Lashiloi agreed to compensate Kinyani one shilling for the broken gate, and also acknowledged that Kinyani had the sole and exclusive right to operate the gate. In his turn Lashiloi demanded ritual purification to dispel the curse with which Kinyani had afflicted him. A goat was to be ritually sacrificed and compensation was to be paid for the curse. They agreed to such a common ritual. Lashiloi was to supply the goat, Kinyani the beer, and both were to take an oath to pledge friendship.

References

Anderson, Benedict (1983). *Imagined Communities: Reflections on the Origin and Spread of Nationalism*. London: Verso

Bailey, F. G. (1983). *The Tactical Uses of Passion*. Ithaca, NY: Cornell University Press

Bohannan, Paul (1957). *Justice and Judgment among the Tiv*. Oxford: Oxford University Press

Bohannan, Paul (1969). 'Ethnography and Comparison in Legal Anthropology', in *Law in Culture and Society*, ed. Laura Nader, pp. 401–18. Chicago: Aldine

Bourdieu, Pierre (1977). *Outline of a Theory of Practice*. Cambridge, London, New York: Cambridge University Press

Bourdieu, Pierre (1984). *Distinction: A Social Critique of the Judgement of Taste*. Cambridge, Massachusetts: Harvard University Press

Brenneis, D. (1988). 'Language and Disputing', in *Annual Review of Anthropology*. Palo Alto, California: Annual Reviews, Inc

Comaroff, John and Roberts, Simon (1981). *Rules and Processes*. Chicago: University of Chicago Press

Fish, Stanley (1989). *Doing What Comes Naturally*. Durham and London: Duke University Press

Geertz, Clifford (1983). 'Local Knowledge: Fact and Law in Comparative Perspective', in *Local Knowledge*, pp. 167–234. New York: Basic Books

Gluckman, Max (1955). *The Judicial Process among the Barotse of Northern Rhodesia*. Manchester: Manchester University Press (2nd edn: 1967.)

Gluckman, Max (1965). *The Ideas in Barotse Jurisprudence*. New Haven and London: Yale University Press

Gluckman, Max (1969). 'Concepts in the Comparative Study of Tribal Law', in *Law in Culture and Society*, ed. L. Nader, pp. 349–73. Chicago: Aldine

Goody, Jack (1977). *The Domestication of the Savage Mind*. Cambridge: Cambridge University Press

Gulliver, Philip H. (1963). *Social Control in an African Society*. London: Routledge

Gulliver, Philip H. (1965). 'Anthropology', in *The African World: A Survey of Social Research*, ed. R. Lystad, pp. 57–106. New York: Praeger

Gulliver, Philip H. (1969). 'Dispute Settlements without Courts: the Ndendeuli of Southern Tanzania', in *Law in Culture and Society*, ed. L. Nader, pp. 24–68. Chicago: Aldine

Gulliver, Philip H. (1971). *Neighbours and Networks*. Berkeley and London: University of California Press

Gulliver, Philip H. (1979). *Disputes and Negotiations*. New York: Academic Press

Gulliver, Philip H. (1988). 'Anthropological Contributions to the Study of Negotiations', *Negotiation Journal* 4: 247–66

Habermas, Jurgen (1979). *Communication and the Evolution of Society*. Boston: Beacon Press

Habermas, Jurgen (1984). *The Theory of Communicative Action*, Vol. 1. Boston: Beacon Press

Habermas, Jurgen (1989). *The Theory of Communicative Action*, Vol. 2. Boston: Beacon Press

Hamnett, Ian (ed.) (1977). *Social Anthropology and Law*, ASA. Monograph No. 14. London and New York: Academic Press

Malinowski, Bronislaw (1951 [orig. 1926]). *Crime and Custom in Savage Society*. New York: Humanities Press

Marcus, George E. and Fischer, Michael M. J. (1986). *Anthropology as Cultural Critique*. Chicago and London: University of Chicago Press

Moore, Sally Falk (1978). *Law as Process*. London: Routledge and Kegan Paul

Moore, Sally Falk (1985). 'Dividing the Pot of Gold', *Negotiation: The Quarterly of Effective Dispute Settlement* 1, 1, 29–43

Moore, Sally Falk (1986a). *Social Facts and Fabrications: Customary Law on Kilimanjaro 1880–1980*. Cambridge: Cambridge University Press

Moore, Sally Falk (1986b). 'Legal Systems of the World: An Introductory Guide to Classifications, Typological Interpretations, and Bibliographical Sources', in *Law and the Social Sciences*, eds Leon Lipson and Stanley Wheeler. New York: Russell Sage Foundation for the Social Science Research Council

Moore, Sally Falk and Myerhoff, Barbara (1977). 'Introduction', in *Secular Ritual*, eds S. F. Moore and B. Myerhoff, pp. 3–24. The Netherlands: Royal Van Gorcum

Steiner, Christopher B. (1993). *African Art in Transit*. Cambridge: Cambridge University Press

Tambiah, Stanley J. (1990). *Magic, Science, Religion and the Scope of Rationality*. Cambridge: Cambridge University Press

Unger, Roberto (1976). *Law in Modern Society*. New York: Free Press

Chapter 3

Civilization and its Negotiations

Laura Nader

Introduction

Writings on the anthropology of law often rest on notions of social evolution. These works often place dispute-resolution forums on a scale, so that self-help and negotiation are commonly placed at the starting-point on an evolutionary continuum towards civilization. Then, with development, societies are shown to move along from these bilateral means, to mediation, arbitration, and adjudication (see Hobhouse, Wheeler and Ginsburg 1930). These same works consider the presence of courts as a sign of societal complexity, or evolution, or development, or all of these, while the simplest societies lack mediation (see Hoebel 1954).

In the 1960s, social scientists even referred to a 'standard sequential order' of legal evolution – each stage constituting a necessary condition for the next (Schwartz and Miller 1964). And in the 1980s, some historians argued that colonial powers considered the development of courts in Africa with third-party mechanisms to be part of their civilizing mission (Chanock 1985). During the same colonial period, the International Court of Justice was promoted by its proponents as the apex of forums for settlement of international disputes by means of adjudication and arbitration, a position ideologically consistent with the works of evolutionary social theorists. However, since the post-colonial 1960s period, there has been a gradual ideological shift away from courts for dispute-handling accompanied by a preference for 'softer', non-adversarial means, such as mediation or negotiation, which by the 1980s and 1990s have come to be considered more civilized processes by those developing the rhetoric of disputing (see Nader 1989).

In this paper, I argue that preferences for ranking dispute-resolution forums change with the 'civilizing mission' of major power-holders. Indeed, from a preliminary sampling of international negotiation in water disputes, it appears as if the ranking preference for dispute-handling forums changes to mirror the distribution of international power. The interests of power-holders (in this paper dominant nation-states) are furthered by an entrepreneurial spirit among interested professionals such as negotiators.

A number of writers, including myself, have documented the ideological shift (Nader 1989) from adversarial forums (courts) to alternative forums (arbitration, mediation, negotiation) within the United States. In this preliminary paper I move the discussion to the international arena, where the scene is striking in its similarity to that of the US Alternative Dispute Resolution (ADR) movement of the 1970s and 1980s – a move which requires an understanding of the elastic nature of definitions of 'civilized' behaviour.

In a chapter on 'The Standard of "Civilization" and International Law' (Gong 1984) Gerrit W. Gong summarizes the discourse on international law in the first few decades of the twentieth century. He makes an interesting point (ibid., p. 55) at the start:

> In the minds of the nineteenth-century international lawyers, 'civilization' became a scale by which the countries of the world were categorized into 'civilized', barbarous, and savage spheres. The legal rights and duties of the states in each sphere were based on the legal capacity their degree of 'civilization' supposedly entitled them to possess....the nineteenth-century publicists, and the international legal texts they penned, declared that 'civilized' states alone were qualified to be recognized with full international legal status and personality, full membership in the Family of Nations, and full protection in international law. Significantly, the authority to determine the jural capacity of the states in the barbarous and savage spheres also belonged of right to the 'civilized' states.

Gong makes a key observation about mid-way when he notes:

> Like Sisyphus, the less 'civilized' were doomed to work toward an equality which an elastic standard of 'civilization' put for ever beyond their reach. Even to attain 'civilized' status, as Japan was to discover, was not necessarily to become equal. The 'civilized' had a way of becoming more 'civilized' still (ibid., p. 63).

Gong believes the 'new' standards of civilization are related to new human rights standards (ibid., pp. 91–3) and standards of modernity and scientific progress (ibid., pp. 92–3). In an earlier paper (Nader 1989) I argued a further point: that, in the latter part of the twentieth century, a new standard of 'harmony' now ranks adversarial behaviour as somehow less 'civilized' than negotiating behaviours. Just as ADR in the United States moved the rhetoric from justice to harmony, so too at the international level the notion of 'mature' negotiation has been replacing the World Court as the 'standard of civilized behaviour'.

In his book *Disputes and Negotiations – A Cross-Cultural Perspective*, Philip Gulliver (1979) elaborates the distinction between negotiation and adjudication, the key criteria being the presence in adjudication or the absence in negotiation of a third-party decision-maker. He sees negotiation as 'one kind of problem solving' (ibid., p. xiii), the purpose of which is to discover mutually acceptable outcomes in disputing through means of persuasion or inducement. His attempt was meant 'to show that patterns of interactive behaviour in negotiations are essentially similar despite marked differences in interests, ideas, values, rules and assumptions among negotiators of different societies' (ibid., p. xv). By his own admission, Gulliver focuses his attention on the process of negotiations, although recognizing that a dispute and its negotiation occur in broad cultural contexts and social situations. He also notes that 'a fuller understanding of negotiations will be achieved when they are considered in their full socio-cultural context' (ibid., p. 270). It is toward such a fuller understanding of negotiation that this paper is directed.

Gulliver is mainly dealing with intra-societal, rather than international, data, whether he examines dispute negotiation among the Arusha of Tanzania or labour–management relations in the United States. His identification of negotiation is sharpened by comparing joint decision-making (negotiation) with adjudication or unilateral decision-making. His stance is more or less detached while focusing on non-judicial means of resolving disputes, seeking the common patterns that characterize interactive behaviour in negotiations. Gulliver does not appear to valorize or rank one mode of problem-solving over another, nor does he see mediation or negotiation as non-confrontational processes. Such a stance is by no means universal, as others *do* attach preference to specific forums, often conflating process and outcome.

Thus, in the international context, two distinct standards of how 'civilized' nations settle disputes have been advanced by Europeans and Euro-Americans. Before the 1960s, the dominant rhetoric held that it was more civilized to *adjudicate* disputes using third-party judges from the World Court. Gerrit Gong (1984) and others describe this attitude, which is embedded in anthropological, sociological, and jurisprudential theories of legal evolution. The more recent rhetoric (post-1960s) views *negotiation* between two parties as more 'civilized' or at least more 'mature' or more harmonious. As a more 'humane' standard, negotiation stands in contrast to the rule-of-law standard mentioned above.

The valorization of negotiating that has been part of the dispute-resolution rhetoric since the early 1970s represents a shift in what (in terms of law) it means to be civilized. Why did this shift occur? What are the implications of this change? When representatives of a more powerful party claim that weaker adversaries prefer less developed, civilized, or humane methods for settling disputes, it behoves us to probe further. Gerrit Gong provides us with an observation on the elasticity of the standard of civilization which allows the 'civilized' to stay a step ahead of the less 'civilized'. Edward Said, in the context of the 'East' and the 'West', calls this a 'flexible *positional* superiority, which puts the Westerner in a series of possible relationships with the Orient without ever losing him the relative upper hand' (1978: 7). What both Gong and Said acknowledge is that the valorization of one cultural form over another is all too frequently linked to imbalances in power or in other words, now that the 'primitives' have courts, we move to international negotiations, or ADR.

In the present context, it appears that a new standard of international negotiations is being promoted as the older standard of adjudication/arbitration in the World Court has become less useful to the more powerful nations of the world. The older standard lost its utility since the emergence in the 1960s of new nations, many of them 'Third World' nations ready to use the International Court of Justice to represent new interests. It is even more interesting that the pendulum swing from adjudication and the rule of law to a valorizing of negotiation and harmony coincided with the development of ADR in the United States and its export abroad, often in the guise of expanding democracy through law.

What follows are: (1) introductory notes on the World Court, illustrating *why* it no longer appears to be useful to stronger nations; (2) a description of the professional culture of international negotiators, whose activity illustrates *how* the negotiating standard has been promoted; and (3) key points of a series of international water disputes to show how the alleged positional superiority of harmony practice plays itself out for the benefit of the stronger disputant. The concluding remarks (4) suggest that valorizing negotiation and harmony above the rule of law is part of the radiation of ADR. It functions to hold the line on power redistribution, and is reminiscent of other neo-colonialist attempts to maintain and increase hegemony by means of civilizing (or development) missions.

From the World Court to International Negotiating Teams

The International Court of Justice is the supreme court for international law. The Court is situated at the Hague, having inherited the precedents of the Permanent Court of International Justice, which was a part of the League of Nations. At present, the Court operates under statute as part of the United Nations Charter organized after the Second World War. The Court consists of fifteen independent judges elected by the Security Council and the General Assembly of the United Nations. Although a series of US presidents supported US membership in both courts, others (including members of the US Congress) voiced concern that national sovereignty would be threatened. The US joined in 1946. Since that time, there have been important changes in the Court's composition and in the types of cases it considers. For example, in 1946, two-thirds of the judges were either Americans or West Europeans. With the addition of over one hundred states (many of them post-colonial 'Third World' states), the World Court now consists of judges who are often sympathetic to the causes of the newer 'Third World' nations (Franck 1986: 36).

According to Thomas Franck, the influence of the Third World in the World Court began to take effect after 1964 (ibid.: 37). A number of decisions, which ruled in favour of 'Third World' and post-colonial states, reflected the influence of these 'newly-recognised "forms of civilization"' (ibid.: 37). For example, in 1966 the Court ruled in favour of Liberian and Ethiopian plaintiffs, and against South Africa; in 1974, New Zealand and Australia were favoured in a decision against France; and in 1984, Nicaragua filed suit against the US, which withdrew from the case when it was apparent that Nicaragua had a legitimate claim (ibid.: 37).

Shortly thereafter, in 1985, the Reagan administration withdrew the US's 1946 agreement voluntarily to comply with the compulsory jurisdiction of the World Court, which effectively ended any serious US commitment to its viability. This was perhaps the most visible continuation of a wider United Nations tendency: for a decreasing percentage of member states to submit to compulsory jurisdiction (ibid.: 49). This phenomenon has been described by one legal scholar as 'the Court's vanishing clientele' (ibid.: 47). A gradual diminishment of jurisdiction, coupled with an inability meaningfully to enforce its decision, clearly have limited the Court's role in adjudicating international disputes. Furthermore, the Soviet Union in the mid-1960s and the US in the mid-1980s, both charter members of the World Court, have both withheld dues, thereby abdicating their financial responsibility and evincing a mood of indifference to international law.

The instrument which Calvin Coolidge described as 'a convenient instrument to which we could go, but to which we could not be brought' (ibid.) was no longer convenient, possibly because of its role in several major controversies such as the Iran-hostage issue, the use of the CIA to attack Nicaragua, the Iran–Iraq conflict, the Afghanistan war, the Vietnam–Kampuchea war (Yoder 1989: 116–19). In sum, the US commitment to international law and the International Court of Justice has, for the most part, been declining. The Third World presence in the Court has made it generally less beholden to 'developed' nations since the late 1960s, and as a result there has been a gradual divergence between the Court's decisions and the national interests of the developed countries. As the interests of the 'developed' world are at stake, fewer countries are willing to recognize the jurisdiction of the World Court. Thus the US shift in 1986 was away from compulsory jurisdiction. Interestingly, this new trivialization of international adjudication came about at the height of the 'ADR explosion' in the United States and its attacks on domestic adjudication. In addition, a number of 'Third World' countries have also refused to recognize the court's jurisdiction because they are unwilling to surrender their newly gained national sovereignty.

The recent stimulus for international negotiation teams sprang from a different source than did the International Court of Justice, although negotiation is part of the work of the United Nations. During the Reagan years and the decade before Reagan, there was a movement in the United States away from adversarial processes for dispute settlement and towards dispute management by the use of 'alternative dispute resolution' (ADR). It was an attempt to stem the 'rights movements' of the 1960s – a pacification scheme in part. In the 1970s, the role of the Chief Justice of the US Supreme Court Warren Burger was pivotal in highlighting the rhetoric about what is civilized behaviour in dispute processing: 'Our distant forebears moved slowly from trial by battle and other barbaric means of resolving conflicts and disputes and we must move away from total reliance on the adversary contest for resolving all disputes ...' (Burger 1984). His remedy was privatization, to move toward taking a large volume of private conflicts out of the courts. An ADR profession was born and institutionalized. The prime focus was on organizational expansion, with implications for profitable new jobs for professionals, and a new source of repression for American citizens (Grillo 1991).

International Negotiators

Who were these new professionals, and what was new about them anyway? ADR professionals come from a variety of fields – law, economics, psychology, political science, therapy – very few from anthropology. What was new was not so much that they were practising mediation, arbitration or negotiation – after all, such modes of dispute-processing had been around for a long time, and in the US as well. What some had in common was a distaste for a confrontational adversarial process, for courts as a way to handle the problems of the masses (or we might say the uncivilized), for justice by win–lose methods. Indeed, one of the few anthropologists practising alternative dispute-resolution, William L. Ury (1990), describes 'primitives' as having 'softer', non-adversarial means: '... there is little or no evidence that our hunter and gatherer ancestors were as warlike as we have imagined them to be. Indeed, they may have been more peaceful than we who call ourselves "civilized". Such "primitive" cultures may have lessons to teach us about dispute-resolution.' In a light piece called 'Dispute Resolution Notes from the Kalahari', Ury concludes with the statement: 'Indeed one might argue that the existence of courts and police in a society is an indicator not of compliance with socially-arrived-at dispute settlements but rather of lack of compliance' (ibid.: 238). Some were against the adversarial mode because it was thought to be uncivilized for the civilized élites. So for example, people in this category would prefer to handle interpersonal, neighbourhood, environmental, consumer, women's cases by ADR means, often arguing it was more dignified, respectful, and fairer. Others would prefer to handle inter-corporate cases by ADR means because adversarial processes were less gentlemanly and more costly than ADR.

At the time I thought I was witnessing a forum fetish – the non-rational preference of one forum over another for purposes of dispute-processing. Gradually, I began to interpret such preference as part of a moving escalator in the civilizing mission, activity commonly associated with assertions of superiority. What had been thought to characterize a primitive level of development – negotiation – was now civilized, and what had been thought to be civilized – litigation – was not.

Probably the most well-known international negotiator of recent US history is former President Jimmy Carter. Carter published an address on negotiation in a book entitled *Negotiation: The Alternative to Hostility* (1984) in which he states his position. Basically he agrees with and echoes Chief Justice Burger's publicly proclaimed position: litigation is an 'unnatural process'; negotiation is the absence of litigation or war. In summarizing the number and diversity of negotiations that he was personally involved in, he observes that negotiations have become increasingly more prevalent as a means of conflict-resolution than in previous decades. He refers to the most well-known issues: the Panama Canal Treaty, Salt II, majority rule in South Africa, securing the release of hostages in Iran, peace in the Middle East, relations with China. Carter is practised in his advice and clearly indicates a flexible framework. He concludes in a manner that recognizes power differentials: 'Although military, economic and political strength certainly favours the more powerful side, the matter of simple justice is a counterbalancing factor. Once the talks begin, there is at least some presumption that a final agreement will be fair to all affected people.' Jimmy Carter was speaking from practice, experience, and an inclination towards peace that may have been based more on his religious beliefs than on his notions of justice in a civil society.

Negotiation studies in the academic world start from a different position. The economists who developed process models proceeded with an assumption of 'rational' actor–negotiators who were engaging in maximizing their outcome in negotiation. Another approach sought a model that would take into consideration the so-called unconscious factors, factors related to situation and individual differences, some of which were based on culture. The latter group is said to be based in social psychology (Janosik 1987), but in fact has borrowed, although in a jumbled manner, much from anthropology, and usually without attribution. Indeed, the culture-negotiation literature is quite extraordinary, mainly because it is so confused about what culture is and how important it is to negotiation. For example, one article (Rubin and Sander 1991) argues that '... attempts to resolve disagreements through negotiation increasingly require sensitivity to the possible contributing role of cultural differences' (p. 249). In the same article, culture is referred to as culture/nationality, '... the set of attitudes and behaviours that are broadly generalizable across a national or cultural grouping, and which tend to persist over time'. Yet the same authors see gender, race and age as additional factors that come into play in negotiation, and conceptually separate from cultural issues.

In another book, *The Practical Negotiator* (Zartman and Berman 1982), in a chapter on 'Structuring Negotiations', the authors observe: 'It is difficult to conclude ... that there are dominant cultural influences on negotiations ... [since] by now the world has established an international diplomatic culture that soon socialises its members into similar behaviour' (p. 227). The same authors ask 'How can cultural behaviour be used or neutralized?' (p. 227) and then note that '... there is a whole cultural area that is real but only peripheral to the understanding of the basic negotiating process, and this relates to language, cultural connotations, social rule and taboos, and other aspects of communication'. While showing that Asians are different negotiators from Germans (elastic versus zero-sum), and from English (who are non-zero sum), they conclude that it is 'still better to find a formula, it is still necessary to define details, and within those needs it is still important to communicate to the other party in signals that he understands' (ibid., p. 229). Here, then, culture is being used as an ideological tool.

A more global view is that of Victor Kremenyuk, who describes 'The Emerging System of International Negotiations' (1988). Kremenyuk observes (as did Jimmy Carter) that international negotiation attracts the attention of many interested parties at home and abroad; consequently this affects the process of international negotiation. When Kremenyuk speaks of an emerging *system* of international negotiation, he is recognizing that international negotiation is 'in the process of acquiring new and important functions' (ibid., p. 212). Kremenyuk is not referring to the mere number of international negotiations, but to the growing interaction among international forms that is occurring with increasing frequency. He attributes the growth to a number of reasons: the growing interdependence of nations and of disputable issues among them, the increasing failure of traditional conflict-resolution devices such as the military, and the realization that negotiation may be the only possible institutionalized and codified way to resolve international disputes in the absence of a real alternative (ibid., p. 213). Nowhere is there mention of the International Court of Justice. Instead the author focuses on the main function of a system of negotiation, 'that it should contribute to the stability and growth (optimization) of the system ... The more efficient the functioning of each international negotiation, the more stable and durable is the whole system of international relations' (ibid., p. 215). He concludes with the comment that the role of international negotiation is no longer a government-to-government activity, but rather an international function of government, non-governmental organizations, public figures, etc., the main goal of which is international stability. While international stability may be a good thing, it can also mean injustice and continuing inequities. It seems that the author is seeking to replace the International Court, without explicit mention being made of its replacement, by international negotiation. Stability and efficiency are prominent themes not justice.

In sum, the programmatic social science literature on negotiation is a conglomeration of disciplinary styles, concepts, and content, the total of which sometimes appears both confused and confusing. However, it is somewhat interesting as an example of interdisciplinary borrowings with an absence of the standards of any particular discipline. For example, negotiation and mediation are sometimes conflated, negotiation is equated with bargaining, power differentials are often ignored, culture is confused with social structure, ethnocentrisms are common, and there is little consideration given to the possibility that the dispute may necessarily lead to zero-sum outcomes (especially where material resources are concerned). The overall implication in much of the literature is that anything can be negotiated, and the concepts of anthropologists such as Gulliver are being used as controlling processes.

The literature gets truly interesting when the analyst deals with the detail of empirical instances. It is in these specific cases that all mention of 'civilized' conduct drops away, and is replaced by phrases like 'mutual learning', 'information-sharing', 'harmonizing', and 'co-operation'. Zero-sum settlements become 'hostile', and information, analysis and solution get in the way of 'constructive dialogue'. Under such conditions, mind-games become a central component of the negotiation process, and toxic poisoning is transformed into a 'perception of toxic poisoning'.

In the following section, some of the water-resource disputes surveyed are indicative of the transition of dispute-resolution forums that was suggested earlier, away from adjudication/arbitration and towards negotiation. The progression is best reported in the case of the Danube River Basin, and moves from (1) procedures of international adjudication/arbitration, to (2) basin-wide planning where river basin commissions deal co-operatively, to (3) bilateral agreements resulting from international bargaining, to (4) non-governmental organizations operating across political and bureaucratic boundaries and working towards the institutionalization of international co-operation (Linnerooth 1990). The transition found in these Danube cases illustrates the progression from third-party adjudication/arbitration, to informal bilateral arrangements, to 'institutionalized' co-operation through negotiation. Such a transition mirrors the 'privatization' of justice through ADR centres in the United States in a genuinely striking manner (see Nader 1989: 282–5).

In the next section, on international river disputes, the progressions noted above become apparent. As we see, many of the authors writing on international negotiation imply that there exists a 'universal diplomatic culture' of negotiators, a common culture of national governmental administrators, the international 'scientific community', and environmental groups (Linnerooth 1990: 637; see also Zartman and Berman 1982: 226). What is claimed to be universal is, I claim, a hegemonic perspective on disputing, one developed in the United States during the seventies and exported world-wide, a hegemony that I refer to as 'harmony ideology', and whose primary function is pacification (Nader 1990).

International River Disputes

In a manuscript written in the 1960s and published in 1978, Lon Fuller, then Professor of Jurisprudence at Harvard Law School, wrote about 'The Forms and Limits of Adjudication'. Fuller discussed adjudication in the broadest sense: 'As the term is used here it includes a father attempting to assume the role of judge in a dispute between his children over possession of a toy. At the other extreme it embraces the most formal and even awesome exercises for adjudicative power' (Fuller 1978: p. 1). He asks, 'What if any, are its proper uses?' Fuller argues that disputes that can be reasoned through logical argument are appropriately adjudicated, thereby becoming an issue of infringed rights or an accusation of guilt (ibid.: pp. 368–9).

Only a very few international water disputes have been settled by adjudication. The *Lake Lanoux* case between France and Spain is the classic example from the late 1950s. When John Laylin and Rinaldo Bianchi wrote about 'The Role of Adjudication in International River Disputes' (1959), both authors were engaged in resolving two international river disputes by negotiation. At the same time, they believed that adjudication could play a useful role in finding solutions for such disputes. They point out what is peculiar to sharing waters of an international river. Firstly,

> the geographical position of one riparian often is such that it can adversely affect the rights of others without acting outside its own boundaries. A lower riparian has for instance, certain advantages, not enjoyed on the high seas, over the shipping interests of an upper riparian or non-riparian; similarly an upper riparian has an advantage over, say, the irrigation interests of a lower riparian.

Although their paper was written over forty years ago, it addresses the issue being raised in this paper – that without the possibility of third-party decision-makers, the more powerful disputant can use ADR negotiation to greater advantage. There is a most striking parallel to the argument I was making in 1979 in discussing disputes between producers and consumers. 'Disputing without the Force of Law' (Nader 1979) biases the decision in the favour of the more powerful. Laylin and Bianchi make the same argument in their concluding section, and set a standard for debate about the choice of forum in what follows:

> At a time when the forces of law and order need ever increasing recognition in the international arena, the notion that states willing to submit international river disputes to adjudication are ill advised has a strange ring indeed. For those who are bent on promoting the rule of law in international relations, the cry of inadequacy of courts in this field betrays a nostalgia for a fast-fading conception of international law in which naked power holds greater sway than recognised principles of justice (ibid., p. 49).

They continue to argue that adjudication can play a constructive role in removing obstacles to agreement, something that has been overlooked by those who strongly oppose reference of river disputes to impartial third-party determination. Those who oppose third-party determination focus on the positive advantages of agreement, as if negotiation is the *only* desirable means to settlement.

Laylin and Bianchi make their case for the usefulness of adjudication in reference to the *Lake Lanoux* case. Lake Lanoux lies within French territory and is fed by waters rising in France. It empties into a tributary which crosses into Spain. France contemplated utilizing the waters of Lake Lanoux in projects that would affect the flow of water to Spain. From 1917 to 1929 France and Spain were unable to come to agreement over French development plans. In 1929, 12 years after the beginning of the dispute, both countries signed an agreement under which they agreed to submit unresolved disputes either to arbitration or to adjudication by the World Court, an agreement which they have since utilized. Laylin and Bianchi's description of the conflicting rights of upstream vs. downstream nations, as well as the more obvious right of a downstream nation to enjoy an adequate supply of water, seems to point to a disagreement that was framed in terms of rights. After being cast in these terms, the dispute was successfully adjudicated by a regional tribunal consisting of judges from several European nations. As Lon Fuller (1978) has noted, adjudicated disputes frequently become either issues of violated rights or accusations of guilt. In the *Lake Lanoux* case, the dispute was presented as a question of infringed rights, and consequently lent itself to settlement by adjudication.

When cases that should be adjudicated are negotiated, as illustrated in Laylin and Bianchi's vignette (ibid., pp. 39–41) about a 1940s dispute between the US and Mexico over the Colorado River, the explicit connections between international law and the World Court, water rights, and the advantages of negotiation become obvious. The authors indicate that many US Senators, in a debate over whether or not to act unilaterally, were emphatic about the desirability of negotiating a rapid settlement: one senator states, 'I say that we should be advised thereby and not lose one day in stopping Mexico from building up any future right [to Colorado River water]' (ibid., p. 40). Here we see that 'efficiency' in negotiation can really mean minimizing losses. Interestingly enough, Senator Tom Connally (an active participant in the US Senate debate on the World Court) instructs the stenographer to keep *this* debate off the record: 'Lift your pen, Mr. Reporter' (ibid., p. 40). Connally must have realized how cynical the process of friendly negotiations might appear in the *Congressional Record*.

The tone of the Danube River Basin case as synthesized by Joanne Linnerooth (1990) is in complete contrast to Laylin and Bianchi's reasoning. Her article links the issues of negotiation (using the formulaic language common to contemporary writings on negotiation) to international water rights, with special reference to pollution in the Danube. Linnerooth recognizes the power imbalances between upper- and lower-riparian countries, but takes the view that the more powerful upstream nations are at a disadvantage if they agree to negotiate 'cooperative [water quality] policies', while weaker nations are at an advantage. Linnerooth does not acknowledge the possibility that the opposite may be true – namely, bilateral negotiation may put the stronger nation at a bargaining advantage *vis-à-vis* the weaker nation. Indeed, she argues that 'some compensating advantage or incentive for the upper riparian states is a prerequisite for co-operation' (p. 643). She seems unaware of other cases where no enticements to negotiate were necessary. In these kinds of cases upstream nations often simply wish to minimize their losses by avoiding a trial (or third-party involvement) that would prove them to be in the wrong, as was for example the cases of India in 1977 (Begum 1988) and the US in the 1940s Colorado River dispute with Mexico (Laylin and Bianchi 1959).

Linnerooth, like many other international negotiating 'professionals', implies that there is a 'universal negotiating culture' or what she calls a 'common culture' composed of national government administrators, international scientific communities, and emerging environmental groups (ibid., p. 637). The language Linnerooth uses in describing how conflicting, adversarial interests might be negotiated is revealing: 'mutual learning' and 'information-sharing', as my research assistant notes, sounds more like marriage counselling, not unravelling conflicts over river pollution. Therapy talk is a strong influence in ADR. Her 'negotiating culture' gives little consideration to disputes that *are* in fact zero-sum. Linnerooth does not seem to be looking for the limits of negotiation, because in her view anything can be negotiated, even if 'perceptions' must first be moulded: '... among groups with different perceptions of the problem ... a fundamental shift will be necessary to orient negotiation support away from "information, analysis, and solution" to providing the very mechanisms necessary for a constructive dialogue' (ibid., pp. 658–9). The literature on dispute resolution in fact gives us little reason to believe that the stronger nation is going to exert the patience or consideration to 'learn' or 'share' without the force of law, the threat of litigation, or the presence of mutually recognized authority.

The Danube River Basin is an interesting example because it is one of the most international river basins in the world. The Danube is Europe's second largest river, with eight riparian countries bordering (including Germany, Austria, Czechoslovakia, Hungary, the former Yugoslavia, Romania, Bulgaria, and the former Soviet Union). The Danube also transfers water from the non-riparian countries of Albania, Italy, Switzerland, and Poland. Eight countries spanning Eastern and Western Europe have declared the need to co-operate on confronting the mounting problems of water pollution. The Danube Declaration is non-binding, a step towards a more co-operative ecosystem approach to the management of the river. The contemporary central issues are the deteriorating quality of the water and demands for exploitation of the river for the generation of electrical energy. The Danube River Basin is home to over 70 million people, people of different cultures and economic prosperity who have different standards on water quality. The rich upper riparian countries use the Danube primarily for industrial and waste disposal and energy purposes. The lesser-developed lower riparian countries use the river for drinking water, irrigation, fisheries, and tourism (ibid., p. 636). As Linnerooth notes, there is a 'mismatch between countries which would benefit from pollution control and those with the resources for providing this control' (ibid., p. 636).

Recognizing the power asymmetry between upstream and downstream nations and recognizing also the poorly defined issue of water pollution, Linnerooth nevertheless proposes co-operation through bilateral, stepwise negotiations. She believes that it is 'unlikely that mini-governments with the power to legislate and implement river basin policies across national boundaries will emerge. The role of transboundary commissions in defining negotiating agendas, linking issues, and facilitating the negotiating process may, on the other hand, have considerable potential promise' (ibid., p. 648). Yet forums do not just 'work' or 'emerge' naturally. They work because forces behind them want them to work. Nevertheless, she continues to argue that in the absence of an international river basin authority, mechanisms for collaboration are most likely to be mainly bilateral agreements and international bargaining, which are increasingly influenced by non-governmental organizations operating across political and bureaucratic lines. 'Win–win' bargaining is to be accomplished by those who share 'a certain professional rationality and thus a common overall frame of the issue' (ibid., p. 657), or what she calls 'limited-authority committees' (ibid.). Negotiating participants may 'translate the border' – its imagery, social expectations, jurisdictional responsibilities and processes, as well as the differences in resources (ibid., p. 659, note 108). In short, what Linnerooth proposes is the transition from third-party litigation/arbitration and enforcement, through informal bilateral arrangements, to the non-governmental institutionalization of international co-operation (in other words the 'privatization' of international justice), arguing that expanding the authority of the Danube Commission will not work in the absence of an international river basin authority.

Within Spain and Portugal, the allocation of water is a less involved case than the Danube, but nevertheless raises some of the same questions regarding asymmetry of power and upstream–downstream issues. In the *Lake Lanoux* decision, France was the stronger nation, yet Spain succeeded in the arbitration. In the current situation between Spain and Portugal, Spain is stronger than Portugal, and has the advantage of having learned a lesson (as the weaker party) from the *Lake Lanoux* case: if you are an upstream nation, do not agree to adjudicate a water dispute.

According to Joseph Dellapenna (1992) the surface water in the Iberian peninsula may be an opportunity for co-operation or a source of conflict. Basically the situation is this: approximately 70 per cent of Portugal's surface fresh water comes from rivers that arise in Spain, while Spain receives virtually none of its surface fresh water from Portugal (Dellapenna 1992: 807). Thus, Portugal is at a severe disadvantage *vis-à-vis* Spain, with limited means of persuading Spain to take its interests into account. Exacerbating the problem are the increased pollution of waters coming from Spain and the Spanish plan to place their only nuclear waste disposal site along the Duero/Douro river just above the Spanish–Portuguese border. The proposed nuclear waste facility at Aldeadávila will be less than one kilometre from Portugal, and any contamination of the river will end up in Portugal. Given that Spain has the worst record of non-compliance with European Community environmental directives of any nation in the Community, Portugal has a right to ask why they must share the risk of disposing of another country's nuclear wastes. Furthermore, the Portuguese construction of the Algueva Dam on the Guadiana River to provide irrigation, hydroelectric generation, and urban and industrial water-supply is threatened by Spanish activities upstream. The Guadiana River rises in Spain, where the Spanish have developed their own irrigation project. Spanish plans would undoubtedly deplete the waters before they reach the reservoir for the Algueva Dam. Portugal has been unwilling to challenge Spain, although the 1927 convention provides for recourse to the International Court of Justice should the parties fail to agree. However, thus far, there has been no implementation of a judicial award.

The profile from Dellapenna's writing emerges as follows: the European Community (of which both Portugal and Spain are members) seems reluctant to get involved, and advises bilateral negotiation (ibid., pp. 806, 823). But Portugal's weak approach in dealing with Spain would not bode well for a fair bilateral settlement, literally because of the freshwater power differential between the two nations (ibid., pp. 806, 812, 822). Although a

1927 convention signed between Portugal and Spain provides for recourse to the World Court, this has not been a considered option. In fact, Dellapenna does not advocate the World Court as a solution, because he sees for a fact that Spain is in clear violation of customary international law; rather, he believes that a legal regime should be created to manage the common waterways (ibid., pp. 813–25). It is law rather than negotiation that he recommends.

ADR recommendations are almost never rule of law. Two articles that were featured in the Fall 1991 issue of *Natural Resources Journal* both deal with southern California water agencies and the plan to line proportions of the All-American Canal with concrete in order to reclaim water that currently leaks from the canal into a transboundary groundwater aquifer. However, the Valle de Mexicali, one of the richest agricultural regions in Mexico, relies on this groundwater to support its crops. The Mexicans are protesting against the lining project as a violation of the 1944 Colorado River Treaty. Douglas Hayes, the first author, implores both the US and Mexico to negotiate, and turn the dispute into a 'win–win' solution (ibid., p. 816). Hayes chides Mexican officials for threatening international litigation in the World Court or the International Court of Justice at the Hague (p. 824). He continues: 'Such a development goes against the grain of ordered, controlled, international management of resources' (p. 824). His main argument is that the international tribunal 'would "force" the litigants to equitably apportion these waters anyway. The United States and Mexico should seek to co-operate ... without the coercion of an international tribunal' (p. 824). Hayes assumes that 'equitable apportionment' would be interpreted in the same way in negotiations as it would in an international tribunal. He concludes that the dispute 'provides both countries the opportunity to act rationally, logically, and humanely' by negotiating. There is no hint that international tribunals might follow substantive notions of justice embodied in *law*. Thus the contempt for law here is total.

The second author, J. Roman Calleros, a researcher from Mexico's El Colegio de la Frontera Norte, wants to pursue the problem by advocating the equity issue. He does not take a procedural approach, and he does not advocate litigation. He is simply insistent on Mexico's right to its share of the water. He estimates monetary damage, and notes that calls for solutions 'from president to president as is the custom in these recurring controversies along the northern Mexico border' (p. 834), are a rather fragile and temporary method of resolution. Calleros believes that an information base is 'extremely important for our representatives' because it will allow them to negotiate on the basis of objectively verifiable data – a long way from Linnerooth's suggestion that perceptions of conflict should be altered.

In an article to which reference has already been made Dellapenna (1992) points out that even clearly dominant states hold back in taking all the water needed for fear of retaliation against the state's own water facilities, and he cites the instance of the Jordan Valley. Even in the midst of various phases of Middle East conflicts and wars over the last fifty years 'tacit cooperation has been the almost unbroken rule between Israel and its neighbours, particularly Jordan' (ibid., p. 805). Israel and Jordan are the primary users of the waters of the Jordan, which satisfies one-half of their combined demands (Neff and Matson 1984). The other riparian states are Lebanon and Syria, whose use of the Jordan waters is minor in comparison to that of the others, satisfying about 5 per cent of their total water demand. Conflict over the Jordan River results from a complex hydrological structure shared by four states, and from the hostilities between these four states. The Arab–Israeli conflict has overshadowed efforts to reach agreement on joint utilization of the waters.

The Jordan River is a complex system: the Dan River, which originates in pre-1967 Israel, discharges into the upper Jordan; the Hasbani River, which originates in south Lebanon, discharges into the upper Jordan; the Banias River, which originates in the Syrian Golan Heights, discharges into the upper Jordan; the Yarmouk river, which forms the border between Syria and Jordan, discharges into the lower Jordan. In the first half of the 1950s a number of water allocation plans were devised with the active involvement of a third party, US ambassador Eric Johnston, leading to the Unified Plan. The Plan was accepted by the technical committees from both Israel and the Arab League, although neither of the groups was able formally to commit itself to the Plan for domestic political reasons. In the absence of 'impartial monitoring' these water allocation plans deteriorated.

A series of unilateral actions followed. Both countries began development projects, and Israel completed the National Water

Carrier project in the mid-1960s. In 1967 and by means of war Israel occupied the Golan Heights and the West Bank, which effectively gave them control of the Jordan headwaters and the Yarmouk River. Thus the situation went from mediated negotiations to unilateral action to violent conflict, without any consideration of an adjudicated settlement – this in spite of the success of the *Lake Lanoux* case during this time-period. Neff and Matson (ibid., p. 45) discuss 'secret negotiations' mediated again by the US between Jordan and Israel. Apparently a series of such meetings took place in the early 1970s as well.

The statistics that Neff and Matson present (ibid., pp. 45, 47–8) indicate the gross inequities present in the consumption of water by Israel and by the settlers on the West Bank. As the authors indicate, these inequities border on the infringement of human rights. According to one source, the Palestinian average in some areas of the West Bank has gone down since the beginning of the *Intifada* to less than 44 litres per caput per day – 'less than the United Nations reckons is necessary for maintaining minimal health standards' (Lowi 1992: 43). Like the *Lake Lanoux* case, this issue can be presented in terms of violated rights, specifically of human rights. For this reason, the Jordan River dispute would seem to be an appropriate case for adjudication.

A final case (see Begum 1988) refers to the long-standing Ganges River dispute between East Bengal/Bangladesh and India, and gives a clear example of the politics of international negotiation, and the advantages of bilateral negotiation for the stronger party. The Ganges river flows from India into East Bengal, and the Ganges River Basin supplies it with much of its fresh water. In the early 1950s the Indian government began planning the construction of the Farakka Barrage, a dam which would divert water from the Ganges River into the Bhagirathi–Hooghly River via a feeder canal. Pakistani officials wanted to be included in the process of developing the Ganges River, but the Indian government continued its unilateral planning. Finally, in 1957 and 1958, Pakistan proposed forming a joint development committee, and also proposed that the United Nations should be involved in the process. The Indian government flatly rejected all proposals. In 1960 they finally agreed to begin bilateral negotiations with Pakistan, but by 1961 India had already begun construction of the Farakka Barrage, justifying their unilateral action by publicly stating that the waters of the

Ganges belonged exclusively to India. East Bengal during this period was marginalized.

The Ganges water dispute had long been a concern of the primarily agrarian people of East Bengal (which became Bangladesh in 1971). After a series of failed negotiations, the government of Bangladesh brought the case before the General Assembly of the UN in September of 1976. The United Nations seemed very reluctant to get involved in this case. The situation became entirely focused on the increased stability of the Bangladeshi government and on the unilateral action of India to withdraw the Ganges water at Farakka. The Bangladesh Supreme Court Bar Association expressed a deep concern at the unilateral and arbitrary withdrawal of waters of an international river by India. This action was followed by protests from all parts of the country.

At the United Nations, Bangladesh's request to include the Farakka Barrage in the agenda of the General Assembly was opposed by India, who argued that it was a 'bilateral issue of [an] "essentially economic" nature' (ibid., p. 169). The UN did clarify both positions at an international forum: India could not get moral support for pursuing a policy of unilateral action, while Bangladesh, being one of the poorest countries of the world and heavily dependent on foreign assistance, had little clout to use in the international arena. However, as India had adhered to the principle of 'bilateralism', India had to prove that such negotiations could bring about a solution without third-party mediation (ibid., p. 172). Ultimately, it seems that a change of government in India made a difference. Although a five-year agreement was reached in 1977, a final resolution has not been achieved.

Each nation has its own preferred solution to the problem. Bangladesh's solution would involve Nepal's participation, while India would like to keep the issues of water strictly between itself and a weaker Bangladesh. As described by Khurshida Begum (ibid., pp. 204–14), 'peaceful' negotiations, strictly bilateral, are a hegemonic tool for India. Over the course of the negotiations a series of 'discrepancies' between the facts reported by India and Bangladesh reveals exactly the purpose for which court trials are used – disagreements of fact. As Laylin and Bianchi have noted (1959) these could be resolved through a third party, or experts independent of the disputants. Also, the serious effects of water shortage claimed by Bangladesh would seem to put this case on the level of human rights violation rather than merely a political tug-of-war in the process of hammering out these agreements. Once again, we are reminded of Laylin and Bianchi's arguments for 'The Role of Adjudication in International River Disputes' (1959) as a means of balancing power discrepancies, while recognizing that adjudication cannot be simply equated with a better outcome for weaker parties.

Concluding Comments

In 1991 the *American Journal of International Law* published an editorial titled 'The Peace Palace Heats Up: The World Court in Business Again?'. The author, Keith Highet, announces that the Hague is busier than ever. Its docket is jammed. Nobody forecast such activity. The voices against the Court have been strident, particularly amongst those supporting the policies of the United States in Central America in the 1980s. The author lists nine new cases brought before the full court in the previous two years, only about half of which are clearly between unequal powers. Furthermore, even 'unpopular' states like Libya and Iran are resorting to World Court adjudication, since this is probably one of the few ways of settling an international dispute without the risks of power play.

In the same editorial the author notes that the United Nations Law of the Sea has a provision for the formation of a specialized tribunal – the so-called Hamburg Court. Such a duplicative tribunal, the author continues, might not be necessary in the light of the fact that the World Court will be undertaking a large number of these cases soon and setting precedents for future Law of the Sea cases. However, the Hamburg Court has strong proponents – the five permanent members of the Security Council – who support this 'alternative solution to existing litigation before the full tribunal' of the World Court (ibid., pp. 653–4). These powerful states are, according to Highet, 'as ever uncomfortable with the [World] Court's activities' (ibid.).

The editorial concludes with the idea that perhaps the developed nations are in support of The Hamburg Court because they would have a stronger hand in it. He believes that the real work of the World Court over the next decade 'will be the reconciliation of the interests of developing countries with those of the developed countries ...; however, in the nine recent cases, the litigants have represented a wide range of middle-level powers, not the greater powers' (ibid.). Thus the piece is hardly reassuring on the role of the World Court as power-equalizer.

In a recent journalistic piece W. T. Anderson (1993) speaks about 'Governing the World without Governments', noting that there is a 'demand for a new system of governance', as national governments, inter-governmental organizations and the United Nations fail. 'Global governance' he calls it. The strong interest in alternative systems suffers from a lack of introspection about the alternative experiments to date, experiments biased towards the powerful. Words like 'global civilization' sound grand; but, as I have indicated in this paper, the 'civilized' – the network of global intellectuals, businessmen, and activists that Anderson speaks about – have a way of diminishing institutions that may function as power-equalizers.

What is so powerful about professional cultures is their built-in protection against participating professionals examining the underlying assumptions of their trade. In the literature on 'modern negotiation' there is little to indicate that 'modern negotiators' are critically examining their trajectories or assessing the broader significance of their work. They write more like 'true believers', avoiding controversy even at the cost of self-reflection, which would necessarily involve understanding the historical and socio-cultural context in which a newly re-civilized negotiation serves as hegemonic power. P. Gulliver could afford to focus on the process of negotiation to the exclusion of broad cultural contexts and social situations as long as the subject-matter was intra-societal and micro in scope. However, in the arena of international power-brokers the purpose of negotiation may not be problem-solving, but control.

Acknowledgments

The author wishes to thank Roberto Gonzalez for his help in researching this paper, and for his critical thoughts about the central ideas. I also appreciate critical reading by Jenny Beer and Ayfer Bartu, and am grateful to Angelle Khachadoorian for preparing the manuscript.

References

Anderson, W. T. (1993). 'Governing the World without Governments', *Pacific News Service*, June 21–25

Begum, K. (1988). *Tension over the Farraka Barrage: A Techno-political Tangle in South Asia*. Stuttgart – Wiesbaden: Steiner Verlag

Burger, W. (1984). 'Annual Message on the Administration of Justice', Warren E. Burger, Chief Justice of the United States at the Mid-year Meeting, American Bar Association, February 12, 1984

Calleros, J. R. (1991). 'The Impact on Mexico of the Lining of the All-American Canal', *Natural Resources Journal* 31(4), 829–38

Carter, J. (1984). *Negotiation: The Alternative to Hostility*, Macon, Georgia: Mercer Press

Chanock, M. (1985). *Law, Custom, and Social Order: The Colonial Experience in Malawi and Zambia*, Cambridge: Cambridge University Press

Dellapenna, J. (1992). 'Surface Water in the Iberian Peninsula: An Opportunity for Co-operation or a Source for Conflict?', *Tennessee Law Review* 59(4), 803–25

Franck, T. (1986). *Judging the World Court*. New York: Priority Press Publications

Fuller, L. (1978). 'The Forms and Limits of Adjudication', *Harvard Law Review* 92(2), 353–409

Gong, G. (1984). *The Standard of 'Civilization' in International Society*. Oxford: Clarendon Press

Grillo, T. (1991). 'The Mediation Alternative: Process Dangers for Women' *Yale Law Review* 100, 1545–610

Gulliver, P. H. (1979). *Disputes and Negotiations: A Cross-Cultural Perspective*. New York: Academic Press

Hayes, D. (1991). 'The All-American Canal Lining Project: A Catalyst for Rational and Comprehensive Groundwater Management on the United States–Mexico Border', *Natural Resources Journal* 31(4), 803–27

Highet, K. (1991). 'The Peace Palace Heats Up: The World Court in Business Again?', *American Journal of International Law* 85(4), 646–54

Hobhouse, L. T., Wheeler G. C., and Ginsberg M. (1930). *The Material Culture and Social Institutions of the Simpler Peoples*. London: Chapman and Hall

Hoebel, E. A. (1954). *The Law of Primitive Man*, Cambridge, Massachusetts: Harvard University Press

Janosik, R. (1987). 'Rethinking the Culture–Negotiation Link', *Negotiation Journal* 3(4), 385–95

Kremenyuk, V. (1988). 'The Emerging System of International Negotiations', *Negotiation Journal* 4(3), 211–18

Laylin, J. G. and Bianchi, R. L. (1959). 'The Role of Adjudication in International River Disputes: The Lake Lanoux Case', *American Journal of International Law* 53(1), 30–49

Linnerooth, J. (1990). 'The Danube River Basin: Negotiating Settlements to Transboundary Environmental Issues', *Natural Resources Journal* 30(3), 629–60

Lowi, M.R. (1992). 'West Bank Water Resources and the Resolution of Conflict in the Middle East', Occasional Paper Series of the University of Toronto Project on Environmental Change and Acute Conflict, Number 1, 29–60

Nader, L. (1979). 'Disputing without the Force of Law', *Yale Law Journal* 88, No. 5 (Special Issue on Dispute Resolution), 998–1021

Nader, L. (1989). 'The ADR Explosion: The Implications of Rhetoric in Legal Reform', *Windsor Yearbook of Access to Justice* 269–91

Nader, L. (1990). *Harmony Ideology: Justice and Control in a Mountain Zapotec Village*. Stanford, California: Stanford University Press

Neff, T. and Matson, R. C. (1984). *Water in the Middle East: Conflict or Cooperation?* Boulder, Colorado: Westview Press

Rubin, J. and Sander, F. A. E. (1991). 'Culture, Negotiation, and the Eye of the Beholder', *Negotiation Journal* 7(3), 249–54

Said, E. (1978). *Orientalism*. New York: Pantheon Books

Schwartz, R. D. and Miller, J. C. (1964). 'Legal Evolution and Societal Complexity', *American Journal of Sociology* 70 (2), 159–69

Ury, W. (1990). 'Dispute Resolution Notes from the Kalahari', *Negotiation Journal* 6(3), 229–38

Yoder, A. (1989). *The Evolution of the United Nations System*. New York: Crane Russak

Zartman, I. W. and Berman, M. R. (1982). *The Practical Negotiator*. New Haven, Connecticut and London: Yale University Press

Chapter 4

The Contentiousness of Disputes

Elizabeth Colson

Disputes and the Myth of the Harmonious Community

Why have disputes continued to dominate so much of the description of social interaction which provides the essential data for social anthropology? Probably because, although they may seem to be out-of-the-ordinary events, they nevertheless mobilize support systems, highlight social cleavages, and are argued in terms of general morality. They thereby provide insights into how people think about their social universe under circumstances which minimize the distorting impact of the observer's presence: these are people getting on with business whose outcome is of importance to themselves in circumstances where they are responding largely to their perception of the reactions of other members of their own community.

But the context in which all this takes place, I argue, has aroused expectations that the outcome of a dispute leads to reconciliation and the restoration of a social harmony considered to be the ideal condition for human beings (Gulliver 1979: 168–9). Ritualized settings, formulaic language, the appeal to generally accepted values to justify claims, and the common practice of marking the outcome with a ritual affirmation or symbolic statement signifying that contestants are again in amity associate the negotiation or adjudication of disputes with religious rituals that unite communities for common purposes that transcend the individual concerns from which disputes arise. Moore, for instance, writes of the utility of viewing 'proceedings of dispute settlement as ceremonies of situational transformation' (Moore 1977: 159). From this it is an easy jump to the assumption that the outcome of disputes, like the outcome of rituals, should be the creation of a community of individuals at harmony with one another.

The very term 'dispute settlement' carries connotations that matters at issue have been dealt with and will no longer disturb normal relationships. Gulliver decided to avoid the term for that very reason, recognizing that the outcome, even in negotiations, where the process is one of contestants reaching some agreement they can live with, was likely to include a residue of antagonism and sometimes bitter hostility between rivals (1979: 78–9, 169, 184). It was the easier for Gulliver to dispense with the term because he was primarily concerned with processes of negotiation, drawing upon his experience among peoples such as the Turkana, Jie, Arusha and Ndendeuli, who at the time of his fieldwork in the 1940s and 1950s relied primarily upon moots to deal with disputes, and regarded courts and adjudication as foreign devices imposed by an alien administration (Gulliver 1955, 1963, 1971). He provides no term to subsume processes of both negotiation and adjudication. I, therefore, like most other anthropologists, continue to write of 'dispute settlement', but with the stipulation that 'settlement' obscures the dynamics of conflicting interests and personal animosities that are not made to go away when a judgement is announced or a bargain is made.

Formalized settings, so characteristic of moots and courts, permit contestants to meet without physical violence and have their say no matter what method of settlement is adopted – direct negotiation, mediation, or adjudication. Formality reminds contestants that they are operating in a public arena where they are dependent upon others for support and are subject to the coercive power of public opinion, not the least effective being that of their own cohort of supporters. In adjudication, formality both symbolizes the status of those who give judgement and legitimates their decisions (see, for example, Moore 1977: 185). Arguments must be phrased in terms that appeal to generally held community standards when contestants try to justify their actions (Gulliver 1979: 192). As Max Gluckman put it, contestants, mediators and adjudicators all try to present themselves as both reasonable and upright (Gluckman 1955–6).

Formal procedures and the enunciation of moral standards and community values by contestants, mediators and adjudicators mean that disputes are aired in circumstances that have much in common with religious rituals, which also mobilize social units, but in a context that dramatizes their interdependence and the necessity of transcending individual and group interests to achieve common goals. Rituals inevitably stress the values of co-operation, common interests, and harmony that transcend, rather than underwrite, the divergences that in fact organize human communities.

The degree to which anthropologists and others have dealt with dispute settlements as though they were rituals that should and perhaps must end in the suppression of contending interests and the restoration or confirmation of harmony, reflects no doubt the fact that we developed our approach by looking at dispute settlement in societies whose members had multiple on-going relationships with one another and recognized that they were mutually dependent in activities vital to their very existence. Those so dependent, it was argued, cannot be in continuous open conflict. Disputes, therefore, must either be settled or contained in some fashion. Gulliver has argued that sedentary populations, unlike pastoralists, who need never settle disputes because they can move away from those with whom they are at odds, 'must devise and follow institutions and processes to cope with the comparative permanence of residence and thus of association. There must, for example, be fairly efficient means by which disputes are dealt with, sealed off, or made otherwise tolerable, among people who cannot avoid each other and are to some degree interdependent' (Gulliver 1975: 379). Much the same argument had also been made by Colson (1953) and Gluckman (1955a,b). It is taken as a given that contention is the enemy of community, though this overlooks the interest that people take in public displays of contention that break the monotony of daily life. Fallers, for instance, describes the Soga courts in Uganda as 'popular places in which to loiter while enjoying the contest' (1977: 58), and I have found Gwembe Tonga in Zambia keenly interested in the disputes of their neighbours without feeling that these necessarily threaten their own interests.

Disputes are dramatic. They are pursued with rhetorical displays in the attempt to gain support and undermine the opposition. Disputes interest members of the community for the very reason they have interested Gulliver and other anthropologists: to them they are both theatre and real contests that test relative strengths and weaknesses and provide a mapping of the social forces with which they themselves contend. But we may value harmony more than they, given that anthropologists for the most part come from societies where there is so little sense of community that quarrels do threaten the social fabric in ways incomprehensible to those who do not think that social relationships are based upon good feeling. Nader, who has pioneered work on the use of an ideology of harmony as a means of social control, has suggested that the emphasis upon the necessity for maintaining harmonious relationships is in fact a western construct derived from Christianity (Nader 1990: 291). Certainly, anthropological emphasis upon the importance of harmony received a powerful impetus from the work of Victor Turner, who informed his anthropology with his Catholicism. He stressed the role of ritual as a response to the human desire for oneness, for what he called *communitas*:

> Essentially communitas is a relationship between concrete, historical, idiosyncratic individuals. These individuals are not segmentalized into roles and statuses but confront one another rather in the manner of Martin Buber's 'I and Thou'. Along with this direct, immediate and total confrontation of human identities, there tends to go a model of society as a homogeneous, unstructured *communitas*, whose boundaries are ideally coterminous with those of the human species (Turner 1969: 131–2).

Turner believed that such a condition was achieved only momentarily 'and it is the fate of all spontaneous *communitas* in history to undergo what most people see as a "decline and fall" into structure and law' (1969: 132).

Law, Turner implies, is the antithesis of *communitas*: settlement of disputes therefore moves contestants back towards oneness. Given the ritualized nature of moots and courts, it is all too easy to concentrate on the rhetoric of the case and thence move to the position that law has as its ultimate aim the creation of *communitas*, that is amity among contenders, rather than equity or some other outcome.

Gluckman, who did much to advance the study of disputes, stressed this aspect of adjudication. In his work on Lozi jurisprudence, he found that judges in the courts of Barotseland (in what is now Zambia) took as one of their principal aims the reconciliation of the parties when these were in 'a relationship which it is valuable to preserve' (1967: 78), and he praised Lozi judges for their attempts 'to enforce upright conduct as well as legal obligations' (p. 191). He described social life among the Lozi as ideally consisting of

> a mutual give-and-take, distinguished by amiability, generosity, and benevolence in reciprocal cooperation. Naturally life does not run this smoothly and quarrels are frequent. Some quarrels come to court. As we have seen again and again, the court does not confine its enquiry to the single element in the relationship which is the subject of the legal claim, but enters into considerations of justice and morality which arise from the relationship as a whole (p. 197).

Gluckman assumed that other African courts, as well as courts in other regions where people quarrelled with known face-to-face opponents, were likely to pursue the same ends, but Fallers challenged that assumption when he found Soga courts placing greater stress upon 'applying the law' than upon 'settling the trouble' (1977: 59). In Gwembe District, Zambia, where most disputes still arise among kin and neighbours, over the last three decades dispute setttlement is seen as appropriately dealing with the issues at stake rather than the nature of the relationships of the contenders, except perhaps in cases of marital dispute.

Moots and courts cannot create a harmony that lasts outside their context, any more than rituals or indeed any more than a witchfinder's campaign against sorcerers and witches can overcome more than momentarily, if then, the anger, greed, humiliations and fears that fuel the suspicions that bring a witchfinder into the community. Kopytoff (1980: 206, 210) advises anthropologists not to attribute a greater healing power to rituals than would their own participants, who are well aware that rituals that purport to cleanse individuals and communities are 'perpetually vulnerable to the everyday battering of reality'.

Gulliver recognized that hostilities survived ritual affirmations of agreement or submission ending the particular case. Moore writes of disputes ending but anger persisting (1977: 186), while I have found the same thing to be true among Gwembe Tonga. Gluckman on his return to Barotseland in 1965 was able to follow up subsequent developments among contenders in a number of the cases he had recorded in the 1940s. He found that despite the court's efforts at the restoration of good relationships, some litigants had remained as hostile as ever, and disputes continued to erupt among them (1967: 434–5). The 'everyday battering of reality' subverts the desire of the court to restore harmony, just as it subverts the harmony sought through rituals. The very embeddedness of law in social life ensures this (Starr and Collier 1989).

Anthropologists have abandoned theories of social structure that assume social integration, and now deal with social life as a creative process rather than as a steady state or equilibrium in which all elements work together for good. Yet the attention given to dispute settlement and its setting assumes that the appropriate outcome to negotiation or adjudication is the restoration of good relationships. Gluckman came to see that a focus upon the setting of dispute settlements inhibited an understanding of disputes as social processes: he had not investigated how disputes had developed or 'how the judicial decisions had, or had not, influenced social relationships' (1967: 371). He obviously thought that they should.

Yet I find that when Gwembe Tonga appeal to 'the law' they seek a remedy for a particular ill rather than a recipe for getting along with their neighbours or kin, even though they phrase their arguments as appeals to common understandings of appropriate action under such and such circumstances. The handling of dispute settlements as though these were rituals of reconciliation reflects such Western clichés as 'little birds in their nests agree' and 'thou shalt love thy neighbour as thyself'. It also masks the realities of the social coercion that maintains some semblance of peaceful co-existence despite on-going antagonisms. Observation of various Gwembe Tonga communities over the past forty years has given me a sense of what lies below the surface amiability. As I have written elsewhere 'I now look around a neighbourhood gathering and wonder at the tough-minded determination that keeps hostilities from surfacing and disturbing the business of living' (Colson 1974: 44). The same point has been made by other anthropologists who have long familiarity with particular communities.

As Gulliver has shown, it is quite possible for people to have little interest in pursuing disputes if they have no reason to continue to interact with one another. It is also possible to refuse to contest a perceived wrong if contesting is not socially acceptable, as is true among Southern Baptists in the United States (Greenhouse 1989). Such avoidance of open disputes is called 'lumping it' by Nader and Todd (1978: 9), using a term first proposed by Felstiner. If people carry their quarrels into a public arena, they do so because they expect to gain something from the encounter, if only the humiliation of the opponent. Gulliver has pointed out that the disputing process by its very nature leads people to think about and formulate points of tension with their opponents (1979: 128). Whatever the official outcome of a dispute, antagonists depart having formulated for themselves good reasons for on-going distrust and dislike.

Disputing in Gwembe District, Zambia

Gwembe Valley, a portion of the Middle Zambezi Valley, is occupied largely by speakers of ciTonga. Until 1958 they lived on either bank of the Zambezi River or in small tributary valleys in the escarpment hills of the high plateaus of Zambia and Zimbabwe. Here I deal only with those who live within Zambia. In 1958 the impounding of the Zambezi by the Kariba Dam created Kariba Lake and displaced over 60,000 people, 37,000 of them on the Zambian side of the river.

I first visited Gwembe Valley in 1949, when I attended and recorded several sessions of the court of Chief Chipepo. In 1956 Thayer Scudder and I began our longitudinal study of Gwembe District (Scudder and Colson 1979). We have visited the district repeatedly, the last visit being in 1992. We have followed the effects of resettlement, the impact of Zambian Independence in 1964, the euphoria associated with rapid economic development in the early years of independence, and the malaise that set in with the decline of the Zambian economy after 1973. During the years of the 1970s, when the District was a base for 'freedom fighters' against European control in Zimbabwe and was subject to commando raids in return, we were unable to visit the valley, but did meet with people then settled elsewhere and remained in correspondence with villagers, a number of whom kept records for us. We now have some sense of the dynamics of Gwembe life over a period of thirty-six years: those who were adolescents when we first met them are now the senior members of their communities. We have listened as people quarrelled, heard various accounts from different contestants, been present at village moots and at hearings in what were once called Chiefs' Courts or

Native Authority Courts but are now known as Local Courts (Colson 1976). Frequently we know enough about the prehistory of a dispute and the characteristics of the contenders to appraise what is happening in much the same way as fellow villagers.

Since the early 1970s, various villagers have kept diaries for us. Their records tend to be accounts of disputes or of acts that are provocative. They may think this is what is wanted, although they have been asked to include economic and demographic information, instances of co-operative assistance, accounts of rituals and a variety of other matters, as well as accounts of quarrels and public disputes. The records suggest that the incidence and seriousness of disputes increased as economic pressures increased after 1973 (Scudder 1983, 1984), but this may be a recording artefact due to the increasing willingness of assistants to show us the seamy side of their communities, and perhaps also to the increasing ease with which they have come to write. Several facts, however, emerge clearly from their diaries and our own field notes: the incidence of violence is high, especially since the great increase in brewing and consumption of beer from the 1960s on; most people have unresolved quarrels with others in their village and neighbourhood, though only some people repeatedly pursue their sense of outrage into a formal complaint, and enmities once in place continue. Endemic hostility affects how individuals deal with each other, but others can work around this.

In 1956, Gwembe Valley was somewhat isolated from the rest of Zambia and Zimbabwe, though its men went out as labour migrants, and few outsiders visited the region. Now road transport and wirelesses link Gwembe villages with Zambian urban areas, the district economy is closely tied to the national economic regime, and its people are involved in national political struggles. In 1956 few had attended even primary school; by the late 1970s every village had a number of residents with some secondary schooling; by the 1990s some village youths had gone on to university and had travelled widely. Meantime the solidarity of kinship groups has declined as villagers look to money to supply goods and services once provided for through local exchanges. The penetration of the state became progressively more evident as police and other agents of the national government were stationed in the district. They provide an alternative to suits in the village and local court. Serious crimes, such as homicide, assaults leading to serious injury, and cattle theft, are matters for police investigation and are heard outside the district in a magistrate's court, although villagers may make their own judgements about such matters and either press or refuse to press for conviction.

Despite these changes, matters of dispute among villagers remain strikingly the same. In 1956, people argued about cattle damage to growing crops, land encroachment, inheritance, elopement and impregnation damages, marriage payments and marital difficulties, slander, including implicit accusations of sorcery, theft, physical violence exploding at beer drinks, and the rights of senior people over the labour of younger men and women. All of these matters continue to engage them, although today they are more likely than in 1956 to dispute over matters of debt, and the availability of roads and guns has vastly increased the scale of armed robbery by men associated with town gangs who raid village shops and herds of cattle.

What has changed are the procedures whereby disputes are aired and evaluated in the public forum. In 1956 the chosen forum was usually a neighbourhood moot, in which contenders presented themselves as members of kinship groups which confronted each other, with senior men from each group stating and restating the grounds of contention and what might be an acceptable solution (Colson 1960: 171–6). Those dissatisfied with the moot could summon an opponent in the chief's court, instituted by the colonial administration, but even then they found it expedient to recruit the support of kin, who accompanied them to the court and sat as guarantors of their testimony. In the 1960s moots became less common except where matters that needed discussion were unlikely to lead to much debate. Other matters were heard by village headmen sitting with several elders, with the hearing modelled on the formalities of the chief's court, now called the local court. The members of that court in turn were instructed by officials in the Ministry of Justice, who were trying to develop a unitary court system for the whole of the country. The headman's court used some of the formality of the chief's court, contestants were told to stick to the point and not probe into other aspects of their relationship, and the judgement was on a particular issue. But, as Moore has pointed out for the Chagga (1977: 185), everyone in the village knew all about the matter and had an intimate knowledge of the contestants before they entered the court, since villages usually have 200 and 300 residents of all ages who have numerous kinship links with each other.

It is difficult to explain the preference for the headman's court over the moot except on the assumption that villagers increasingly saw themselves as individuals who ought to be free to act on their own initiative unencumbered by the necessity of recruiting the support of kin. The forced relocation of 1958 undercut the authority of political leaders who were seen as powerless to prevent the move. This affected the willingness to listen to headmen. Village hearings were also affected by the new prevalence of beer brewing, since cases were often heard when all participants had been drinking, formal procedures rarely controlled angry contestants, and hearings often ended in turmoil. Chiefs also lost public support, but they retained their court messengers and the backing of the official hierarchy and could enforce decisions. Those intent on pursuing grievances beyond the first explosion, therefore, usually continued on to the chief's court.

It is interesting that whereas the American legal system in recent years has encouraged contestants to resort to negotiation or arbitration, Gwembe Tonga after long experience with negotiation have shifted to adjudication. Moots were effective arenas, and negotiation worked reasonably well when negotiation took place between assembled lineages rather than the particular parties to the dispute. The system inhibited contestants from pursuing trivial disputes: matters had to be serious before kin support could be recruited. Once the moot opened, the contestants were pressured as much by the decisions of their nominal supporters as they were by the arguments of their adversaries. Negotiation works better when group representatives rather than angry litigants carry the brunt of the argument, and the latter are forced to moderate demands by the willingness of their supporters to compromise. The majority of participants in the moots of the 1950s were present as a duty and had no particular reason to pursue a quarrel to the point where it inconvenienced themselves if they could get some kind of agreement. Recalcitrant principals faced the threat that henceforth their kin refused to be involved.

As Gwembe villagers have increasingly emphasized the right of an individual to make decisions about person and property without the intervention of kindred and have repudiated the old joint obligation for the delicts of their kin, they have turned to the court, to which they come as individuals but which restricts their freedom of action by its own procedures and the threat of the power of the state if they disrupt its formality or refuse to accept decisions. At the same time, however, they are free to bring opponents into court on matters which once would have been seen as too trivial for action, precisely because they need only ask the village clerk for a summons, to which the opponent must respond. Disputes become a means of publicizing minor offences, as well as grievances arising out of real conflicts of interest. This has happened despite the fact that village courts are rarely willing to pronounce the moral judgements once thought to be characteristic of dispute-settlement in local African courts.

Initially, as already noted, they suffered from the disaffection with government associated with the forced resettlement, which affected local politics. People were not at all inhibited about abusing headmen to their faces, even in their courts. In the 1970s and 1980s, when Zambia was a one-party state under the United National Independence Party (UNIP), elected branch and section party leaders replaced the headman with his counsellors as both judicial and administrative functionaries. The courts they held followed models set by the local courts, but the power to enforce decisions came from their position as party officials. Gwembe Tonga in general were opposed to UNIP, but they recognized that it had the power to make things distinctly unpleasant for those who challenged its position. Disrespect to its local branch and section chairmen when these were functioning as party officials could be interpreted as a challenge to the party itself (Habarad 1988). When Zambia shifted to a multiparty state in 1991 and UNIP was defeated in the national election of late 1991, the party ceased to provide a framework for local government and adjudication. Instead the new national government reinstituted a system based on a hierarchy of village, chieftaincy, district, and province, much as in the late colonial period. Headmen once again had jurisdiction at the village level. The office by then was held to be elective, but headmen were usually chosen from the lineage assumed to have the right to provide a headman for the village, and they are men, or the successors of men, who were headmen before the party system began to provide the formal structures of local governance. As a rule they, and the counsellors they select, have less education than many younger members of the village, and of course a longer history of misdeeds. Young educated men and women do not like being subject to uneducated old men, for whom they may have little respect. The Ministry of Justice, however, considers the headman's court to be the court of first hearing; local courts with jurisdiction over all villages in a chieftaincy are staffed with counsellors and clerks who have been through training courses, but they now require litigants to come with letters of referral from a headman's court.

In the early 1990s, therefore, villagers who want a complaint heard have to dispute with one another in the headmen's courts, which are scaled-down versions of local courts. The headman is associated with two counsellors who conduct the hearing, a clerk who records the case, and messengers who summon defendants and keep order. Both plaintiff and defendant pay a hearing fee. They must stand or sit in a fashion which symbolizes submission to the superiority of the court members. When a judgement is handed down, they are told that appeal is possible to the local court. Penalties for particular offences are standardized: so much, say, per head of cattle invading a field before harvest. It is the plaintiff who defines what the case is about in his or her original complaint, registered when the summons is taken out. The court may decide at any stage that there is no case, but it does not redefine the dispute as falling under some other unacceptable category of behaviour, as was true of local courts in the 1950s. The only time the court defines the nature of a case is if it cites someone for failure to show proper respect or for failure to pay a judgement. Either is considered an attack upon the court itself, and so subject to a fine. Fines, along with the hearing fee of the loser, belong to the court, whose officials may use the money to buy beer, with which they regale themselves after the hearing. Since decisions deal only with the merits of a particular claim, a common outcome is a decision that the case is a 'wash-out', either because the court can find no issue that it regards as relevant or because the contestants are unable to produce adequate witnesses. Contestants do not necessarily consider this a failure if the purpose of the suit was finding a forum in which to embarrass an opponent. The headman's court is therefore a place where community values find expression in terms of moral evaluations of contestants, but these are made primarily by the contestants themselves, and have the consequences of embittering their relationships when they are not seen merely as pure rhetoric appropriate to the context.

Contestants may try to induce the court to reprimand their opponents and lecture them on the need to reform, but headmen and counsellors are usually inhibited from doing so. They dispense with lectures. They are adjudicators, not moral exemplars. While court members hold official positions defined as comparable from court to court, they are also ordinary members of the village community, and known all too well in their own persons. Most headmen and counsellors of whom I have record have committed most of the offences for which they might reprimand disputants. They have been guilty of procrastination in meeting their debts, including bridewealth payments and other obligations, and fighting at beer drinks. They have been accused of theft, violence against kin and neighbours, including homicide, slander and sorcery. None of this prevents them from judging the evidence presented, deciding whether the complaint has been substantiated, and announcing the appropriate compensation or fine to be paid.

A Case in Point

The case presented here was chosen because it illustrates many of the points made above, and precisely because it is an instance of someone trying to use the court as a moral forum to deal with 'the trouble' rather than 'the case'. It was heard in 1992 in a headman's court composed of the headman, regarded as ineffectual and alleged to have killed his two predecessors with sorcery, a senior counsellor notorious for fighting who had badly injured his mother in a drunken tantrum, and a second counsellor also with a history of fighting at beer drinks. Both counsellors were classificatory sons of the headman. The court clerk was delinquent in his marriage payments, and two messengers both had outstanding claims against them. In fact, the court was representative of the village men. The court met regularly on a Sunday, and usually heard a number of cases, which might be brought by either men or women.

On this occasion, the plaintiff, a man of fifty-three years, was one of the more prosperous villagers, but also known as someone who never had been able to overlook any threat to his dignity. The defendant was a thirty-five-year-old man, the son of the senior counsellor, who had returned to the village two years earlier after a career in the national police force. He came back to the village only because he was ill, and still wanted very much to return to the police and urban life. Like his father he had a reputation for fighting, and had also shown his contempt for village ways and village elders, whom he thought of as unsophisticated bumpkins. Within the month before the case was heard, he had publicly insulted his father and beaten his mother, sister, and wife. He had also been summoned on this day by the headman's close kinswoman for verbal abuse, but since she failed to appear the case went unheard. Both men were classificatory grandsons of the headman, but kinship links between them are so remote they are never invoked. Before the hearing opened, village opinion had already judged the case: the defendant was guilty of the charge, but the plaintiff should have treated their particular quarrel as trivial.

After the men had deposited their hearing fees there was some discussion as to whether they should be made to sit on the ground or given the dignity of stools. They were given stools, probably because one man was an elder who had held political office, while the other had been in the police. Later this courtesy was pronounced a mistake, since it placed the contestants too much on the same plane with court members; they should have been made to symbolize their submission to the court by sitting on the ground in the normal fashion. The clerk asked the plaintiff to state his case, and he told in detail of how the defendant's ox had come on several evenings to his cattle pen, that this had worried him because he might be held liable if something happened to it, and that he had protested to the defendant, who came for it one evening, about the propriety of allowing cattle to roam like this. The defendant responded with strong abuse (*kutukila*) and called him an ignoramus. He, the plaintiff, had therefore summoned the defendant, because it is wrong for a young man to abuse an elder in this fashion, and the court should reprimand him before he caused more problems. The defendant was then asked to speak. He admitted being at the plaintiff's homestead, but insisted that he had responded appropriately, telling the plaintiff that it was natural for his ox to go after the plaintiff's cows since men follow after women, cocks after hens, and oxen after cows. Thereafter, he said, the plaintiff had used words of abuse towards him and told him that he stank because of illness.

After a long silence, the clerk asked for witnesses. The defendant named his father, the senior counsellor, and this was noted by the clerk. The plaintiff named his three wives and an elder distantly related to himself. They were told to return with their witnesses at the next session of the court one week later. As this was being sorted out, the defendant tried to interrupt and was told to keep quiet when others were speaking. At this he began to shout abuse at the court for taking a nonsense case: he had already spoken to the plaintiff's chief witness, who said he knew nothing of the matter. Thus, since he was not here, the case should be dismissed. In any event the court was no court; he from his police experience knew all about courts and this was nothing like the magistrates' courts with which he was familiar. The court told him again to be quiet and ruled that the case was recessed until the following Sunday. The defendant left shouting insults. The plaintiff smiled happily and commented, 'You see!'

One week later, with the witness elder still refusing to attend, the court dismissed the case on the grounds that the plaintiff's wives and the defendant's father were biased witnesses. Each man was made to pay a small fine and told to live in peace. The fine, of course, was a symbolic statement of disapproval. The plaintiff was thought to have been intemperate in pursuing a case of verbal abuse, while the younger man was recognized as having behaved badly. But the court did not attempt to justify the fines on these grounds, nor did it expect the men to live in peace. The plaintiff, however, had rather effectively warned the defendant off from further visiting his homestead. He also saw himself as fully compensated for his investment in the case when he was able to inform the headman that the court had been wrong in dismissing the matter; already the defendant had beaten an elder in the next village whom he had heard commenting regretfully on recent wife-beatings when he thought that his own recent behaviour was under comment.

Conclusion

Negotiation and adjudication can settle particular claims, because moots and courts have the means to persuade contenders to accept a verdict, whether this is an agreement reached through bargaining in the moot or laid down by a court. They have much less success in convincing contenders that they are in the wrong, and they do little or nothing to heal ruptured social relationships or abate anger and contempt. The hearing, in fact, formulates and publicly states discontents which may previously have been latent. However much disputes and their settlement are conducted in a rhetoric of community values appealing to something like *communitas*, what people learn from them is much more pragmatic information: the limits of community tolerance for different kinds of behaviour under a variety of circumstances, an appreciation of how particular individuals respond to provocation, and some mapping of the changing alliances that form the basis for daily interaction.

Acknowledgements

Field research has been supported by the Rhodes-Livingstone Institute, and its successor the Institute for African Studies, University of Zambia; the Social Science Research Council; the National Science Foundation, and the John Guggenheim Foundation.

References

Colson, Elizabeth (1953). 'Social Control and Vengeance in Plateau Tonga Society', *Africa*, 23(3): 199–212

Colson, Elizabeth (1960). *The Social Organization of the Gwembe Tonga*. Manchester: Manchester University Press

Colson, Elizabeth (1974). *Tradition and Contract: The Problem of Order*. New York: Aldine

Colson, Elizabeth (1976). 'From Chief's Court to Local Court', in *Freedom and Constraint* ed. Myron Aronoff, pp.15–29. Amsterdam: Van Gorcum

Fallers, Lloyd (1977). 'Administration and the Supremacy of Law in Colonial Busoga', in *Social Anthropology and Law*, ed. Ian Hamnett, pp. 53–76. London: Academic Press

Gluckman, Max (1955–6). 'The Reasonable Man in Barotse Law', *Journal of African Administration* 7: 51–5, 127–31; 8– 101–5, 151–6

Gluckman, Max (1955a). *The Judicial Process among the Barotse of Northern Rhodesia*. Manchester: Manchester University Press

Gluckman, Max (1955b). *Custom and Conflict in Africa*. Oxford: Basil Blackwell

Gluckman, Max (1967). *The Judicial Process among the Barotse of Northern Rhodesia*, 2nd edn. Manchester: Manchester University Press

Greenhouse, Carol (1989). 'Interpreting American Litigiousness', in *History and Power in the Study of Law: New Directions in Legal Anthropology*, ed. June Starr and Jane F. Collier. Ithaca: Cornell University Press

Gulliver, Philip H. (1955). *The Family Herds*. London: Routledge & Kegan Paul

Gulliver, Philip H. (1963). *Social Control in an African Society*. London: Routledge & Kegan Paul

Gulliver, Philip H. (1971). *Neighbours and Networks: The Idiom of Kinship in Social Action among the Ndendeuli of Tanzania*. Berkeley, CA: University of California Press

Gulliver, Philip H. (1975). 'Nomadic Movements: Causes and Implications', in *Pastoralism in Tropical Africa*, ed. Theodore Monad, pp. 369–86. London: Oxford University Press

Gulliver, Philip H. (1979). *Disputes and Negotiations: A Cross-Cultural Perspective*. New York: Academic Press

Habarad, Jonathan (1988). 'Neighbourhood and Nation among the Tonga of Gwembe Valley, Zambia', Unpublished paper presented at the annual meeting of the American Association of African Studies

Kopytoff, Igor (1980). 'Revitalization and the Genesis of Cults in Pragmatic Religion: The Kita Rite of Passage among the Suku', in *Explorations in African Systems of Thought*, eds Ivan Karp and Charles Bird, pp. 183–212. Bloomington, Indiana: Indiana University Press

Moore, Sally Falk (1977). 'Individual Interests and Organisational Structures: Dispute Settlements as "Events of Articulation"', in *Social Anthropology and the Law*, ed. Ian Hamnett, pp. 159–88. London: Academic Press

Nader, Laura (1990). *Harmony Ideology: Justice and Control in a Zapotec Mountain Village*. Stanford: Stanford University Press

Nader, Laura and Todd, Harry (1978). 'Introduction' in *The Disputing Process: Law in Ten Societies*, eds Laura Nader and Harry Todd, pp. 1–40. New York: Columbia University Press

Scudder, Thayer (1983). 'Economic Downturn and Community Unraveling: The Gwembe Tonga Revisited', *Culture and Agriculture*, 18: 16–9

Scudder, Thayer (1984). 'Economic Downturn and Community Unraveling, Revisited', *Culture and Agriculture*, 23: 6–10

Scudder, Thayer and Colson, Elizabeth (1979). 'Long-Term Research in Gwembe Valley, Zambia', in *Long-Term Field Research in Social Anthropology*, eds George Foster et al., pp. 227–54. New York: Academic Press

Starr, June and Collier, Jane (1989). 'Introduction: Dialogues in Legal Anthropology', in *History and Power in the Study of Law: New Directions in Legal Anthropology*, eds June Starr and Jane Collier, pp. 1–28. Ithaca, NY: Cornell University Press

Turner, Victor (1969). *The Ritual Process: Structure and Anti-Structure.* Chicago: Aldine Publishing Company

Chapter 5

Gentlemanly Values: Contesting Corruption Accusations in the Cities of London and Lagos in the mid-1950s

Christina Johnson

In this chapter I seek to contribute to our understanding of the ideological character of the relationship between power and knowledge. I shall explore its development in a colonial milieu, as the sun was setting on Empire, in relation to standards of public behaviour upheld in the metropole. I shall touch on its capacity to structure the field of action of others.

My objective is to analyze concepts of public morality embedded in the rules of procedure of Tribunals of Inquiry held in Lagos and in London. The Crown appointed Sir Hylton Foster-Sutton, QC, to preside over a quasi-judicial Tribunal of Inquiry (1956) in Lagos to investigate allegations that Dr Nnamdi Azikiwe, Premier of Eastern Nigeria, had behaved corruptly. In the following year the Crown appointed Chief Justice Hubert Lister-Parker, QC, to investigate accusations that part-time directors of the Bank of England had used inside knowledge of the forthcoming rise in Bank Rate to advantage their private banks.

I show how a gentlemanly code of public morality constituted an ideology, a ruling class's (moral) theory of power as it should be practised, and so I consider some ways in which this code informed procedures to test the accused's credibility, the accuracy and veracity of his evidence, and thus shaped judgements regarding those deemed to have abused ('corrupted') the norm. In both cases the Tribunals' official objective was to establish whether servants of the Crown, men of public affairs, had misused inside knowledge of government decision-making 'for the purpose of private gain' (Nigeria 1957a: 4). In both locations concepts embodying ruling views of society, of persons, and of the exercise of power pertinent to society exercised a structuring effect on Tribunal discourse.

Tribunals constitute a delimited space, a forum, within whose walls unfold in miniature the conflicts of the macrocosm; they are 'concerned with relative power and the struggle to control scarce resources' (Gulliver 1979: 270–1). Here I shall show how, *pace* Gluckman (1955: 35), in the microcosm accuser and accused 'work' with words; using the English language, some struggle to uphold, others battle to change the 'agreed' meanings of key concepts (i.e. 'truth', 'honest man', 'self-interest', 'fairness') that constitute Tribunal discourse and rules of procedure in the colony and the metropole.

In this chapter I also reveal some ways in which a ruling élite deployed gentlemanly values both to uphold its pre-eminence in the City of London, the British Empire's financial nerve centre, and in addition to construct 'black Englishmen' supportive of British influence in the developing modern states and capitalist economies of Africa. In effect, at this macro-level, gentlemanly norms authorized financial and political practices intended to uphold a gentlemanly élite's dominance at home and overseas.

The State and 'Public Man'

In Western political thought the modern State is an institutionalized *public* order exercising impersonal sovereign power (Held 1983: 1). Its emergence in the pre-industrial and industrial eras has been closely linked to capital accumulation and the rise of class society on the back of empires (Anderson 1974; Wallerstein 1979). In Britain modernizing, mercantile elements emerged who claimed they represented a greater national identity, and so they struggled long to democratize State power and render it more accountable than hitherto. Historic compromises eventually resulted in measures intended to uphold the political norm that men engaged on State duties must subordinate private (pecuniary) interest to the greater, national good. This century gentlemanly élites holding – indeed, often inheriting – positions of power in government, the City, the Army and the Church of

England moulded themselves in 'public man's' (*sic*) image. Thus men of affairs accused of using their public position to their private advantage are called 'corrupt', not only because they may be shown to have flouted the rule, but because dereliction of duty reveals 'public man' to be something of a myth, part of an ideology that actually serves the interests of a ruling minority. Widespread belief in allegations of corruption subverts the principle that the State serves the public good. Gentlemanly values portray 'public man's' exercise of power as just, and therefore synonymous with the greater, national interest. In this view the proper exercise of public power is synonymous with the public good.

Some academics seem to have accepted English gentlemen's word that their exercise of power promotes the national interest. These writers concur with the gentlemen rulers that British public institutions were cleaned up earlier this century, and distance current conditions from the 'old corruption' of the English landed aristocracy (cf. Wraith and Simpkins 1963). On the other hand, some scholars like to emphasize the distinctiveness of African corruption, with its bases in strong vertical ties between patrons and clients often divided by economic class but of the same ethnic, religious and home community. In the absence of an impersonal, impartial State, patrons are obliged to deliver the tangible rewards of office to their constituencies (Ward 1989: 1). And so some European writers incline to 'the brutal truth ... that African corruption is home-grown' (Isaac 1987: 10). This kind of power is said to be synonymous with patronage, with selfish (ungentlemanly) behaviour that subverts the greater, national interest. It is as if Africans alone have a deep predilection for corruption, in the past and the present; as if external Western concepts and practices of corruption – long in the making, simultaneously shaping and shaped by capital accumulation – have played little or no part in State formation in Africa.

In actual fact, since the 'reforming' 1880s, periodic allegations that distinguished men of affairs have behaved 'improperly' have pushed British governments to pass legislation which sought to restrict the direct misappropriation of public funds (i.e. embezzlement, see GB 1949: 1) and to restrain the indirect acquisition of pecuniary advantage through insider dealing (*Chambers Encyclopaedia* 1950: 246). This anti-corrupt-practices legislation was also applied in far-flung outposts of Empire by the colonial administration against 'corrupt' African civil servants, and sometimes indeed against its own British employees (Lugard 1906; Lawal 1986: 6–15). I argue that rules of procedure instituted under this legislation, especially the Rules of Evidence (1921) Act, reflected gentlemanly norms of 'public man' that advocates applied when questioning witnesses and assessing evidence. Tribunals of Inquiry into allegations of corruption, both at home in the City of London and in the colonies, thus defined 'the truth' and how to find 'it' in terms of their own gentlemanly values and practices.

Two Tribunals in the 1950s

In this chapter I examine the voluminous Bank Rate Tribunal Proceedings to show some of the ways in which taken-for-granted and so barely elaborated notions of 'public man' utilized during the Tribunal's hearings in London (1957) contrast with more explicitly formulated definitions voiced during marathon sessions before the Foster-Sutton Tribunal in Lagos a year earlier (1956). In London, for example, witnesses and counsel were in such close agreement about 'public man' that his attributes tended to be taken for granted in spite of the fact that witnesses' evidence reveals a number of ways in which they had deployed the 'old boy' network, utilizing ties of marriage and kinship, club membership and other informal sources of solidarity to circumscribe the field of decision-making of others in the Bank of England and the Cabinet. Overseas, in the Nigerian city of Lagos, Tribunal counsel (British and Nigerian) applied the same rules of procedure, but asked witnesses very specific questions so as to establish whether they had in fact behaved as gentlemen of public affairs. Counsel compelled witnesses to demonstrate that they were indeed 'black Englishmen'.

In both instances, the Tribunals exercised structural power within the formal context of quasi-judicial hearings. Thus gentlemanly notions concerning the characteristic conduct of 'corrupt man', on the one hand, and virtuous 'public man' on the other, inhered in the concepts which made up the legal rules. Tactical power consisted in manipulating the ambiguity of certain concepts so as to demonstrate that one was speaking 'the truth', and that one's accusers were not (Gluckman 1955: 57). Quasi-judicial procedures thus played a part in structuring ideological and political relations between British élites and their Nigerian counterparts.

City and Empire

Major changes in the structure and functioning of the British State, in the sheer weight of the State's financial contribution to the economy, and to popular perceptions of 'proper' relations between 'public' and 'private' domains occurred in the aftermath of the Second World War. The Labour Government under Prime Minister Attlee (1945–51) nationalized the Bank of England (1946) in order to obtain greater control over the country's financial decision-making, but it remained closely linked to and influenced by City of London merchant banks (Hanham 1959: 21). In the mid-fifties the Bank's Court of Directors and certain City finance houses continued to recruit from south-eastern and Lowland Scots families educated at Eton and Oxbridge, and with a strong record of military service for King and country in at least one, and often two, World Wars.[1]

Senior City men and Conservative Party officials linked greatly increased State expenditure, sluggish manufacturing productivity, high wage costs and rising inflation rates to external pressure on sterling and a steadily weakening pound (Mathews, Feinstein and Odling-Smee 1982). August 1957 saw a sharp rise in rates of currency and deposit withdrawals, and a continuing decline in Britain's gold reserves (GB 1958a: 10638). This was serious, because member countries of the sterling area fixed their currencies in relation to the pound, and held some or all their reserves in sterling (Cain and Hopkins 1993: 76–82). Manufacturing industry's painfully slow growth and inability to increase the volume and value of exports so as to offset spiralling import costs added to inflation pressures. City men also noted in early 1957 that currency instability and a general lack of confidence in sterling, together with low interest rates, was promoting more interest among buyers of gilt-edged stocks.[2]

In August 1957 pressure on the pound, aided and abetted by yet another devaluation of the French franc (*The Times* 20.9.1957: 7), and on Britain's gold reserves had increased so greatly that fears were raised of a major collapse of confidence not only in sterling but also in gold (*The Times* 19.9.1957: 10; 3.10.1957: 10). In late 1957 'worst case' scenarios were seemingly confirmed when the German bank rate was cut from 4.5 per cent to 4.0 per cent on 18 September 1957, while the British bank rate remained at 5.0 per cent. In early September the pound fell to a new all-time low against German and dollar currencies. As one patrician banker later informed the Bank Rate Tribunal, bankers in North America were very worried indeed 'that the whole faith in this country was disappearing ... and it was a critical situation' (GB 1958a: 7343). There were 'ugly rumours of devaluation'. At such times it was important that finance houses 'keep liquid' and, if in possession of gilt-edged securities, sell them (GB 1958a: 3850). Long-term gilts had become a risky investment, because they tied up capital at unchanging rates of return at a time when markets were becoming more volatile and major European traders (France, Germany, Belgium) were raising and lowering interest rates. In Britain City merchant and clearing bankers advocated a renewed credit squeeze, tighter control over government expenditure, 'other measures to fortify the pound' (Proc. 1958: 2), and abandonment of the current policy of 'funding by stealth' to counter market pressures forcing downwards gilt-edged values (*The Times* 2.7.1957: 9). Some, like the Lord Kindersley – Chairman both of the merchant bank, Lazard Bros. and of the country's most venerable insurance company, the Royal Exchange Assurance, a director of the British Match Corporation and also a part-time director of the Bank of England who was related by marriage and by blood to some of the country's leading political families (Lupton and Shirley Wilson 1959: 40–2) – secretly lobbied the Deputy Governor of the Bank of England to raise the Bank Rate. He saw this as quite proper for, as any gentleman might, he assumed that his beliefs about the parlous state of the pound were identical with the national interest. He told the Bank's Deputy Governor 'very forcefully that Bank Rate had got to be raised and raised properly' (GB 1958a: 7392).

Pressure on sterling deposits also emanated from a new quarter, the British colonies of West Africa, whose English-speaking, urban-dwelling élites were demanding the right to withdraw Marketing Board deposits in London to fund economic growth and public investment in indigenous banks. Nigerian nationalists led by Dr Nnamdi Azikiwe were especially assertive on this point. In their view the British (Barclays, Westminster) and South

African (Standard Chartered) clearing banks, which controlled the Bank of British West Africa, pursued profits to the benefit of Britain and so held back Nigeria's progress.

However, calls for tighter money would mean higher interest rates, and these, it was expected, would effect a depreciation in the price of gilts (GB 1958a: 1811). When the Bank Rate was raised on 20 September to 7 per cent it was at its highest since 1921 (*The Times* 20.9.1957).

It was subsequently alleged that several men in the public eye, including the afore-mentioned Lord Kindersley, had 'improperly disclosed' the decision by the Bank, Treasury and Cabinet to raise the Bank rate from 5 per cent to 7 per cent to 'maintain the internal and external value of the pound', and had used inside knowledge 'for the purpose of private gain' (GB l958b: 9). The Home Secretary R. A. Butler appointed Lord Justice Sir Hubert Lister-Parker to be Chairman of a Tribunal to investigate allegations of improper disclosure of inside information for private gain.

'Public' and 'Private'

It is plain from the Tribunal Proceedings that gentlemanly values in the 'square mile's' most respected merchant banks hinged on 'character'.[3] Thus the principal founder of Morgan-Grenfell, a merchant bank with which some leading witnesses before Bank Rate Tribunal were closely associated as shareholders and directors/chairmen, had insisted that 'for a private banker, an unsullied reputation for plain dealing is the only guarantee of continued prosperity'. In those days 'The integrity of the partners was unquestioned' (Hobson 1990: 91). Furthermore, men who held important positions in the Conservative Party, in Cabinet or the City usually enjoyed private means, and so, it was believed, could be relied upon to place public service before pecuniary gain, and to influence the Court of Directors of the Bank of England from a disinterested position. Thus at that time, in the 1930s–1950s, gentlemen bankers believed that 'the paramountcy of the reputation of the house over personal enrichment was beyond question' (Hobson 1990: 1–2, 79–80).

Indeed the Attorney-General, Sir Reginald Manningham-Buller, the Crown's senior counsel, seemingly still believed in this dictum so completely that before hearings commenced he declared in his opening statement that there was absolutely no evidence to support the allegation that a leading player 'had improperly disclosed information given to him in the course of carrying out his political and financial duties' (GB 1958a: 1231). In fact all persons suspected of such disclosures – by however small a hint – claimed they were innocent of such improper behaviour on the grounds that they did not discuss business matters in the company of non-privileged others, even when they were admittedly hard at work analysing sterling's current malaise and lobbying for more effective action to 'fortify the pound' (GB 1958a: 1550, 1770). Reluctantly, perhaps fearful that 'the truth' would come out that they had indeed discussed possible rises in Bank Rate, witnesses insisted they had engaged in no more than 'loose conversations' about sterling's problems. Lord Kindersley, for example, had had several such conversations with partners and friends – some were seen by eagle-eyed City journalists 'taking coffee together in the Pall Mall clubs', possibly the Reform Club (GB 1958a: 649; 6051, p. 158). And Lord Kindersley did admit he had discussed the Bank Rate with the Deputy Governor and Governor of the Bank of England as they rode in chauffeur-driven cars to and from the City.

Denials of improper disclosure focused on gilt-edged sales by three companies – Lazard Bros., the Royal Exchange Assurance and Jardine-Matheson – which rumour alleged had used advance information of the decision to raise Bank Rate in order to profit by engaging in massive sales. The Royal Exchange Assurance's investment adviser admitted 'I cannot recall any sale of gilt-edgeds in a single day which accounted to so high a nominal figure', for on 17 and 18 September upwards of £10 million sales were made on the Stock Exchange. Witnesses representing these companies admitted they or their partners had authorized the sale, but invariably they maintained that 'It was a coincidence as opposed to consultation' that Lazard and the Royal Exchange sold gilts so heavily on 17 and 18 September (GB 1958a: 6874); that is, they asserted that no one had planned intentionally to make a profit prior to the Bank Rate's being raised. Actually, Lazard and Co. sold over £1 million worth, a very large amount indeed at that time, representing no less than half their gilt-edged holdings. But Lazard's Chairman and Managing Director, Lord Kindersley, maintained that 'he only learnt of the sales after they had been made', because it was another partner with responsibilities for gilt sales who had dealt with the matter. His partners conceded later that they assumed he had known, but they had refrained from asking him openly to avoid 'embarrassing' him (GB 1958a: 6057). When asked by the Attorney-General what he would say if asked by a partner 'Shall we sell gilts?' the second Baron Kindersley responded that 'a man in that position ... has got to try and give a view which he would have held if he did not have the secret information'. 'He has got to try and divorce himself from that knowledge?' 'Yes' (GB 1958a: 2771; 4777). Helpful as ever to his eminent witnesses – he was after all a fellow-Etonian, Oxbridge-educated, and a member of some of the most exclusive Pall Mall clubs – the Attorney-General asked Kindersley 'Do you allow the knowledge you have in your mind to influence a business decision?' (GB 1958a: 7551–2). The latter replied that not to do so was the 'ideal' at which he aimed; he had only found 'Secret knowledge, conflicting or making it difficult ... in other business interests' on about ten to twelve occasions while a director of the Bank of England (GB 1958a: 7567); and always, as an ex-officer in the Scots Guards, who had fought with great distinction and gallantry in two World Wars, he was motivated to fight for 'British interests'.

Possibly these gentlemen financiers sincerely believed that they did successfully distance their private pecuniary interests from information imparted to them in the course of their public duties as directors of the Bank of England. After all, they held dear such principles as that 'all seven partners [of Lazard Bros.] have absolute confidence in each other', so that decisions were usually 'arrived at in principle' and frequently not minuted (GB 1958a: 7328). Notionally, each partner assumed responsibility for his own area of decision-making, based on expert knowledge of a specific financial function, and so separated himself from the decisions of the others. Likewise, said Lord Kindersley, 'It is an unwritten law in Lazard – it has been ever since I have been a Director of the Bank of England and for the 32 years my father was – that you do not talk about that kind of thing with the person dealing with it' (GB 1958a: 7549).[4]

William Keswick, a leading member of the wealthy Dumfries family and Managing Director of the profitable Hong Kong-based family company of Jardine-Matheson and a director of its London affiliate, Matheson and Company, had also ordered the sale of large amounts of the company's gilt-edged stocks. Before this decision, Keswick had travelled 'up' to Dumfries to join one of his two brothers at a 'special grouse drive which had been a feature of our lives every year' (GB 1958a: 3966). The party had included Nigel Birch, the Economic Secretary to the Treasury. But Keswick maintained 'we try as much as we can not to deal with business matters' (GB 1958a: 4249). The Attorney-General was ostentatiously eager to display his knowledge of grouse-shooting practices, referring in his questions to 'butts', 'drives', 'counting the bag' and other customs (GB 1958a: 3545). William Keswick made amends for his brother's reluctance to talk other than in ambiguous terms by confirming that 'while we were counting the bag', he and his brother (also a director of Matheson and Co.) actually had discussed 'the squeeze' and how it might be tightened by increasing the Bank Rate (GB 1958a: 3548). He said that they had decided in between drives, while at their butts, to recommend that they off-load all their company's gilts, though as a British company they should support British bonds and the pound (GB 1958a: 3813, 4001). Thus they felt that the 'old boy' network in the City helped busy men to take decisions quickly and in confidence (Cohen 1974: xxiii). Later they could 'consult' the relevant committee or board.

This informal decision-making throws an interesting light on several witnesses' claims that decisions to sell gilts 'emerged', almost without words, on account of long familiarity with the situation. As William Keswick said of his company's decision to off-load large amounts of gilts on 18 September, 'we drifted to the decision' (GB 1958a: 4342). Each man informed the Tribunal that he could read his brother's/partner's mind, so extended discussions were unnecessary. Lazard Bros. did not keep formal minutes of meetings, because they knew one another so well and trusted one another; people carried 'a great deal in their head and memory' (GB 1958a: 3692, 5294). A Lazard partner, with a notable mixture of metaphors, said 'One plays this tune according to ear and if you think the waves are running high you tend to want to get liquid' (GB 1958a: 6916).[5] Another Lazard man explained that he did not do research into figures because 'one felt what was going on' (GB 1958a: 5920–1). A third partner stressed how much he hated looking at 'deposits and liquidity figures' (GB 1958a: 5541). Witnesses were reluctant to quantify in detail their decision to sell gilts in the two days before Bank Rate was raised.

A gentlemanly sense of making important decisions by semiconscious processes, at work and at play, may explain why partners emphasized the need to separate their role in Lazards' financial decision-making from that of their Chairman. Lord Kindersley was placed in a delicate position on account of his position as a director of the Bank of England. Partners then sought to place a fence, as it were, between Lord Kindersley's knowledge obtained through his position as a Bank of England director and the information he used in financial decision-making at Lazard Bros. They did so by refraining from asking him 'embarrassing' questions.

Certainly dereliction of duty in this respect was hidden from public view behind the veil of secrecy imposed on Club members by the 'rule' that no member can mention a fellow member's name outside Club portals without his express permission. Thus, information that a government announcement on the Bank Rate was expected 'was given in a club', so 'it is obviously not possible to mention the person's name without his consent' (GB 1958a: 1916). Indeed, the Tribunal Chairman (Sir H. Lester-Parker, QC) agreed with a distinguished witness, Sir John Braithwaite, Chairman of the Stock Exchange 'I know it is *distasteful* to mention names' (GB 1958a: 1861; my italics). The witness did not deny the happening, but refused to cite the announcer's name.

The Attorney-General found that there was no direct evidence to support the belief, widespread in City, political and Club circles, that Lord Kindersley did use his secret knowledge for the benefit of Lazard Bros. and other companies he chaired. Rather, Lord Kindersley had 'conducted himself with complete honesty and propriety during a period when he might at any moment have been placed in an *embarrassing* position' (GB 1958b: 20; my italics).

Had the Tribunal's hidden agenda, then, been to carry out a whitewashing job? Reviewing the evidence before him the Chairman had found that the principal witnesses had demonstrated 'complete propriety and honesty' (*The Times* 22.1.1958: 8); Lord Kindersley and others had shown they had not used confidential knowledge gained in the course of public duty to their own or their companies' private financial advantage. The Chairman therefore concluded that he hoped the Tribunal's findings would work 'not only to maintain, but actually to enhance, the reputation of London for financial integrity' and thus 'the national interest'(GB 1958b: 39).

Lupton and Shirley Wilson's (1959: 32 ff.) data indicate that 70 per cent of Ministers in the Tory government, as well as of senior civil servants, had been to Oxbridge, as had 50 per cent of Directors of the Bank of England. The 1957 Tribunal Proceedings (GB 1958a) revealed that several leading players belonged to leading banking and landed families: ties of kinship and affinity pertaining to the private sphere were reflected in multiple directorships in the public sphere. Their companies had sold shares before the change in Bank Rate: had they thus misused their inner knowledge of government and Bank of England decision-making to make a private windfall? The Tribunal decided that, though they were placed in an extremely awkward position, nothing improper had occurred (GB 1958b: 16; 39).

Upholding the Line on the Periphery: The Foster-Sutton Tribunal

A year earlier, the Premier of Eastern Nigeria had been accused by highly placed men of depositing public funds in the African Continental Bank (known as 'Zik's Bank'), in which he and his family had controlling interests. It was alleged he had advantaged himself, his friends and family. Responding to persistent pressure to establish 'the truth', in August 1956 the Secretary of State for the Colonies, Alan Lennox-Boyd, appointed a Tribunal of Inquiry of four distinguished men (only one of whom was Nigerian), chaired by the Chief Justice of the Federation of Nigeria, Sir Stafford Foster-Sutton. They were to abide by precedent and hold hearings in the English language, open to the public in Lagos. Their terms of reference were to investigate allegations that Dr Azikiwe's conduct had been impugned, both as a private individual and a public person of high standing, through 'abuse of office and corruption in connection with the deposit and investment of public monies of the Eastern Region in the African Continental Bank in which Dr. Azikiwe had a substantial pecuniary interest' (Nigeria 1957b: 1). They were to determine 'the truth'. A key question was: 'Has Dr. Azikiwe, with a motive of personally enriching himself ... used his power or influence knowingly to bring about that end?' (Nigeria 1957a: 966).

At this period, Nigerian nationalists were pushing the British into constitutional preparations for a transfer of political power to a democratically elected government in 1960. Part of the build-up to independence included more rapid economic growth, which the new political élites wanted to pay for with funds that had been saved by the cocoa, palm oil and groundnut marketing boards. The southern nationalist parties sought to make credit available to entrepreneurs for commercial ventures, to farmers eager to expand into cash-crop production, to would-be manufacturers of, for example, clothing, soft drinks, white bread and other urban 'luxuries' of the time. Influenced by Keynesian policies of state intervention to secure economic growth, they wanted to achieve a 'New Deal' in Nigeria by creating statutory corporations to implement industrialization. As Azikiwe informed the Tribunal, his party, the National Convention of Nigeria and Cameroon, wished to appoint party men who would implement party policy (Nigeria 1957a: 800; 21553). But they could do little to implement these grand designs without substantial funding.

They were blocked by the British banks – the British Bank of West Africa (BBWA) and Barclays D C and O – which dominated the Nigerian financial system. Some witnesses said the expatriate banks served 'the selfish interests of ... shareholders' through international trade and 'refused to lend to the African' (Nigeria 1957a: 841; 22374). Furthermore, as Azikiwe argued before the Tribunal, he and other nationalists knew that these funds were held in the UK to the advantage of the British balance of payments. He questioned the 'public morality' of the ex-Minister of State for the Colonies, Lord Harlech, a director of BBWA, as well as that of other high-ranking men of state (i.e. the Rt. Hon. Heathcote-Amory, the Minister of Agriculture; the Prime Minister, the Rt. Hon. Anthony Eden; and the Marquess of Salisbury), who journalists claimed were directors of two of the 'big' four banks which owned the BBWA (*Daily Times* 9.08.56: 9; Nigeria 1957a: 841; 22374–380). These men and others like them were among 'the Molochs of Great Britain' declared Azikiwe; they were influencing friends in the Colonial office who had allegedly instructed the Governor of the Eastern Region to eschew developing indigenous banking in order to protect the BBWA as a 'depository of government funds, from which source it earns the bulk of its profit' (*Daily Times* 21.07.56: 1). Azikiwe and his ministers wished to 'repatriate' these monies and use them to develop indigenous banks, so they could do for the Nigerian entrepreneur 'what expatriate banks would hesitate to do' (Nigeria 1957a: 13; 761; 20761).

Before this the Action Group (AG) had pressed for, and had obtained control of, some £2 million of the £16 million belonging to the former Cocoa Marketing Board. The AG deposited this £2 million in the Western Region-based National Bank, established in 1933, to increase its liquidity–deposit ratio and to make credit available to entrepreneurs (Azikiwe 1961: 209–10). The Eastern Region had no such similar national bank. However, it did produce palm oil and kernels, and was due to 'inherit' some £8 million from the Palm Oil Marketing Board. The Eastern Region government wished to use some of this money to develop a national bank, and decided to fund 'Zik's bank', the African Continental Bank, albeit covertly, because it was still a private bank. Under this plan they would fund the bank with public monies drawn from the Marketing Board and parked temporarily in an 'independent' body, the newly established Finance Corporation. In early 1955 the Corporation duly received over £2 million from the Marketing Board, and was thus empowered to challenge the 'virtual monopoly created by two leading (expatriate) banks'.

Dr Azikiwe was accused of abusing the 'trust' placed in him by the Eastern Region Governor, a theme taken up vociferously by rival nationalists as 'a prima facie breach of trust ... regarding the transfer of £2 million' to Zik's bank (*The Times* 21.8.56: 8). Critics said Dr Azikiwe and his Minister of Finance had broken 'a gentleman's agreement' to the effect that no funds should be transferred until 'after consultation with, and with the approval of, Executive Council' (Nigeria 1957b: 38).

It was thus alleged that Azikiwe had allowed his private pecuniary interests to corrupt, even destroy, his public duty as a man of state to protect public funds. The Secretary of State for the Colonies had informed Dr Azikiwe when they had met in London in November 1955 that in Britain it would be 'quite unthinkable ... for a bank set up by a Chief Minister to receive £1 million from public funds to keep it solvent' (Nigeria 1957b: 159). In late 1956 the Eastern Region Governor Sir Clement Pleass – when described by Azikiwe as 'obdurate and old-fashioned' – had persuaded the Colonial Secretary of State, Alan Lennox-Boyd, to appoint the Foster-Sutton Tribunal to 'ascertain the truth' about the allegations (Report 1957: 207). The Tribunal was to determine whether 'any persons holding ministerial office or other public office has infringed the standards of conduct demanded of the holder of such office' (Nigeria 1957a: 1).

In his defence Dr Azikiwe argued that these allegations were a smokescreen by British imperialists working in the interests of the British Bank of West Africa – owned by four clearing banks – i.e. Lloyds, Westminster, National Provincial and the Standard Bank of South Africa – which was fighting secretly to maintain its monopoly hold over banking in Nigeria (Nigeria 1957a: 22218). According to Dr Azikiwe not only had [British] overseas banks 'usually restricted credit facilities among Africans' (Nigeria 1957a: 13), but they had appointed to their Boards former governors and secretaries of state for the colonies (Nigeria 1956: 4–7). Azikiwe and his followers believed the real issue was 'a struggle between British imperialism and Nigerian nationalism' (*The Times* 21.8.56: 8). As he had said so pointedly, the struggle for real independence against British monopolies 'was being conducted under the pretence of *public* morality' and his presumed *private* immorality, through the colonial government's appointment of a Tribunal of Inquiry into allegations of corrupt practices on his part (*The Times* 28.7.1956: 6; my italics). Furthermore, he maintained, by acquiescing in these proceedings, the nationalist movement had allowed the British to impose the gentlemanly ideology, that a political struggle was really all about a 'public man's' alleged private immorality.

The 'Honest' Man

Foster-Sutton abided by precedent in advising the Tribunal he chaired that as 'this is an Inquiry, and not in any sense a trial, witnesses will be the witnesses of the tribunal and not of any interest or person ... There is no plaintiff, and no defendant, no prosecutor, no accused. You are a fact-finding tribunal' whose proceedings are open to the public (Nigeria 1957a: iv). A Tribunal of Inquiry could not impose criminal penalties, but it could recommend that a person found to have committed 'improper conduct' – i.e. a Minister of the Crown who failed to relinquish his private financial interests on assuming office – be excluded from holding office.

Tribunal Chairman and Counsel alike reiterated throughout the fifty-day-long Inquiry in Lagos the importance of witnesses telling 'the truth' to the Tribunal, of being honest, of demonstrating that they had unequivocally put public duty before private interest in their role as men of state. Sir Stafford Foster-Sutton (Chairman) and senior expatriate Counsel expected distinguished Nigerian witnesses to *prove* they were telling the truth. In the words of a senior silk addressing the Premier of Eastern Nigeria, it was counsels' duty in cross-examination 'to test the credibility of your evidence ... its accuracy and its veracity' (Nigeria 1957a: 836). He asked 'Dr. Azikiwe, it is right is it not, that you, at the outset of your Ministerial career, and through it have set a very high standard of conduct in relation to such matters as corruption or conflict of private interest in public duty ... Would you not be anxious to be judged by those same high standards?' The witness replied 'That is why I submit myself to this Tribunal' (Nigeria 1957a: 22215).

One low-ranking witness, Dr Azikiwe's assistant, one Nwosisi, complained to the Chairman, Foster-Sutton, about [white] Counsel, 'who's rude to me. I wouldn't have it, he is too rude ...'. Later in response to another apparently insulting question, Nwosisi retorted 'I am surprised you ask me such a question. Do you think I am a child to tell lies here? I do not come here to tell lies ...' (Nigeria l957a: 448; 11752). The *coup de grâce*, perhaps, was administered by Dr Azikiwe, who replied thus to Counsel's twice-put question as to whether he was 'telling the truth': 'With respect to the Tribunal I may say I would not say I resent it but I did not expect you would put that question to me. I am speaking on oath ... After all, I know that this is a Tribunal and a quasi-judiciary. What I am saying here is what I will say even if it is a criminal trial' (Nigeria l957a: 7687; 20900). Asked by Counsel whether in promoting the cause of indigenous banking he was 'wholly actuated by the consideration for the public welfare, and not at all by the consideration of [his] own private advantage?', Azikiwe had replied 'Yes' he was acting in 'the public interest'. 'I am not interested in any profit' (Nigeria 1957a: 21186, 21190, 21219).

The honest man is thus one who makes a manifest distinction in his public behaviour between his official duties and his private interests. Azikiwe agreed with [white] Counsel that no 'Minister ought to put himself ... in a position to afford his official influence in support of any contract in regard to which he has an undisclosed private interest' (Nigeria 1957a: 22216). Dr Azikiwe denied he had done anything wrong. He maintained that when he had been appointed a Minister of State, that is Premier, he had resigned from his directorships and Chairmanship of the African Continental Bank, but had retained his shareholdings in the Zik Group of companies and the bank (Nigeria 1957a: 2). Dr Azikiwe also agreed, though, that 'the moment he ceased to be Premier, he would be able to go straight back to this Bank which has been fed with public funds during his tenure of office' (Nigeria 1957a: 21142). Indeed, one witness felt that Azikiwe had 'reversionary rights' to return to the African Continental Bank: his resignation of his directorship was no sacrifice (ibid.).

Yet honesty was also a key theme in conversations which witnesses to the Tribunal reported had taken place at important meetings setting up the Eastern Region Finance Corporation, the vehicle for transferring over £2 million of public monies to the African Continental Bank. The Eastern Region Minister of Finance warned his colleagues in Cabinet against 'selfishness, parochialism and short-sightedness' and added that if the members of the Corporation would 'work hard as a team *honestly* and incorruptibly, the Corporation would achieve success' (Nigeria 1957a: 10; my italics).

In this discourse, the honest man, whether white or black, needs to acquire the gentlemanly art of separating his personal and public relationships with another man. As Azikiwe said of a conversation he had had with the Governor of Eastern Nigeria: 'We have disagreed on a number of points but these are *honest* differences of opinion, but in our personal relationship nothing has come between us. You have taken me into confidence and I have taken you into confidence' (Nigeria 1957a: 21143; my italics).

The Tribunal, too, saw itself as guided by 'its quest for the truth'. Its standard of behaviour was the British political concept of the 'honest man', one who is always in the public eye, who gives principled priority to his obligations to the public and who can handle public policies without regard to his private financial interests. The Tribunal affirmed of the (expatriate) Secretary of the Eastern Region Executive Council convened by Governor Pleass: 'We have no doubt that Mr Saville was a witness of truth'. (Nigeria 1957b: 15; 49), but found that as 'trustees of public monies' the Chairman of the Finance Corporation and Secretary Okoye were 'in dereliction of duty' (Nigeria 1957b: 42, 202). Having struck several blows for the British concept of conduct required of servants of the Crown, the Tribunal concluded that 'Dr. Azikiwe was being less than candid with us in the early stages of his evidence' (Nigeria 1957b: 16; XX). He had known all the way along of the 'rescue' contract between the bank and the Finance Corporation – after all, his had been the invisible hand at the helm – but he had hidden it from the crucial December 1954 meeting of the Eastern Region Executive Council (Nigeria 1957b: 17). In its Report, the Tribunal found that Dr Azikiwe's silence in the company of political colleagues had encouraged them to focus on his abortive negotiations in 1956 with a British bank (Martin's) to rescue the ailing African Continental Bank. In their view the investment of public funds in the Bank had been achieved by several sleights of hand based on secrecy: neither Executive Council nor the Finance Corporation Board had been informed.

The Tribunal summed up: Dr Azikiwe had allowed the Governor and Executive Council to remain 'in complete ignorance of the fact that ... the policy of the Finance Corporation of investing a large sum in the African Continental Bank was ... initiated ... by Dr. Azikiwe and his colleagues' (Nigeria 1957b: 39; 175–6). In an additional act of duplicity, the Tribunal alleged, Dr Azikiwe's government had issued a White Paper 'to give the investment transaction a cloak of respectability, which he did not think it otherwise possessed' ... 'although the Bank operated at a loss, yet it was solvent' (Nigeria 1957b: 40; 180). 'That statement (was) false' (Nigeria 1957b: 39; 176). The Chairman's Report on behalf of the Tribunal had concluded 'Dr. Azikiwe ought to have relinquished his financial interest in the Bank ... he was guilty of misconduct as a Minister in failing to do so' (Nigeria 1957b: 42; 197). That Dr Azikiwe had failed to give up his interests in the bank for almost three months following his election as Premier suggested to the Tribunal that he had indeed accorded priority to his own financial interests over those of the Eastern Region and its tax-payers. Clause III of the Finance Corporation–African Continental Bank agreement stipulated that on 'a net assets basis when all this money had gone into the Bank from the Finance Corporation the existing shareholders had now got shares worth on that basis 13s. or 14s. each, compared ... with no value before that date' (Nigeria 1957a: 19; XX). Whether or not Dr Azikiwe returned to the bank, he and his family and other pre-1956 'rescue bid' shareholders had benefited considerably from the investment of public funds. In the Tribunal's eyes, a Premier had tainted himself and his administration with the pecuniary.

In Search of the Truth

Honesty continued to be a critical theme in Nigerian political culture and practice in the aftermath of the Foster-Sutton Tribunal. Some felt the Report had failed to home in directly on persons involved in the transfer of revenues from public departments to private banks and individuals; it had tacitly exonerated them. One Minister in Nigeria said the 'Report of the Tribunal has fallen short of the expectations of *honest*, reasonable people' (*The Times* 21.1.1957: 4).

In England, too, publication of the Bank Rate Tribunal's findings led some to query the gentlemanly assumption that City and national interests were always identical (*The Times* 5.2.1958: 10). Subsequently, the British Prime Minister, the Rt. Hon. Harold Macmillan, appointed Lord Radcliffe QC to constitute a committee to study the functioning of the Bank of England and other financial institutions in the City in situations where some men are directors of the Bank as well as of their own private companies. The Committee was necessary, Prime Minister Macmillan informed the House of Commons, to secure 'the *integrity* of members of the Government and Party officials', to defend 'the *honour* of those against whom individual insinuations have been made ... [in] circumstances when issues of *private honour* and *public import* are concerned' (*The Times* 4.2.1958: 4; my italics). Macmillan was himself related to some witnesses before the Tribunal, including the Governor of the Bank of England, and he too assumed that City interests and advocacy of tight monetary control were synonymous with the national interest.

It is possible that the Prime Minister had taken the highly unusual step of appointing the Attorney-General to the Tribunal so as to encourage the Chairman and counsel to frame questions in a way that would assist leading witnesses to construct bland replies. Had not witnesses answered 'no', when they should have answered 'yes' to some questions? Had not these witnesses sought to avoid further questioning about access to inside information, especially discussions between the Governor of the Bank of England and the Chancellor of the Exchequer on the Bank Rate? (Devons 1959: 2). A Labour politician, addressing the House of Commons in a major debate on the Bank Rate Tribunal's Report, doubted whether the Attorney-General had sought to 'wholly ignore his *personal* interests, and [sought] to serve to the best of his ability the *public* interest, and that alone' (*The Times* 4.2.1958: 4; my italics). Consequently some felt the Attorney-General had acted like a 'cad' or a 'stooge' (ibid.). A Labour politician doubted, too, the truth of witnesses' assertion that 'an absolute coincidence' or 'inspired anticipation' (GB 1958b: 3; GB 1958a: 2-3) accounted for the fact that of 11,000 registered companies only four had sold gilts on any scale in advance of the Bank Rate's being raised, and that all four were connected with two Bank of England directors, the Lords Kindersley and Bicester, who were also Chairmen or Managing Directors of the companies in question (*The Times* 22.1.1958: 13). Just because they were deemed eminent gentlemen, had they not been let off the hook by other gentlemen, including the Attorney-General and the Prime Minister? Would not these honourable gentlemen continue to run the Bank of England like 'a sovereign state' even though it was a nationalized industry? In Whitehall and the City, then, establishing the 'truth' required witnesses to demonstrate they had not used confidential information obtained in the course of their work as Directors of the Bank of England to advantage their finance houses (*The Times* 20.12.1957: 4; 4.2.1958: 4). Elsewhere, it was suspected that the Lords Kindersley and Bicester, and William Keswick, had probably been less than candid. Indeed, the very ambiguity of their answers fuelled the widespread suspicion that their inside knowledge had been advantageous. They had declined to reveal the extent of the intermeshing of their private lives with their public positions and associated class interests.

Gentlemanly tactics were to place trusted partners, politically influential friends and relatives on the boards of finance houses, major corporations such as Vickers Ltd and Rolls Royce Ltd, the Bank of England and government departments. The Court of Directors of the Bank in the 1950s included men who had either 'inherited' a directorship from their father (i.e. the Lords Kindersley, Catto, Bicester) or would be succeeded by a nephew, son or grandson in the future (i.e. the above mentioned Lords and the Keswick brothers). Equally, some prominent merchant banks had retained a more or less continuous presence on the Court since the 1930s i.e. Lazard Bros., Hambros, Morgan Grenfell. These tactics assumed that, possible differences of opinion notwithstanding, family connections, the 'old boy' network and gentlemanly collegiality would hold firm in the present and in the future, influencing gentlemanly power tactics. My research on the wider networks of Tribunal witnesses points up the significance of City contributions to the Conservative Party in shaping Conservative tolerance of financial scandals (Lazard Bros., Hambros, Morgan Grenfell, for example, have donated handsomely to the Party for many years; cf. Johnson, forthcoming). And Tribunal Proceedings contain ample evidence that witnesses used their social, familial and City–Whitehall connections tactically to influence the Bank of England's decision-making about Bank Rate in particular, and financial matters in general.

In effect the behaviour of these English gentlemen differed little from that of Dr Azikiwe, who had been accused of pillaging marketing board funds to invest in his private bank. Both parties denied they had behaved 'selfishly', or that they had put their own pecuniary interests before public duty (Nigeria 1957a: 984; GB 1958a: 296). In London and Lagos learned counsel saw the need to separate 'want of propriety' and 'improper' conduct which could endanger the depositor's funds both public and private (Nigeria 1957a: 964; GB 1958a: 297). Though there was a sense in the City and Parliament that Lord Kindersley may have 'acted in this matter with some want of propriety as a Director of the Bank of England' (GB 1958a: 297), the Bank Rate Tribunal Chairman found 'he conducted himself with complete honesty and propriety' (GB 1958b: 57). However, the Foster-Sutton Tribunal had found Dr Azikiwe 'guilty of improper conduct' (Nigeria 1957b: 194). It believed that his main motive had been to promote an indigenous bank with the object of liberalizing credit for Nigerians, but it also believed that he was attracted by the financial power his interest in the bank gave him (Nigeria 1957b: 192–4). Azikiwe had been found wanting, a 'black Englishman' without the privileged connections of his judges, and one who therefore had to be even more convincing in responding to questions informed by the gentlemanly ideal of honest 'public man'.

Conclusion

I have suggested that this quasi-judicial procedure for the settlement of disputes (Gulliver 1979) inscribes in a microcosm aspects of a (moral) ideology of the relationships between power and knowledge, its specific representation in a colonial setting, and its more general statement in the metropoles. Tribunals in both locations sought to hold popular perceptions of the powerful in line with official notions of the 'honest man', one who maintains a strict separation between his public conduct and private (pecuniary) interest. Counsel deployed gentlemanly values inhering in the quasi-judicial procedures of Tribunals of Inquiry in Lagos and London to establish 'the truth' and thus to affirm the essential validity of the 'public man' – one who subordinates private gain for the greater good, and conducts himself 'with complete honesty and propriety during a period when he might at any moment have been placed in an embarrassing position' (GB 1958b: 57). Understanding 'corruption', then, requires critical investigation of ruling ideals like the gentleman of public affairs ('public man'). In principle, he upholds the norms of public service without private gain; he therefore lends credibility to the ruling ideology that the State exercises power for the public, national good, over private interests incarnated in civil society.

In 1956–7, as today, at similar moments of crisis the proceedings of quasi-judicial Tribunals of Inquiry show ruling élites exercising structural power in which their actions shape and structure the field of action of others (Wolf 1990: 586). They deploy a moral ideology of the rightful (honest) and wrongful (dishonest, corrupt) man; the latter is a fall-guy, a wrongdoer, whose scapegoat role redeems ruling groups as a whole and consequently protects the potency of the ideology that power is exercised on the majority's behalf.

Notes

1. I constructed a small sample of forty-five men born between 1885 and 1935 eminent in political, administrative and financial affairs at home and in the colonies in the mid-fifties, most of whom knew one another or were on nodding terms in the City and Whitehall as well as in London and Edinburgh clubs, and some of whom were intimately involved in events surrounding Bank Rate. (For further details see Johnson MS.) Data were drawn from *Who's Who* (1957). These men were born into upper-middle-class and lower aristocratic families of south-east England and of the county of Dumfriesshire in the Lowlands of Scotland. All the men had married at least once, and twenty-eight of them, well over half, had married a woman whose father was titled. Most of

the remainder had married one or two rungs up in the county hierarchy – daughters of military men, justices of the peace, and plain country gentlemen of substance and sensibility. The relatively fluid social composition of outer circles of the English and Lowland Scots peerage around a core of long-standing, carefully ranked ancient titles confirms earlier, more general social research into the upper classes and their renewal through daughters who may marry lower status, but wealthy, men (Bloomfield 1955; Lupton and Shirley Wilson 1959; Scott 1982).

2. These are government securities on which interest payments are guaranteed to be met and repaid at par on the due date; in effect, confidence in gilts is secured by a public authority, government, on behalf of private sellers and buyers.

3. Merchant banks are finance houses primarily engaged in accepting foreign bills of exchange, advising companies on flotations and takeovers, underwriting new issues, making long-term loans to companies and managing investment portfolios, funds and trusts.

4. My investigation of the Annual Returns of companies cited in Bank Rate Tribunal Proceedings in relation to men at the time directors of the Bank of England revealed perpetual succession to directorships in major companies in the private sector and in government departments whose function was to promote greater British investment in the Commonwealth. By the early 1980s the recently ennobled Catto (1921), Bicester (1938), Kindersley (1941) and Piercy (1945) families had produced sons appointed over at least two, and sometimes three, generations, to four directorships in the Bank of England, two in the Royal Bank of Scotland, and three in the Export Credit Guarantees Department. In the 1950s they were building up family 'ownership' of a seat on the Board of the Colonial Development Corporation, established in 1948. It goes without saying that during the seventy-year period of my enquiries the Chairmen and Managing Directors of the eminent finance houses of the Lazard Bros., Morgan-Grenfell and Samuel Montagu Banks were recruited from founding families or their close associates; these included the Kindersleys, the Cattos and Bicesters, and the Montagus and Keswicks.

5. Several witnesses resorted to biological analogies when pressed for more specific information. Favourite phrases included: 'entirely natural'; markets 'weaken', 'slip away', 'soften', 'indigestion in the market', 'drifted into the decision to sell gilts'.

References

Unpublished Sources

Companies House, Annual Returns
Vickers Ltd. *Annual Return of Vickers Ltd up to 10 June 1955: 14th day after the Annual General Meeting for the Year 1955. Report of the Directors.* Vol.77, part 1 (6 Parts), 1955.

Government Sources
GB (Great Britain) (1949). *Great Britain. Tribunals of Inquiry (Evidence) Act, 1921. Report of the Tribunal Appointed to inquire into Allegations reflecting on the official Conduct of Ministers of the Crown and other Public Servants, 1948.* London: HMSO (cmd 7616), 1949.

GB (Great Britain) (1958a). *Great Britain. Proceedings of the Tribunal Appointed to Inquire into allegations that information about the raising of bank Rate was improperly disclosed. With the Minutes of Evidence taken Before the Tribunal, December 1957.* London: HMSO, 1958.

GB (Great Britain) (1958b). *Great Britain. Tribunals of Inquiry (Evidence) Act, 1921. Report of the Tribunal appointed to Inquire into Allegations of Improper disclosure of Information relating to the Raising of the Bank Rate.* London: HMSO (cmd 350), 1958.

Hansard (1957–8). *Hansard, House of Commons Debates,* Vol. 581, col. 855–1000, 1957–8.

Nigeria (1956). *Nigeria. Banking Monopoly in Nigeria. Statement made by the Hon. Premier in the eastern house of Assembly on 8th August, 1956.* Enugu: The Government Printer, Eastern Region, 1956.

Nigeria (1957a). *Nigeria. Proceedings of the Tribunal Appointed to Inquire Into Allegations Of Improper Conduct By The Premier Of The Eastern Region Of Nigeria In Connection With The Affairs Of The African Continental Bank Ltd And Other Relevant Matters. August – November 1956, Vol. 1.* Lagos: Federal Government Printer, 1957.

Nigeria (1957b). *Nigeria. Report of the Tribunal appointed to inquire into allegations reflecting on the Official Conduct of the premier of, and certain persons holding Ministerial and other Public Offices in, the Eastern Region of Nigeria.* London: HMSO (cmd 51), 1957.

Nigeria (1962). *Nigeria. Report of the Coker Commission of Inquiry into the Affairs of Certain Statutory Corporations in Western Nigeria.* Lagos: Federal Government Printer, 1962.

Published Sources

Anderson, P. (1974). *Passages from Antiquity*. London: New Left Books

Anon. (n.d.). *The Lynskey Tribunal. Précis of Evidence and Summary of Findings. Compiled from Press Reports. Caricatures by Mounsey (2/-)*. London: No Date

Bloomfield, P. (1955). *Uncommon People, a Study of England's Elite*. London: Hamish Hamilton

Cain, P. J. and Hopkins A. G. (1993). *British Imperialism, Crisis and Deconstruction 1914–1990*. London: Longman

Chambers Encyclopaedia (1950). 'Crime', Vol. 4, pp. 239–46. London: George Newnes

Cohen, A. (1974). 'Introduction: The Lesson of Ethnicity', in *Urban Ethnicity*, ed. A. Cohen. London: Tavistock

Devons, E. (1959). 'The Bank Rate Tribunal: A Symposium. An Economist's View of the Bank Rate Tribunal Evidence', *The Manchester School of Economic and Social Studies* XXVII (1): 1–16

Doig, A. (1990). *Westminster, Babylon*. London: Allison-Busby

Giddens, A. (1986). *Durkheim on Politics and the State*, Stanford: Stanford University Press

Gluckman, M. (1955). *The Judicial Process among the Barotse of Northern Rhodesia*. Manchester: Manchester University Press

Gulliver, P. H. (1966). 'Dispute Settlement Without Courts: the Ndendeuli of Southern Tanzania' in L. Nader (ed.) *Law in Culture and Society*. Chicago: Aldine, pp. 24–63.

Gulliver, P. H. (1979). *Disputes and Negotiations. A Cross-cultural Perspective*. London and New York: Academic Press

Handwerker, W. Penn (1987). 'Fiscal Corruption and the Moral Economy of Resource Acquisition', in *Research in Economic Anthropology* ed. B. L. Isaac, Vol. 9, pp. 307–53. Greenwich, Connecticut: JAI Press Inc

Hanham, J. H. (1959). 'The Bank Rate Tribunal: A Symposium. A Political Scientist's View', *The Manchester School of Economic and Social Studies* XXVII (1): 17–29

Held, D. H. (ed.) (1983). *States and Societies*, Introduction, pp. 1–34. Oxford: Basil Blackwell

Hobson, D. (1990). *The Pride of Lucifer. Morgan-Grenfell 1838–1988. The Unauthorised Biography of a Merchant Bank*. London: Hamish Hamilton

Johnson, C. 'Gentlemanly Values in Decline: Corruption in London and Lagos in the 1980s', forthcoming in *The Politics of Cultural Performance*, ed. D. Parkin, L. Caplan, and H. Fisher. (Forthcoming).

Johnson, C. 'For Love of Money: Gentlemen and Corruption at Home and Abroad'. (MS)

Ikoiwak, E. A. (1983). 'Political Office Holders, Bureaucrats and Corruption', in *Corruption in Development*, ed. F. Odekunle, pp. 82–91. Ibadan: Ibadan University Press

Isaac, B. L. (ed.) (1987). *Research in Economic Anthropology*, Vol. 9. London, Greenwich, Connecticut: JAI Press

Lawal, A. A. (1986). 'Anatomy of Corruption in the British Colonial Service in Nigeria'. Paper delivered at the 31st Annual Congress of the Historical Society of Nigeria, 18–24 May 1986

Lugard, Baron F. J. D. (1906). 'Instructions to Political and Other Officers on Subjects Chiefly Political and Administrative'. Xerox copy. London, 1906.

Lupton, T. and Shirley Wilson, C. (1959). 'The Bank Rate Tribunal: A Symposium. The Social Background and Connections of "Top Decision Makers"', *The Manchester School of Economic and Social Studies* XXVII (1): 30–51

Matthews, R. C. O., Feinstein, C. H. and Odling-Smee, J. C. (1983). *British Economic Growth, 1856–1973*. Oxford: Oxford University Press

Odekunle, F. (ed.) (1983). *Corruption in Development*. Ibadan: Ibadan University Press

Scott, J. (1982). *The Upper Classes, Property and Privilege in Britain*. Basingstoke: Macmillan Press

Sullivan, G. (1985). 'Fraud and the Efficacy of the Criminal Law: a proposal for a wide residual offence', *Criminal Law Review* 616–30

Ward, P. M. (1989). *Corruption, Development and Inequality*. London: Routledge

Wallerstein, I. (1979). *The Capitalist World Economy, Essays*. Cambridge: Cambridge University Press

Wolf, E. (1990). 'Distinguished Lecture: Facing Power – Old Insights, New Questions', *American Anthropologist* 92: 586–96

Wolff, K. (ed.) (1950). *The Sociology of Georg Simmel*. London: The Free Press of Glencoe and Collier-Macmillan Ltd

Wraith, R. and Simpkins E. (1963). *Corruption in Developing Countries*. London: Allen and Unwin

Newspapers
Daily Times (Lagos)
The Times (London)
The Financial Times (London)

Chapter 6

The 'Inhabitants' vs. the 'Sovereign': A Historical Ethnography of the Making of the 'Middle Class' in an Irish Corporate Borough, 1840-1

Marilyn Silverman

The centrality of ethnography to the discipline of anthropology continues to be reiterated – by new tropes and through contested meanings – both from within the discipline (e.g. Comaroff 1992; Wolf 1990) and from outside (e.g. Giddens 1984: 284). Given this simultaneous centrality and contentiousness, it is helpful to look to the work of a particular practitioner and to draw from it both broad patterns and specific concerns which can continue to inform the discipline and the doing of ethnography. In the ethnographic corpus produced by P. H. Gulliver, and through his theoretical viewpoints, we can in fact find such broad themes and particular interests, even as his writings necessarily changed over time, along with anthropological paradigms and vocabulary.

Overall, Gulliver's work has displayed his firm commitment to the ethnographic analysis of material relations and social change in small-scale locales contextualized in wider arenas and historical understandings with the aim of, and underpinned by, theory. Nested in these broad themes, however, have been several narrower foci which have provided him with the vehicles for addressing them. These narrower concerns can be summarized as interdependent dualities, and they have permeated, in different ways and with different degrees of emphasis, the numerous analytical ethnographies which he has produced. They are the simultaneity of 'conflict' and co-operation, of disputes and dispute-management, and of individual action and the formation of collectivities.[1] In the present chapter, I explore aspects of these narrower concerns in the spirit of the broader patterns which have typified Gulliver's work.

Methods, Concepts, Questions and Problems: An Ethnographic Endeavour

In 1979 Philip Gulliver and I began a joint project in the Republic of Ireland in a town and its rural hinterland.[2] By contrast with field conditions in East Africa, Gulliver found extensive archives and an established historiographic tradition. He also encountered essential differences as compared with, for example, such 'simple milieux' as Ndendeuli settlements in Tanzania. The latter were small (32 to 42 households), unstratified, economically undifferentiated and actualized by 'relationships, especially those which involved rights and obligations ... framed within the powerful idiom of kinship' (1977: 37). In contrast, the Irish research locale contained 507 households differentiated by strata (lifestyle) and class (access to the means of production). It was these differences which structured rights and obligations, whilst kinship played a more muted role, although it contributed to the reproduction of class differences and provided an emic map for daily social interaction (Gulliver and Silverman 1990). In other words, 'kinship linkages' in Thomastown did not cause differential access to the means of production; nor were they 'representations of exchange relationships' as amongst the Ndendeuli, nor the basis for 'both cooperation and competition' in the public sphere (Gulliver 1977: 38–9).

Nevertheless, the public sphere in Ndendeuli and in Thomastown were strikingly similar in at least one respect. Neither possessed corporate groups of the kind which elsewhere structured relations of 'conflict' and co-operation, gave rise to disputes and processes for their management, and prescribed fundamental affilations and, therefore, the composition and actions of collectivities. In both Ndendeuli and Thomastown, politics and collective action were diffuse – actualized out of situational events and out of the intersection of, on the one hand, individual and collective lived experiences and, on the other, material interests. Thanks to Gulliver's work (1971, 1977), we know how this operated along the kinship nexus in several 'simpler milieux' at the times he did his research. How, though, did it operate in Thomastown? To answer this question, I first look at the methods, concepts, questions and problems which relate particularly to aspects of our research in Thomastown and to the historicity of the locale.

The 'Body Corporate': Thomastown Borough in History

The town of Thomastown was founded in about the year 1200 as a military base for Norman colonial consolidation in that part of south-eastern Ireland and, importantly, as a trading depot at the head of navigation on an inland river system which connected both it and Kilkenny city, about 15 miles upriver, to world markets. The foundation charter of the town, and later royal charters too, gave numerous rights to the borough's inhabitants: to collect tolls, to hold markets and a court and, after 1553, to be 'for ever, ... a body corporate' (Parliamentary Paper 1835: 573–4) and to send two members to the Irish parliament (Pilsworth 1951: 37). A surviving folio from 1693 lists the freemen and burgesses of the borough at the time. The Corporation had, as its 111 members, 'gentlemen', 'merchants', 'boatmen', artisans, 'yeomen' and a 'labourer'. Clearly the borough in the seventeenth century was a highly stratified place. Indeed, the centrality of class in south-eastern Ireland has been noted more generally. Of County Kilkenny, Cullen wrote: 'To a degree rare in Ireland it is possible in the case of Kilkenny to look at social problems without the complicating intervening factors of race and religion' (1990: 288).

In 1802, an observer described Thomastown at the time:

> The want of any resident officer of the corporation ... is greatly felt, there being no person to quarter soldiers, abate nuisances, to regulate weights or markets; ... the corporation courts too, if held according to charter, might be of great service, as the cheapest and the most convenient mode of redress, for those within the liberties (Tighe 1802: 464).

This decay in the 'body corporate' was hardly surprising. Penal laws introduced at the turn of the eighteenth century meant that 'Catholics could not sit in parliament or, between 1728 and 1793, vote in parliamentary elections. They were [also] excluded from municipal corporations' (McCracken 1986: 37). After 1728, then, most of the town's inhabitants could not take part in Corporation business or be appointed to the Corporation. Instead, those who became freemen and burgesses were non-resident Protestants who, by 1740, had been appointed by, and owed political loyalty to, a county Tory family, the Davises, whose main concern was to control the borough's two parliamentary seats. Members of the 'body corporate', in other words, were non-residents and uninterested in local affairs. This lack of interest increased after 1800, when the Act of Union abolished the Irish parliament and the Corporation's parliamentary seats.

In 1833, four years after the anti-Catholic penal laws were themselves abolished, a Parliamentary Commission investigated the state of municipal corporations in Ireland. Its findings in Thomastown echoed Tighe's assessment three decades before. According to the Commissioners, the Corporation 'consists of a Sovereign and Burgesses of the Town of Thomastown' and although 'the charters mention a provost, recorder, town clerk, serjeants at mace and other officers, none such are appointed'. Moreover, the Commissioners

> could learn little as to the proceedings of this corporation; the sovereign [Sydenham Davis] was the only person connected with it who attended our Inquiry; he stated that he had been appointed deputy sovereign in 1818, and sovereign ... [in] 1823, and had continued sovereign since that period; but that he had little acquaintance with the affairs of the corporation. A Local Court was held here by him from the time he was appointed deputy sovereign, until about two years ago, with a jurisdiction limited to sums not exceeding 40s. Irish. ... [However] after petty sessions had been established in the town, the business of the court lessened considerably, and all proceedings in it have been abandoned for the last two years. ... We had no evidence that the corporation ever had any Property in lands. Although a Market and Fairs, with Tolls, are granted to the corporation, and tolls are still collected, the corporation do not receive or claim them.

Instead, the tolls were collected by Lord Carrick, who leased them from the owner Sydenham Davis.

> The collection of these Tolls is a source of much disturbance in the town, and their legality is disputed. There are no municipal regulations here. The Streets are repaired by county presentment in the usual way. ... We were informed that the continuance of the corporation was of no advantage to the town, and that it never did any benefit to it (Parliamentary Paper 1835: 574–5).

Clearly, the 'body corporate' barely functioned. Essential services in the town were provided by state agencies – the petty and quarter sessions (law) and county juries (public works). Moreover, Corporation property, its land and the tolls, had been appropriated by the Davis family, whilst the Corporation's remaining functions, particularly the town court, were either moribund or controlled by Sydenham Davis, the local representative of that family.

In 1840, state policy encouraged municipal corporations to elect local commissioners, under an Act of George IV, to set values on local property and collect rates, and to carry out public works. Efforts by some of Thomastown's inhabitants to implement this policy exacerbated tensions in the town and gave rise to a political fracas. Much of it was recorded in a Corporation minute book which has survived and in several newspaper accounts of the time. Other archival materials supplement these, providing multiple points of entry into the dispute and background materials on the people and the structures.[3] It is the historical ethnography of this dispute which I explore in this chapter.

Historical Experience and the Making of the 'Middle Class'

The particular historical experiences of Thomastown lend themselves to a certain kind of method (archival) and to the use of certain concepts (e.g. class). These allow me to explore, as Gulliver did very often, an empirical event (a dispute and its management), agency and class formation (individual and collective experiences), and the intersection of material interests and political alliances ('conflict' and co-operation). However, this particular event also allows me to pose questions which are somewhat different from those that often concerned Gulliver in his African work, precisely because Thomastown was a class-based locale for which some ethnographic fragments have survived from the distant past. One of these questions is the anomalous positioning, and nature, of the so-called middle class.

The problem of describing class structure in capitalist societies in a way which incorporates those who are neither bourgeoisie (exploiters) nor labour (exploited) has been the basis of important and lengthy debate in Marxist sociological theory. Professionals and self-employed producers are empirical examples of categories and people who do not fit the bi-polar structure of traditional Marxist analyses (Wright 1989: 24). In the absence of an agreed-upon approach to class structure which fits these categories in, the linked issues of class formation, struggle and consciousness also have been obscured (Wright 1989: 272).

> Somewhat analogously, from the perspective of social history, is that most extraordinary of absences in British historiography, the making of the middle class. In effect the middle class leaves the stage of social-historical analysis somewhere between the 1790s and 1832, and does not really re-enter it until the defeat of Chartism, and then more as a socio-cultural abstraction represented in certain administrative, religious and philanthropic practices than as a carefully specified social phenomenon (Eley 1990: 38–9).

In Thomastown in 1840, the dispute in the Corporation mobilized, in various ways and differing degrees, not only bourgeois capitalists and labourers, but also townspeople who occupied anomalous occupational positions: a landlord, a tenant-farmer, clergy, professionals, retailers and artisans. Their actions and inactions reflected, simultaneously, their lived experiences and material interests, and therefore give insight into the formation of collectivities: how those who occupied certain structural locations became political agents and actualized the interrelated processes of class formation, struggle and consciousness in a particular place and time. More particularly, through the dispute, we can see the 'middle class' as a social phenomenon – how and why it formed itself as a class for itself – in one small town in the mid-nineteenth century. Second, certain alliances and coalitions emerged as part of the disputing process: individual and collective 'conflict' and co-operation were simultaneously interlinked and mutually interdependent. Finally, the dispute itself had a particular history: its trajectory – its outbreak and management – was governed by how agency and class dynamics, and 'conflict'/co-operation, intersected and were made to intersect in Thomastown at the time. Thus, in analysis of this event, I try to show the simultaneity of individual actions and the formation of collectivities, of 'conflict' and co-operation, and of disputes and dispute-management. In so doing, I try to make an ethnographic contribution to a current issue – the making of the so-called middle class.

The Dispute: The Inhabitants vs. The Sovereign

In November 1840, as a result of a petition sent to the Lord Lieutenant of Ireland by '21 householders', Sydenham Davis – sovereign of Thomastown Corporation – was ordered to hold a meeting to determine whether the Corporation would adopt or act upon the provisions contained in an Act of George IV which provided for the 'lighting, cleansing and watching of Irish cities and towns, and [the] election of town commissioners for these purposes' (Moody et al. 1982: 308). From the records of this and subsequent meetings, we learn about town politics at the time. We learn how some of the town's inhabitants – of diverse sect and occupation – were brought together in opposition to, or in support of, sovereign Sydenham Davis. Such support or opposition arose from a variety of factors: the personal control which Davis exercised, the condition of local services and the way in which the Corporation functioned, the inhabitants' approval, or lack of approval, of the Act, Davis's alleged appropriation of Corporation property, disputes and alliances in other arenas – and, no doubt, because of long-standing personal animosities and friendships.

Dramatis personae

Local/Parish residents:

Landlord	Sydenham Davis*	(landlord, sovereign of Thomastown Corporation; Protestant)
'Gentleman'	Hutchinson, Edward*	(Protestant)
Farmer	Cantwell, Patrick	(large farm 228 acres, Catholic)
Professionals	Clifford, William*	(bank manager, Protestant)
	Sterling, Myles	(doctor, Protestant)
	McEnnery, Joseph	(solicitor, Catholic)
	Murphy, Fr F.*	(curate, Catholic)
Industrialists	Bull, William*	(flour-mill owner, Protestant)
	Innes, Henry*	(flour-mill owner, Protestant)

	Loughlin, John*	(grist-mill owner, Catholic)
	Nugent, Anthony*	(brewer, Catholic)
	Ryan, Fr James	(tanner, priest, Catholic)
	Ryan, Thomas	(tanner, Catholic)
	Splint, Joshua	(brewer, Catholic)
Retailers	Bishop, Thomas	(publican–grocer–hotelier, Catholic)
	Cronyn, Edward	(grocer–draper, Protestant)
	Devine, Peter	(baker, Catholic)
	Dowling, Patrick	(draper, Catholic)
	Dunphy, Michael	(grocer, Catholic)
	Hoyne, Denis	(hardware, Catholic)
	Kelly, Edward	(grocer, Catholic)
	O'Connor, William	(baker, Catholic)
	Spruhan, John	(publican–grocer, Catholic)
Artisans	Walsh, Edward	(cordwainer, Catholic)
Labourers	Grace, William	(Catholic)
	Morris, Joseph	(Catholic)
	Power, Laurence	(Catholic)
Non-local participants:		
	Bracken, Counsellor	(Kilkenny city; solicitor)
	Ebington, Lord Viscount	(Dublin; Lieutenant-Governor of Ireland)
	Hyland, Michael	(Kilkenny city; solicitor)
	Quinn, James	(Kilkenny city; solicitor)

(* Indicates residence outside the boundaries of the medieval town wall)

The Events: November 1840 to February 1841

At the meeting ordered by the Lord Lieutenant in late November 1840 and held in Thomastown's Sessions House, tanner–priest James Ryan proposed, and retailer Peter Devine seconded, that the Act 'be put in execution so far as cleansing said town'. John Spruhan (a publican–grocer who, as is seen below, was a Davis supporter) then proposed an amendment that the meeting adjourn. Davis, in the chair, asked for a list of £5 householders, that is, those 'entitled to vote within the borough of Thomastown.' According to the minutes, he then proposed that the galleries should be occupied by those entitled to vote [:] the gallery on the right hand to the supporters of the [Spruhan] amendment and the gallery to the left for the opponents of the same amendment and supporters of the original [Ryan/Devine] resolution. This [latter] gallery was crowded to suffocation. ... The chairman proceeded to take the votes and the amendment was decided against by a majority of 86 to 10 and the original motion carried.

It was then proposed by farmer Cantwell and seconded by retailer Devine 'that the following persons do be appointed Commissioners'. By law, all had to be £20 householders. Of those on their list, Spruhan and Davis objected to Fr S. Murphy, millers Henry Innes and William Bull, brewer Anthony Nugent, and Edward Hutchinson, 'gentleman'. Thirteen, however, were 'admitted' without objection: industrialists Fr James Ryan and Thomas Ryan (tanners), Joshua Splint (brewer) and John Loughlin (grist-miller), professionals Myles Sterling and William Clifford, farmer Patrick Cantwell, and retailers Thomas Bishop, Peter Devine, Patrick Dowling, Denis Hoyne, Edward Kelly and William O'Connor.

According to the minutes, Davis 'scrupulously examined every candidate ... proposed' by Cantwell and Devine and 'those whom he rejected ... resided outside the old Corporation bounds or walls'. Interestingly, Davis himself dwelt outside the walls; but he was not running for commissioner. Davis also refused to take any more nominations, arguing that thirteen was sufficient. A motion was then proposed (seconded by Clifford) to adjourn the meeting to the following week 'for the purpose of swearing in the said Commissioners'. Davis refused to sign either the motion admitting the Commissioners or the adjournment motion (Minutes, 27 November 1840).

At the next meeting, ostensibly for swearing in the town commissioners, those attending 'on looking over the Minutes ... found that Sydenham Davis the Chairman came back ... and wrote 'Objected' next to William Clifford and John Loughlin's name'. In addition, Davis apparently announced that he 'did not know what was done' at the previous meeting and had decided, therefore, 'to postpone' the present meeting and not to swear in the new commissioners. He left the chair and the meeting. It was then proposed by James Ryan and seconded by Innes that yet another memorial be sent to the Lord Lieutenant:

> At a meeting of inhabitants of Thomastown cawled by the Sovereign ... the provisions of the 9th George 4th for cleansing said Borough were by a great majority adopted by the five Pound householders. ... Each of the Commissioners were proposed[,] seconded and duly elected by the Majority of ... said inhabitants. ... We the undersigned being the persons appointed by said Inhabitants presented ourselves before said Sovereign ... and he refuses to [swear us in.] ... We having no recourse ... pray your Excellency to issue orders to the nearest resident magistrate to swear us in said office (Minutes, 9 December 1840).

By this time, the newspapers had picked up the dispute. A report in the *Kilkenny Journal* described the above meeting as one of 'respectable people', adding that it had been attended by a Kilkenny solicitor named Bracken. 'It was rumoured that he had been retained by Mr Davis to oppose the election of the commissioners.' According to the report, after 'the minutes of the last meeting were read', Mr Clifford 'offered himself to be sworn in but was told that the sovereign Mr Davis had objected to him. ... Mr. Clifford said that they had been proposed properly and other voices agreed.' Bracken then

> said that several ratepayers had retained him and they were not happy with the appointments as some of those proposed did not reside with the precincts. He refused to name the ratepayers. ... There then followed some argument as to the exact boundaries of the town and these could not be satisfactorily determined. Mr Hyland then asked the chairman to proceed with the swearing in. ... Rev Mr Ryan ... offered himself for swearing in saying that there was no objection raised to him at the last meeting. Chairman [Davis] said he couldn't remember. Chairman then said that the commissioners were not proposed and seconded the last day. This remark was met with voluble protest from many present. ... Chairman [also] denied proposing a resolution at the last meeting that they adjourn and meet on this day to swear in commissioners. This lead to heated remarks by Mr Clifford. There followed much argument with the Chairman denying most of the alleged happenings at the last meeting. He then adjourned the meeting for a fortnight but refused to sign the notice of adjournment. He then left the courthouse to the groans and hisses of the meeting (*Kilkenny Journal*, 12 December 1840).

A few weeks later, a letter appeared in another newspaper which stated that 'very little reliance can be be placed upon [the above-mentioned *Journal* report] as it only gives the sentiments of those who were opposed to the Sovereign fully.' It conceded, however, that

> we [do] learn from the Report ... that the Commissioners appointed in a clumsy and illegal manner on a former day were not sworn in by the Sovereign on the grounds that the proceedings were irregular and not conformable to the Act of Parliament. ... [And] if the mode of election was not legal, how could they levy a rate ... for ... any householder may replevin his goods seized for the rate, and proceed by action against the Chairman or any solvent member of a body so illegally constituted (*Kilkenny Moderator*, 16 December 1840).

At the next Corporation meeting, solicitor Bracken 'entered a protest against all the proceedings passed and to pass on this day'. The protest was signed by, and submitted on behalf of, six ratepayers, only one of whom can be identified. He was Edward Walsh, a cordwainer. It seems likely, too, that the other five also were artisans and that, in this action, they stated their opposition both to the anti-Davis coalition and the Davis faction.[4]

According to the minutes 'Mr Davis [then] said he should proceed to swear in the Commissioners ... and read his list.' However, 'a number of persons came forward to protest against' two of the names which he read out – Joseph McEnnery (solicitor) and Michael Dunphy (retailer) – 'as not being elected on the 27th November and insisted that Mr William Clifford and John Loughlin were the persons proposed and seconded and admitted'. At that point, McEnnery 'withdrew himself and refused to be put on the list', while Dunphy had not attended the meeting. Davis, however, 'refused to swear in Mr Clifford and John Loughlin'. He simply swore in eight others and adjourned the meeting. James Ryan was elected chair of the commissioners and they decided to send the Lord Lieutenant 'a report of the day's proceedings' (Minutes, 23 December 1840).

At the next meeting, with tanner Fr Ryan in the chair, the commissioners not only took care of local business (such as employing the bill man), but they also passed resolutions to ensure orderly conduct (that 'our votes in future should be taken by ballot') and to raise popular support against Davis. Thus, all '£5 householders' were given 'liberty to give their opinion on the subject under discussion' at meetings. The commissioners also decided to incorporate the previously mentioned 'report' to the Lord Lieutenant into the Corporation minutes. It stated that 'thirteen Commissioners were duly elected on the 27th November' but that 'the Sovereign objected to put in nomination any ... who did not live inside the old Corporation wall'. However, the Commissioners pointed out that

> the charter was not confined to the town *intra muros* but include[d] other townlands outside said Walls and that the Sovereign did always and at all times exercise his authority beyond the walls of the town – and that as we intend to extend the benefit of ... the 9th George 4th [Act] to beyond the old walls ... we would wish those ... persons residing [there] as Commissioners[.] ... [W]e do consider it a hardship to exclude those individuals as being the most respectable[,] the most wealthy of our Community and the most efficient to advance the interests of our town (Minutes, 30 December 1840).

By the first week of January 1841, 'no answer' had been 'received from the Lord Lieutenant' and Chairman Ryan wrote again stating 'I consider our future will depend mainly on acting legally'. He queried whether a new election ought to be held, what the number of commissioners ought to be, and whether those now sworn, though not being the number originally elected, could legally carry on Corporation business (Minutes, 4 January 1841). After two weeks without an answer, the commissioners took action themselves. They passed a motion that 'the limits of the town be extended to one Irish Mile from the verge of the Market place of Thomastown and that the benefits of the Act ... be extended thereto'. They elected those to whom Davis had objected because they had lived outside the wall and those, namely Clifford and Loughlin, whom he had refused to swear in. They selected the previously rejected Henry Innes as treasurer, they appointed a permanent clerk, and they chose several of themselves to be 'Valuators of the Borough and suburbs' (Minutes, 13 January 1841).

In the last week of January the Lord Lieutenant's reply was received. It stated that any objection to a commissioner's election had to be decided by the Court of the Queen's Bench, but that, regardless, 'it would be prudent' to fill all vacancies, up to the fixed 13, before taking any administrative actions. The commissioners met. They rescinded all their earlier motions and passed them again to ensure their legality (Minutes, 1 February 1841). The anti-Davis coalition was now firmly in control of town administration.[5]

Class Formation and the Disputing Process

The anti-Davis coalition was broad-based and diverse. But how extensive was its pull and what was its class base? First, from a spatial perspective, the anti-Davis protagonists not only wanted to have the Act applied locally, they also wished to define this local area fairly broadly and to include particular people who lived within it. The Act, however, pertained to legally-constituted corporations. Therefore, to incorporate the wider area and its residents required that the boundaries of Thomastown Corporation be broadly defined – to include an area which extended beyond the boundaries of the now-defunct medieval town wall. The protagonists were explicit in their reasons for wanting this area and its residents: not only did they wish a wide jurisdiction to extend 'the benefits of the Act,' they also wanted as commissioners 'those individuals' who 'were the most respectable and the most wealthy of our Community and the most efficient to advance the interests of our town', including the bank manager and the owners of two modernized flour mills.[6]

Second, from the perspective of class structure, several problems ensue, particularly the vagueness of the boundaries which surround the occupational categories of the *dramatis personae*. All the industrialists exploited labour, as did the farmer but only some of the retailers did so and, except for a groom and house servants, none of the professionals or the so-called gentleman. In that sense, only the industrialists, the farmer and some of the retailers were capitalists, whilst the gentleman was a *rentier* capitalist. In another sense, that of ownership of the means of production, the large farmer and the industrialists 'owned' their land and premises respectively, in that they all had long leases of 199 to 999 years. In contrast, very few of the retailers owned or had long leases to their premises, although they did own the stock to the extent that they were not indebted to wholesalers. The professionals, of course, owned only their skills – as did the artisans, who stayed aloof from the dispute. Finally, the proportions of people from these occupational categories who became involved varied considerably: all the town's industrialists and professionals, less than a quarter of the retailers and certainly not all the larger ones, few of the artisans, and virtually none of the farmers. Conspicuously absent until this point in the dispute were the labourers. It seems then, that what all participants had in common was, first, their importance and wealth as £20 householders and, second, a concern with local services and conditions – with 'advanc[ing] the interests of our town'.

In these concerns, they opposed a member of the landed class, albeit one whose prestige was not high: the *bricoleur* strategy of Davis's father marked him as a *nouveau arriviste* and not part of the county élite, a feature confirmed by the fact that no one from his family was, or became, a magistrate, although they had resided in the town from at least the 1760s. An aspect of this *bricoleur* strategy was that Davis's holdings were scattered. He held, in either freehold or long lease, several labourers' houses in the town and approximately 2,000 agricultural acres and several industrial sites (mills) located in different parts of the parish and of counties Kilkenny and Carlow. However, apart from a 13-acre field which brewer Splint rented from him, Davis held no control over any of the *dramatis personae* because of his ownership of property. Either they rented from other landlords or, in the one other case in which Davis was a landlord *vis-à-vis* an agent (leasing 191 acres to farmer Cantwell), had their tenure protected by a 199-year lease.

Davis also had inherited from his father several debt bonds and mortgages from gentlemen resident elsewhere in the county. This was a type of asset unlikely to commend him to the society of the county landed class. He also had inherited 'the tolls and customs of said town' and this was a source of local discontent as was, we learn later, the inhabitants' belief that his family had appropriated Corporation lands as well as the tolls. Finally, in his actions, Davis did not represent, or make an effort to represent, the landed class in the Thomastown area. He did, however, see himself as 'Sovereign' – as the formal head of the town and its ancient Corporation and as an informal wielder of financial control over some members of the landed class. He had, however, no direct source of power over those agents who joined together against him.

Davis, in turn, was joined only by perhaps 10 per cent of the £5 householders – that is, the ten out of 96 who voted for Spruhan's pro-Davis amendment. Of these, only large retailer Spruhan, solicitor McEnnery and retailer Dunphy were named. The political support of the latter two was not firm, however, for they failed to take part in a crucial meeting.

What emerged in late 1840 and early 1841, then, was a broad-based coalition of 'respectable inhabitants' only some of whom were capitalists, but none of whom were labourers or artisans. Because of their individual organizational capacities, prestige and interests, *and* through actions which actualized these attributes collectively, they can be said to have constituted a self-conscious 'middle class'. Its formation was apparent at the first public meeting called under the Act, because its agents had earlier petitioned the Lord Lieutenant; its consciousness emerged in, through and out of the dispute that constituted its activities, and its struggle was propelled, in large part, by the sheer determination of the main agents – from particular occupational categories and, importantly, from both religious persuasions. In other words, by and through their actions, some inhabitants who occupied particular occupational categories came together as 'a class' to challenge a local landlord who occupied a locally-based, moribund office. In so doing, the agents ignored the important differences amongst themselves – differences of wealth, prestige, interest and religion.

In saying this, it is important to point out that the material interests of the agents, in terms of the various occupational categories from which they came, were not in *conflict*.[7] That is, in Thomastown, industrialists, farmers, professionals and retailers each had *different* concerns but not *opposing* economic or material interests. Certainly in the interpersonal and business domains, some retailers and the two flour-millers, for example, competed amongst themselves. However, no structural attributes of the local political economy located any of these categories as intrinsically in *conflict* with any other. Moreover, the conjuncture of, on the one hand, the legislative Act and, on the other, the inhabitants' shared experiences (a perceived need for public services, antipathy to a local strong man, and an absence of town administration) brought particular people together even as nothing structural kept them apart. In this way, a 'middle class' emerged, that is, a self-conscious collectivity engaged in active struggle. Importantly, these same features simultaneously meant that this class had accepted the hegemony of the state in administrative matters.

What, however, were the 'opposed interests' and the structural cleavages in the local political economy at the time, and why did these not propel the dispute at this stage or figure in the process of class formation? It is quite clear that, during these months, only their bare outlines were discernible. They included the *conflict* between labour and capital, the differing interests of artisans as compared with labour, and the varying material concerns of town inhabitants as distinct from country-dwellers. Indeed, it was the situational and structural absence of these or any other cleavages at that point that contributed to the formation of an urban 'middle class' as a self-conscious collectivity. The town's artisans, as far as the record shows, simply withdrew from the dispute, having expressed their dissatisfaction with all parties. No other *conflicts* or cleavages were apparent. In other words, the disputing process and class formation were both rooted in the political economy of the locality and its historical parameters.

February 1841 to 6 September 1841: Alliances and the 'Middle Class'

With firm control over the Corporation through the Act, agents of the 'middle class' proceeded along two fronts. First, the commissioners kept confronting Davis by collectively pursuing ongoing and older disputes that linked them more firmly to each other and to those of the town's inhabitants who, either by choice or structural constraint, were not part of the coalition. Second, as commissioners, the 'middle class' began to govern the town aggressively. These efforts again brought them into confrontation with Davis and again firmed up their collective consciousness.

One long-running dispute that the commissioners pursued concerned a fishing weir owned by Davis, which allegedly was blocking traffic on the river. The commissioners requested him to come to a meeting 'to account for the nuisance'. Davis refused (Minutes, 19 February 1841). Two days before, James Ryan, Hutchinson and Clifford – all commissioners – had summoned Davis to the petty sessions for obstructing navigation. McEnnery led Davis's defence, stating that the magistrates had no jurisdiction because Davis was sovereign. 'Sultan not sovereign' interjected the plaintiffs' solicitor, James Quinn. McEnnery was overruled. Quinn continued:

As was well-known, Mr Davis was Sovereign of the town but he did not do good for the town. He lived beside the river and had built a wall across it thus preventing navigation of a previously navigable river. The wall also caused floods in the town. Mr Davis, far from being moved by the plight of those he reduced to poverty had, when he advertised his letting of his mill in the Advertiser, put down as an advantage that there was large unemployment in the area and thus workers could easily be found cheaply. He had been summoned about the wall two years ago and had agreed to let Mr Clifford and Mr Bull deal with the matter. When they went about removing the wall however he refused permission.

Two other similar complaints against Davis were then held over until this first one was decided (*Kilkenny Journal*, 17 February 1841).

Unnamed 'inhabitants' then sent a memorial to the Lord Lieutenant. Until 1836, they stated, 'the inhabitants of the town had communication with the sea. ... In that year ... Sydenham Davis ... built ... a wall across the river ... thereby putting an end to navigation.' He was 'brought before Petty Sessions and agreed to remove the wall but later refused to do so'. Then, in 'the summer of 1838, one of the petitioners removed the wall himself at which Mr Davis rebuilt it stronger than before'. Recently, 'the petitioners were advised to proceed on an act of parliament of Henry VIII commonly called the fishery act by memorial to the sheriff of the county'. They not only did this but they also had Davis 'brought before Petty Sessions' yet again, and, also, sent another petition to Dublin.

> The petitioners beg to impress upon his excellency the great hardship caused to the poor by resultant flooding and also the unemployment which is attributable to the obstruction of navigation. The petitioners disclaim any malicious, political or religious motive in making the charges as the petitioners are persons of all shades of political and religious opinion.

The Lord Lieutenant's response was that the petitioners should appeal to the county Sheriff, who 'by the act of Henry VIII has the power to remove obstructions on the river. ... The sheriff should be called upon at once to cause its removal' (*Kilkenny Journal*, 10 March 1841). Interestingly, but not surprisingly, this correspondence was with Henry Innes, flour-miller, treasurer under the Act and 'middle class' agent.

In fact, the town's navigation had been declining from at least the late eighteenth century because of silting and because of competition from other modes of transport. Davis was hardly responsible for this; indeed, he was trying to obtain funding from the state and the gentry to revive it (Silverman 1992a). Moreover, although the wall may have caused flooding, more important was that it interfered with salmon fishing, one of the activities by which many of the labouring class earned part of their livelihood (Silverman 1992b). In other words, these petitions and court cases, phrased in the language of navigation and flooding, were about an attempted alliance between the 'middle class' and local labour. Such language, however, provided both a rationale and a means for appealing to state agencies and the law, whereas fishermen's livelihoods and local poverty did not.

However, some fishery law pertained to weirs. Thus, several months later, Davis was summoned before the Kilkenny Petty Sessions on grounds that the spur wall on his weir was 'highly injurious to the fish in the river'. At the sessions, several labourers gave evidence. It is important to note, however, that they did so both against *and* for Davis. Lawrence Power swore that the wall was 'taken down in ... 1837, according to an order from the magistrates at Thomastown Petty Sessions; it has been built up again since that time'. Joseph Morris deposed that the spur wall was 10 yards shorter a year before. In contrast, William Grace, 'never saw a shorter weir than Mr Davis''. When cross-examined, it was discovered that Grace was employed by brewer Anthony Nugent, who also had an illegal fishing trap 'on the opposite side of the river'. The solicitor for Davis argued that 'the magistrates had no power to interfere with ... private property'. Solicitors Hyland and Quinn countered with 'a hope that the magistrates would protect public right in opposition to individual interest' (*Kilkenny Moderator*, 21 August 1841). The 'middle class' clearly was trying to court, with only limited success, members of a dependent and factionalized working class.

They were also concerned with courting those who lived in the country. They had already begun to govern the town actively. Property values were posted by valuators whom the commissioners selected, tax collectors were appointed and property was defined: 'The sweeping of the Streets and Roads to be left to the inhabitants until ... nine o'clock in the morning ...; after that hour, the manure becomes the property of the Commissioners' (Minutes, 15 February 1841). Delicts and fines also were fixed: 'If any person ... shall take or carry away dirt, dung, etc. ..., for the first offence he shall be fined five shillings – for the second offence, Ten Shillings' (Minutes, 1 March 1841). In line with these concerns and the commissioners' earlier efforts to have their members come from as wide an area as possible, the commissioners decided to investigate 'the limits of the Borough' according to 'the ancient boundaries'. They made 'a respectful appeal to the Sovereign' to hand over 'Charters, Corporation books and documents in his possession'. In this effort, at this point and whilst the commissioners were in firm control, motives also became clarified. The commissioners did not simply wish to extend benefits outwards and incorporate more distant-dwelling residents; they also wished 'to avoid the people from the heavy burthen of taxation which must necesarily fall upon them ... unless we can obtain assistance from those who are able to afford it'. In other words, the wider the jurisdiction, the greater the tax base: 'The Commissioners are under the apprehension that it would cause a severe and useless burden on the Town for the sake of a paltry taxation on the Country ... to take in Such a [limited] Space as they first contemplated'. They therefore posted 'an advertisement ... in the Sessions House requesting any inhabitant of Thomastown' who had any relevant documents to bring them forward (Minutes, 5 and 29 April 1841).

Davis, however, did not think he could 'legally comply' with their 'respectful appeal' and the commissioners 'had no other alternative but to apply to the Courts of records'. They also ordered ordnance survey maps and obtained evidence from witnesses, none of whom could 'throw any light on the subject nor could any of them recollect the old Custom of riding the franchise'. Undaunted, they asked all commissioners 'to bring to their recollection the many instances Wherein the Sovereign did exercise his authority beyond the wall of the Town'. Fr. Ryan suggested 'that there could be no difficulty with respect to the extension ... as it was the Opinion of all he consulted that those living in rural parts as nearly as much benifited by the State of Roads and Streets' and this was 'bound to lighten the taxation on all within'. Using such a rationale, the commisoners then listed, exactly, the widest possible 'limits of the Borough Town of Thomastown'

(Minutes, 29 April 1841). They made a valuation of the entire area and passed a 'rate of 4 pence on premises of the yearly value of £10 and 2*d* on premises of the yearly value of £5' (Minutes, 3 May 1841).

By mid-1841, the commissioners held such control that they unanimously voted that all future Corporation meetings would be held in private, notwithstanding their previous motion that all £5 housholders could attend (Minutes, 7 June 1841). They also announced a new anti-Davis campaign: they would make an effort to inquire into 'corporate property' (Minutes, 7 and 11 June 1841) and five of their number were formed into a committee to investigate the collection of tolls (Minutes, 6 September 1841). This concern with so-called Corporation property was not new. In late 1840, the *Journal* reported that 'the elected commissioners ... are determined to recover any property which may have been alienated from the corporation'. The *Journal*, in order 'to be of service in tracing out the property of the people of Thomastown', reproduced one of its advertisements from 1767: 'To be sold – that part of Dangan Wood growing upon the estate of Thomastown Corporation' (3 December 1840). By 1840, Dangan Wood was owned by Sydenham Davis – as were Thomastown's tolls. Indeed, much of what was reputed to be Corporation property was held by sovereign Davis, inherited from his father.[8]

The process, however, was cut short. In August 1841, the Irish Municipal Reform Act abolished Thomastown Corporation, as it did most others in Ireland and, with it, the commissioners and their powers. As a result, rights to tax and to order public works fell largely under the jurisdiction of county juries controlled by landlords and, after 1850, of a poor law board composed of landlords and farmers. In the half decade after 1841, the press reported few town events that even remotely suggested that a self-conscious, locally-based 'middle class' had continued to pursue its interests: two petitions to raise funds for reviving the town's navigation (1842 and 1846), collections to raise money for a cathedral in Kilkenny (1842) and to relieve local poverty (1846), and two small meetings in 1844 held by Catholic supporters of the O'Connell nationalist movement. Even fewer events were reported over the next three decades, whilst economic depression gradually depleted the number of locally-resident industrialists and professionals (Gulliver and Silverman, in press). In other words, a conscious 'middle class' had formed, for a brief time, and then dissolved.

An Historical Ethnography of the Making of the 'Middle Class'

The dispute which developed in the context of Thomastown's virtually moribund Corporation in 1840 was generated by the conjuncture of state policy and a parliamentary Act, some inhabitants' shared experiences in the town and a politico-economic structure which enabled, and indeed encouraged, people from certain occupational categories to come together. Through their actions, a conscious 'middle class' emerged in opposition to a local landlord and in association with a political economy in which the material interests of the agents were not in *conflict*. More particularly, the 'making of the middle class' occurred *after* the state devolved the possibility of real administrative power to particular and non-antagonistic categories of the town's population (£20 householders), who had to be elected by other less, but still relatively well-off, inhabitants (£5 householders), in a context that contained an active but weak opposition (the sovereign). The 'middle class' was thus actualized, in Thomastown, through a coalition of professionals, retailers *and* industrialists as a result of material conditions and lived experiences as these intersected with state domination at a particular point in time. The class, however, defined as self-conscious through its administrative and legal struggles, was an ephemeral phenomenon in Thomastown, even though the occupational categories which underlay it had deep historical and, in many cases, persisting roots. For the reproduction of the 'class' required a formal administrative infrastructure and the support of the state. When both were removed, its consciousness vanished.

A key feature, therefore, of the 1840 conjuncture and of 'middle class' consciousness was the centrality of state hegemony in administrative and legal matters. Another feature was the effort of this 'class' to bridge two key cleavages in local society: that between labour and capital and between town and country. At the time, labour was dependent, relatively impoverished and factionalized. Efforts to forge an alliance had little impact on workers as a class, but did intensify the antagonism between the 'middle class' and the landlord. Similarly, in accommodating rural agents and extending their control outwards, the 'middle class' simultaneously expanded its tax base and its confrontation with the landlord. All these struggles contributed to the continuation of class consciousness. Meanwhile, as part of these processes, the third cleavage in the town at the time – the separation of artisans both from labour and the 'middle class' – was simply reproduced.

Clearly though, not all members of Thomastown's occupational categories were equally involved in the Corporation dispute. Rather, agents came mainly from amongst the professionals, industrialists and retailers – and, in terms of proportion, mainly from amongst the former two. Agents also were all urban-based: even farmer Cantwell lived in town at the time. Anxious to improve town services to benefit themselves whilst simultaneously spreading the cost, it is hardly surprising that their meetings concentrated on valuing property, setting rates, defining Corporation boundaries and reversing the alienation of what was thought to be Corporation property. Nevertheless, the administrative zeal of the 'middle class' was striking: administration provided the impetus, *raison d'être* and ideology for and of the class.

Once the commissioners were in control, the 'middle class' also provided a hegemonic viewpoint as it set out to incorporate the surrounding urban sprawl and countryside and to circumscribe the sovereign's residual power, which still rested on the corporate rights of the now-decayed Corporation. As the 'middle class' gained ground in these efforts, it simultaneously cultivated an alliance with labour. At that point, however, the state intervened dramatically, with its own agenda *vis-à-vis* local political structures in Ireland. The domination wrought by the 1841 Municipal Reform Act irrevocably removed all possibility of formal administrative control from townspeople and, in the process, destroyed the consciousness of the town's 'middle class' and buried, finally, its 'body corporate'.

Concrete Manifestations, Dualities and Theory

The concerns of sociological theorists with 'class structure' and of social historians with 'class experience' can be investigated through their empirical or concrete manifestations, and some relation between the two can be suggested. In Thomastown in 1840, the occupational structure reflected its particular history: a fundamental division was between labour and capital. Yet the town's commercial function had also given rise to other sociological categories which, although linked generally to an overarching system of capitalist exploitation, took on a local immediacy and empirical importance. In addressing this, I have found it useful to look at particular dualities derived from the work of Gulliver: how individual actions gave rise to a collectivity, how this was actualized through 'conflict' and co-operation, and how both could be viewed through a dispute and its management even as they formed the impetus for its trajectory. I also have found that this enabled me to say something about theory – about the making of the so-called middle class as a social phenomenon and its relation to certain agents who occupied anomalous class locations. In this way, the broad patterns of Gulliver's work continue to inform anthropology: the ethnographic analysis of material relations and social change in small-scale locales, contextualized in wider arenas and historical understandings, with the aim of, and underpinned by, theoretical advance.

Notes

1. Gulliver has used the term 'conflict', like most anthropologists, in at least three ways: in 'the treatment of *inter-personal disputes*, where the *raison d'être* of social action was conflict brought into the public arena' (1971: 188)(italics mine); as *political competition* ('factions may be defined as persisting, non-corporate conflict groups ... involved in competition to protect and promote a succession of interests' [1971: 254]); and as *contradiction* ('There was a fundamental contradiction in Ndendeuli social organisation. ... Egocentric ties conflicted with cluster coordination' [1977: 63]). Nevertheless, he has always been clear as to its interdependence with co-operation or 'co-ordination' as 'two sides of the same coin': on the one hand, 'inherently conflict situations entailed cooperation; and, on the other hand, essentially cooperative interests and action entailed conflict' (1971: 189). In the present paper, I either avoid the term or sign it carefully. I use quotation marks ('conflict') when referring to Gulliver's work and/or any of his three meanings (as dispute, political competition, contradiction) and I use italics (*conflict*) when I use it in the strict Marxist sense of class conflict.

2. Field and archival research in Ireland and Thomastown were carried out over a 14-month period during 1980–1 and then,

intermittently, for another 12 months during the summers of 1983, 1987, 1989 and 1992. Research was funded, at various times, by the Social Sciences and Humanities Research Council of Canada (SSHRC); the Wenner-Gren Foundation for Anthropological Research, New York; and the Faculty of Arts, York University.

3. A Corporation minute book, for the period November 1840 to September 1841, has survived and is located in the Public Record Office, Dublin. Several county newspapers of the period are located in the National Library (Dublin) and in Rothe House and the County Library (Kilkenny city). Complementary materials include parochial records, valuation records, deed memorials, wills and probate papers, commercial directories, British parliamentary papers, etc. These are discussed in more detail in Gulliver (1989).

4. Data on early tradesmen have proved difficult to come by. In the present situation, I have deduced that the six were artisans. I know that they were not farmers, retailers or industrialists and, because they were ratepayers (according to Bracken), they were unlikely to have been labourers. Therefore, they must have been artisans.

5. Until the February 1st meeting, it is not known who produced the minutes. After that time, as a reflection of the new administrative order, they were produced by the hired clerk. Little is known about him. He lived in the town in 1845; by the next valuation (1857), he was no longer resident. He also could not be connected to any local kin via the parochial records.

6. The walls had surrounded about 16 acres. As previously noted, until the 1800 Act of Union most freemen and burgesses had lived some distance away. Moreover, since at least the seventeenth century, townspeople occupied houses on the various roads that led into what had been the walled area. Indeed, the outsiders to whom Davis objected all lived within a few hundred metres of the old walls, as did Davis himself.

7. See Note 1.

8. Contrary to the 1835 Parliamentary Commission report (Parliamentary Paper 1835), the Corporation had owned property outside the walls. At the time of the Cromwellian conquest in 1649, its so-called Liberties contained 1,840 acres. These were confiscated and allocated to the Hewetson family. Davis had bought these lands in the early nineteenth century from a

landlord who had purchased them in 1791 from the Hewetsons. Only in this indirect way, then, had the Davis family appropriated lands. It seems likely, though, that the concern at the time was with the possibility of a more recent and direct alienation by Davis himself.

References

Comaroff, John and Jean (1992). *Ethnography and the Historical Imagination*. Boulder, Colorado: Westview Press
Cullen, L. M. (1990). 'The Social and Economic Evolution of Kilkenny in the Seventeenth and Eighteenth Centuries', in *Kilkenny: History and Society*, ed. William Nolan and Kevin Whelan. Dublin: Geography Publications
Eley, Geoff (1990). 'Edward Thompson, Social History and Political Culture: The Making of a Working Class Public, 1780–1850', in *E. P. Thompson: Critical Perspectives*, ed. Harvey J. Kaye and Keith McClelland. Philadelphia: Temple University Press
Giddens, Anthony (1984). *The Constitution of Society: Outline of the Theory of Structuration*. Berkeley: University of California Press
Gulliver, P. H. (1971). *Neighbours and Networks: The Idiom of Kinship among the Ndendeuli*. Berkeley: University of California Press
Gulliver, P. H. (1977). 'Networks and Factions: Two Ndendeuli Communities', in *A House Divided?*, eds Marilyn Silverman and Richard F. Salisbury, Anthropological Studies of Factionalism. St John's Newfoundland: ISER, Memorial University
Gulliver, P. H. (1989). 'Doing Anthropological Research in Rural Ireland: Methods and Sources for Linking the Past and the Present', in *Ireland from Below: Social Change and Local Communities*, ed. Chris Curtin and Thomas M. Wilson. Galway: Galway University Press
Gulliver, P. H. and Silverman, Marilyn (1990). 'Social Life and Local Meaning: "Thomastown," County Kilkenny', in *Kilkenny: History and Society*, eds William Nolan and Kevin Whelan. Dublin: Geography Publications
Gulliver, P. H. and Silverman, Marilyn. *Merchants and Shopkeepers: An Historical Ethnography of Commerce and Retailing in a Southeastern Irish Town, 1200–1986*. (In press.)
McCracken, J. L. (1986). 'The Social Structure and Social Life, 1714–1760', in *A New History of Ireland (Vol. IV): Eighteenth-Century Ireland, 1691–1800*, eds T. W. Moody and W. E. Vaughan. Oxford: Clarendon Press
Moody, T. W., Martin, F. X. and Byrne, F. J. (eds) (1982). *A New History of Ireland: A Chronology of Irish History to 1976*, Vol. vii. Oxford: Clarendon Press

Parliamentary Paper (1835). *Reports from Commissioners on Municipal Corporations in Ireland.* H.C. 1835, xxvii, p. 573.

Pilsworth, W. J. (1951). 'Thomastown Corporation.' *Old Kilkenny Review* 4

Silverman, Marilyn (1992a). 'From Kilkenny to the Sea – By River, Canal, Tram or Rail? The Politics of Transport in the Early Nineteenth Century', *Old Kilkenny Review* 4, no. 4, 988–1011

Silverman, Marilyn (1992b). 'From Fisher to Poacher: Public Right and Private Property in the Salmon Fisheries of the River Nore in the Nineteenth Century', in *Approaching the Past: Historical Anthropology Through Irish Case Studies*, eds Marilyn Silverman and P. H. Gulliver. New York: Columbia University Press

Tighe, William F. (1802). *Statistical Observations Relative to the County of Kilkenny Made in the Years 1800 & 1801.* Dublin: J. Archer

Wolf, Eric R. (1990). 'Facing Power – Old Insights, New Questions', *American Anthropologist* xlii, 586–96

Wright, Erik Olin (1989). *The Debate on Classes.* London: Verso

Chapter 7

The Milieu of Disputation: Managing Quarrels in East Nepal

Lionel Caplan

Introduction

A great deal of attention in the anthropological literature on legal processes has been focused on the means by which disputes are dealt with in a variety of social settings. The distinction between negotiation and adjudication has been widely employed, and in his work on disputing behaviour Gulliver focuses primarily on 'patterns of interactive behavior in negotiations', arguing that they are 'essentially similar cross-culturally' (1979: xv). He notes, furthermore, that every dispute 'occurs in a cultural context and a social situation that have been previously established' and calls for this wider setting to receive greater attention in the presentation and analysis of disputing behaviour (ibid.: 268–9). In this paper I will examine the content and character of quarrels as they relate to the historical and political circumstances of east Nepal, where they arise, are prosecuted and dealt with. My argument is that this milieu of disputation can only be properly understood against the background of the political transformations which occurred as a consequence of the unequal struggle for power between the long-settled 'tribal' populations and the expanding Gorkha (later Nepalese) state which sought to win control of their remote mountain territories during the eighteenth and nineteenth centuries. I shall focus on two kinds of dispute arising from this new political reality, one relating to land struggles involving the long-settled Limbu people and high-caste settlers who entered the area in the wake of state aggrandizement, the other arising from Limbu marital practices, which become contexts in which cultural identities are debated and reiterated.

The Limbus of East Nepal

The Limbus have been settled in what is now far eastern Nepal (*Pallo Kirat*) for many hundreds of years. Little is known of their way of life prior to the incorporation of Limbuan (Limbu country) into the Gorkha state during the last quarter of the eighteenth century, although there is evidence of a political system based on shifting alliances among powerful household heads (Sagant 1981). Land, which until the latter half of the nineteenth century was plentiful, was deemed to belong to the group of agnatic kinsmen who cleared the forest and brought it under cultivation. It is likely that until the eighteenth century the Limbus, like many 'indigenous' groups of hill dwellers, practised a form of slash and burn, or shifting cultivation. But even with the adoption of plough agriculture, probably as a result of contact with non-Limbu migrants entering their territories, the Limbus retained this system of landholding. The individual had rights to land by virtue of membership in kin groups of ascending order – sub-lineage, lineage, clan, etc. This, and others like it, was probably the ancestral system of land tenure to which the Gorkha ruler attached the label '*kipat*' in the wake of the conquest and unification (see Burghart 1984: 109). When I first encountered them (in 1964–5), Limbus regularly asserted that their forebears had cleared forests, worshipped deities and made them witnesses to their right to have these lands for all time. The grant of a Royal Order (*lalmohar*) by the first Gorkha king in the last quarter of the eighteenth century was seen as state confirmation of this legacy. Kipat was thus more than a system of land tenure; it was the basis of Limbu identity as a people (see also Chemjong 1958, 1966; Melford 1966; Caplan 1990).

Since the principal resource was labour, powerful households sought to attract followers and labourers by marriage and other forms of political alliance, so that the principle of agnation was lightly marked as far as access to land was concerned. In other words, rights to cultivate within the group's territory were granted to Limbu kin and political followers who were not necessarily agnates. All such grants were made in the context of a 'clan-based' economy lacking a concept of private property; the gift of land was not seen as an act of alienation (Gregory 1982).

While the state granted the Limbus a Royal Order to hold their lands under kipat tenure, during the next two centuries it lost no opportunity to reduce the area under this form of tenure by a series of hostile legislative measures. These were designed principally to satisfy the growing demands for land to cultivate by the large numbers of non-Limbu immigrants who had entered Limbuan in the wake of the conquest. Limbus were urged to settle these immigrants on their lands, and since Limbu landholdings were extensive and there was a need for settlers to provide labour, the Limbus conferred land grants on the newcomers, who recognized their dependence on the Limbus by both tributary and ritual offerings.[1] For some time these lands continued to be regarded by all parties concerned – the Limbus, their non-Limbu grantees, and the state – as belonging to the Limbu donors under kipat tenure. The gift of land was not perceived by the Limbus as an act of alienation, since, as I have already indicated, there could be no such concept in a clan-based economy without private property. By the latter part of the nineteenth century, however, the state – dominated almost entirely by members of high castes (see Bista 1991) – introduced legislation which allowed non-Limbu settlers and their descendants to convert into *raikar* tenure – in effect, private property – all lands which had been or would in future be granted to non-Limbus by their Limbu hosts. Gifts were thus transformed into commodities.[2]

In other ways, too, kipat lands were reduced and raikar lands increased by state fiat. For example, the state appointed official Limbu headmen (*subba*) – usually senior lineage figures – to collect taxes on all the lands within their domain (including those granted to non-Limbus), represent the administration to their rural followings, and hear disputes among the latter. For the privileges attached to these duties, the subbas were compelled to surrender large amounts of land to the administration, which transformed these plots into raikar tenure. Again, kipat land was sequestered to support the local militia in the district of Ilam, where my own fieldwork was conducted, but even after the troops began to be paid in cash the land was not returned to the original donors, but registered as raikar, and thus lost to the Limbus. Similarly, Limbu lands taken for the purposes of running the postal services were later converted to raikar. Finally, the establishment by the state of an administrative apparatus requiring registration of land titles, tax revenues, and meticulous (if often inaccurate) record-keeping of all kinds placed the Limbu kipat-hoiders (*kipatiyas*) at a gross disadvantage. The first Limbu inhabitants of the settlements I was acquainted with in the district of Ilam only learned to read and write during the first quarter of this century while serving in the Gurkha regiments of the (British) Indian army. Before this the largely illiterate Limbus relied on genealogies and other kinds of oral tradition to verify and attest to their land rights (as well as on non-Limbu scribes to translate this knowledge into the appropriate written format), a situation which could be and was exploited by both the state and the non-Limbu population to reduce the extent of kipat land.

By the beginning of this century the rate of kipat loss had reached serious proportions, and under intense pressure from the Limbus the state – concerned about the volatility of a remote region – executed a partial reversal of policy, banning the permanent alienation of kipat lands to members of other groups.[3] By this time in Ilam where I did fieldwork, only about 40 per cent of irrigated paddy lands (*khet*) remained under kipat. These developments must be seen in the wider context of the state's concern to abolish kipat and similar kinds of 'tribal' tenure throughout the country, and standardize tenurial arrangements that favoured high-caste populations. McDougal reports that in Rai country kipat had been totally abolished by the 1940s. He suggests that the state was able to exert its will over the Rais more decisively than over the Limbus because the former lived closer to the capital and 'presented less of a united front' (1979: 15). Regmi argues that Kathmandu had less difficulty establishing control over the kipat lands of other ethnic groups not only because these groups were 'less organized and turbulent' than the Limbus, but because they were situated in 'less strategic' areas (1971: 53).

By the time of my first fieldwork in Ilam in 1964–5 the long process of in-migration and Limbu land loss was evident in the settlement configuration. Ilam contained a population of 124,000, the majority of whom were non-Limbus. The Limbus were living in a number of much reduced kipat enclaves, surrounded by and occasionally interspersed with members of (mainly) high castes ('Chetri-Bahuns') who held their lards under raikar tenure, akin to freehold. The Indreni cluster of settlements, north of the district capital, which was the locus of my study, was populated almost entirely by Limbus (80 per cent), whose homesteads and fields were kipat. The non-Limbu minority in the settlements, as well as the population of the surrounding villages (who constituted the majority population in the area), held only raikar land.

Local Land Disputes

This history of land struggle is clearly mirrored in the kinds of recurring disputes (*jagarda* in Nepali) between the Limbus (principally the subbas or headmen) and the non-Limbu settlers (mainly members of high castes) in Ilam that characterized the early part of this century, and had by no means ceased by the time of my first acquaintance with the area in the mid-1960s. Below I summarize two such disputes.

The Case of Dilli Ram vs. the Indreni Subbas

In 1912 Dilli Ram, a Brahmin from a neighbouring settlement, filed a case in the Ilam Court[4] against five subbas from the Indreni settlements, claiming that 19 khets (irrigated paddy fields) which had been cleared, terraced and incorporated within their kipat domains by their forefathers had not been properly registered as the law subsequently demanded. Dilli Ram argued that these lands – which were especially productive – should therefore be made raikar and registered in his name under the rule that if a complainant (*polaha*) can prove his case the property in question becomes his own. The subbas agreed that their common ancestor had indeed cleared the jungle and transformed it into kipat paddy fields, rights which had been enjoyed by the mythical 'Ten Limbus' since their first arrival in Ilam, and confirmed by successive Royal Orders dating back to 1796. While the Limbus had copies of several of these documents, they could not produce the originals, and in any case, argued Dilli Ram, these made no mention of specific fields, but only generally of Limbu rights to enjoy kipat in Ilam.

The subbas' case therefore relied mainly on oral tradition, on claims to first settlement, and on eligibility to lands conferred by generations of labour and occupation. For Dilli Ram, and the court, the crucial issue was written documentation, and in the absence of firm title to these particular kipat fields, the subbas were assumed to have broken the law. In this case – as in many others like it – the decision went against the Limbus. They were fined, and all but one of the 19 fields was declared raikar and awarded to the Brahmin plaintiff as complainant. Several subbas were effectively beggared by the case, and emigrated from the Indreni settlements.

The Case of Dul Prasad's Kipat

Soon after my arrival in the Indreni settlements my attention was drawn to the attempts of Dul Prasad Limbu to recover some of his kipat lands, lost – he claimed – through a deliberate deceit perpetrated by the father of his Brahman neighbour (Krishne) on the blind and illiterate wife of Dul Prasad's father's brother. Since the woman had been childless, Dul Prasad was the heir to the land, and after a long sojourn in India, he returned determined to regain the kipat to which he felt he was entitled. In his petition to the district court, Dul Prasad explained how his father's father had mortgaged the land in 1910 to Krishne's grandfather, who was, in addition to being a well-to-do village resident, a highly-placed official in the Ilam administration. The transaction involved the modest sum of some 80 rupees, although the land concerned included both a large 'dry' field (*bari*) on which maize and millet were grown, and a productive irrigated paddy field. As was the custom, the land was being cultivated by the Brahman creditor until such time as the principal was repaid. Since this had not happened during his lifetime, the Brahman's son (Krishne's father) had 'inherited' the cultivation rights to these same fields, while Dul Prasad's father's brother had in his turn inherited the kipat rights, which were assumed by his widow after his death. Dul Prasad insisted that Krishne's father had persuaded the widow, who was by this time blind, to accept an additional loan (*bard*) of Rs 1000, and to put her thumbprint to a new document which registered the total mortgage at Rs 8000.[5] This was a spurious amount (Dul Prasad used the Nepali term for husk, useless) which the Limbu debtors could never hope to repay, so effectively securing the Brahman's cultivation rights in perpetuity. His petition also made mention of the fact that he was a subba, a headman, one of those respected persons on whom the government had relied in the past to collect taxes and maintain law and order in his domain.

In his counter-petition to the court, Krishne by and large confirmed the sequence of events as set out in Dul Prasad's document, but denied any dishonesty by his father – claiming that the Limbu widow had received the full amount stated in the mortgage paper on which she had placed her thumbprint.

In a variety of informal contexts, however, Krishne admitted that most creditors in Limbuan – his late father included – had, at the time such documents were being drawn up, taken advantage of Limbu innocence and illiteracy to 'add a few zeros' to the amounts actually loaned to the kipat-holders. On the veranda of his house in the Indreni settlements, in the presence of both Limbus and members of other groups, I heard him remark that

> our forefathers [referring collectively to high castes] came here from the west [of Nepal]. This was a Limbu area, and we were welcomed by them. They said 'take this land, and settle'. At first, in our great-grandfathers' time, we respected the subbas, and folded our hands when we addressed them and asked for favours. But later we didn't take care of them. We took their lands and with government help made them raikar. Later, in our grandfathers' and fathers' time, when they needed loans we gave them a little money and took [under mortgage] a lot of kipat land. In those days the Brahmans were a little more clever than the Limbus. So we did this 'other work' as well [i.e. took advantage of Limbu innocence] and became rich.

Krishne insisted that these practices were a thing of the past, and he personally would not countenance such behaviour.

During the first eight months of my stay in the Indreni settlements there were sporadic attempts to resolve the dispute before it reached the court. It was widely recognized that Dul Prasad stood no chance, and furthermore would probably end up having to pay a hefty fine, which would require him to mortgage yet more of his by now meagre landholdings. When several Indreni Limbus heard me ask why the matter was not taken to the Village Council (*panchayat*),[6] which had the authority to hear disputes, their reaction was a mixture of amusement and despair. It was not that they resented the 'law powers' invested in fellow villagers, as Starr reports is the case in the Turkish village she studied (1978:149). Village Councils of one kind or another have been around for a fairly long time in Ilam, and most ordinary villagers regarded the Council as one of several possible forums in which they might air certain of their grievances (see below). Their response can be explained rather by the fact that these Councils have since their inception been controlled by well-to-do members of high castes, and Limbus have understandably not tended to turn for redress to the very persons they regard as having been responsible for their plight in the first place. The Council at the time of my fieldwork was dominated by several Brahmans whose own wealth had been built on kipat lands taken under possessory mortgage from Indreni Limbus. The likelihood of the latters' getting a fair hearing from the panchayat was therefore deemed negligible, and the matter of Dul Prasad's dispute with Krishne was never formally raised in that arena.

Dul Prasad's agnatic kin, several of whom claimed to have lost much of their kipat patrimony through similar experiences of dishonest practice in the past, recognized the hopelessness of his legal case, and urged him to seek a solution out of court. At the same time, several prominent non-Brahmans in the area were encouraging Krishne to negotiate a settlement, and after months of *ad hoc* discussions the parties met to agree a compromise. The meeting took place on market day at the back of a shop in Ilam Bazaar, the district capital – thus away from the Indreni settlements – and out of sight of the many Indreni residents who visit the Bazaar on that day. Apart from the disputants, there were several of Dul Prasad's agnates, a wealthy and highly respected Gurung resident within the boundaries of the Village Panchayat who also had extensive kipat holdings under mortgage (said by most people to have been acquired honestly) and two prominent non-Brahman members of the Ilam District Council. After hearing Dul Prasad's reiteration of his case, all of those present acknowledged the fraud perpetrated on his widowed aunt by Krishne's father, but also underlined the absence of legal proof for his claim. After stressing the need to avoid court costs and fines they turned to the outlines of a compromise. Krishne offered to return some of the dry fields in dispute, but refused to give back the (irrigated) paddy land. After some four hours of bickering, during which time Dul Prasad several times left the meeting announcing he would fight in the courts to save his honour as a subba even if it meant his total ruin, he was persuaded to accept Krishne's slightly improved offer of dry fields, along with the right to cultivate one of Krishne's paddy fields (actually part of Dul Prasad's own kipat holding) at a nominal rent. A document was subsequently written in accordance with this compromise, and the court case was quietly dropped.

Although these talks focused exclusively on finding an acceptable solution to the disagreement over land, there was an additional silent agenda which all participants were aware of but addressed only indirectly. Dul Prasad's petition to the court had been prepared by and with the encouragement of another prominent Brahman resident of the Indreni settlements ('Bishnu') and one of two major factional leaders in the area, the other being

Bishnu's own brother. Bishnu happened to be a close patrilateral relative of Krishne, and was widely acknowledged to be at odds with the latter (as he had been with Krishne's father before him). Faction leaders (and their close allies) were reported to seek out any number of local quarrels (and instigate others) to support, embarrass, thwart, beggar or defeat one of the parties, particularly if the factional opponent was involved with the other side. These faction leaders were therefore in almost continuous dispute, either with one another or with those who might seek to challenge their dominance. I often heard the figure of 150 cases of litigation over the years quoted as the measure of their wealth, power and capacity for stirring up trouble, and it was generally assumed that the only appropriate arenas for such contests were the courts.

By seeking to remove this dispute from the courts, the negotiators not only hoped to save Dul Prasad from serious financial loss, but also to take it out of the factional domain, and so allow for the possibility of compromise. At the same time, of course, participants in these discussions were perfectly aware that, as long as factional leaders continued to exercise their influence over local disputes, solutions reached by negotiation could only ever be partial and ephemeral. In this kind of political context dispute *settlement* is, at best, an uncertain process.

Local Marriage Disputes

I noted earlier how, until the latter part of the nineteenth century, the subbas controlled access to land in Limbuan. By making grants to Limbu dependants and non-Limbu settlers on their domains they stood at the apex of the local political hierarchy. In the course of the struggle for kipat, as we have seen, state institutions – dominated from the start by members of high castes – played a major part in undermining and ultimately overturning this hierarchy of power in favour of what eventually became the majority, non-Limbu population. For nearly a century now the dominant elements in Ilam and other parts of east Nepal have been members of the highest castes.

The Limbus were not only economically and politically marginalized, but saw their ways of life heavily influenced by regnant state ideologies, including a law code based on Hindu beliefs and practices. Along with most other 'tribal' communities they were incorporated into a ritual hierarchy which designated them a 'drinking' (*matwali*) caste and allocated them a place between the 'twice-born' high castes and the lowest 'untouchable' groups. Still, notwithstanding their incorporation into a multiethnic society, and strong cultural influences towards 'Hinduization', the Limbus have retained a strong sense of themselves as a distinct people. I have argued that, with the threat to their lands, kipat became the focus of their identity. With the emergence of a constrasting category of people holding property under distinct and novel (i.e. raikar) tenurial arrangements the Limbus became acutely aware of themselves as 'different'; in the course of this discovery their land assumed highly symbolic significance (see Caplan 1970; 1991).

Limbus were also conscious of the contrasts between many of their own cultural practices and those of the high castes, nowhere more so than in the area of marriage. Bride theft or capture was the prevalent 'traditional' form of marriage among the Limbus as among other 'tribal' populations in east Nepal (Sagant 1970; Allen 1987). In the Indreni settlements a significant proportion of the adult population had been married in this way, and even in the 1960s young men were apt to abduct or 'steal' unmarried girls (usually but not always with their consent), often after drinking and dancing together. With equal if not greater frequency women already married, though probably not yet mothers, would leave their husbands and join other men – as their first or subsequent wives – in new domestic unions.[7]

But if Limbu unions continued to result from the wilfulness of young people, there was a contrary tendency – of more recent vintage – which followed the high castes in arranging the first marriages of children. At the time of my first fieldwork as many as two-thirds of initial Indreni marriages had been arranged by parents, although not a few of these were ended when women went away with other men (usually in the early stages, before any children had been born). The arrangement of marriages was certainly as favoured by wealthy members of the Limbu community – many of whom were Gurkha ex-servicemen – as by prominent non-Limbu resident in the area, as well as government officials, all of whom were members of the dominant higher castes. The latter took meticulous care in organizing their own affinal alliances, and exercised tight control over daughters and daughters-in-law. Whatever the nature of the personal tie between husband and wife among the high castes, the relationship was acknowledged as formally unequal and based on the control of the latter by the former. More importantly, the bond between the two families was hierarchical and distant.

By contrast, both affinal links and gender relations among the Limbus were more nearly egalitarian, despite an increasing stress on arranging unions.[8] Because of this, and because of the marital fluidity resulting from the behaviour of young people, the relations between affines were often fraught and conflictual. Their marital practices therefore generated an almost endless series of open disputes, requiring considerable time and effort to defuse and resolve. In the following section I describe one of the numerous 'trouble cases' which occurred while I was in the Indreni settlements. What I want to draw attention to is how, in the process of settling these quarrels, Limbu identity claims are restated.

The Case of Harka Moti's Adulterous Marriage

Harka Moti, the daughter of Chandra Bahadur Limbu, had been wed several months previously to a man from a village about a day's walk away. The marriage had been arranged by the two families, who were already known to one another through various affinal bonds linking the two settlement areas. As was not uncommon, Harka Moti had returned after the wedding to her natal household (*maiti ghar*), where she was to live for a time until her husband's family fetched her to her new home. During this period Harka Moti, like most of the other unmarried or newly married daughters of the village, spent many evenings in the company of young men and women drinking and taking part in *dhan nac*, or 'paddy dance'. In the course of one such evening she danced with a young man from the district of Panchthar to the north, who was visiting his married sister in the Indreni settlements. That night she 'disappeared', and it became clear in the course of the following day that she had returned with him to Panchthar.

The news spread quickly to her husband's family and several days later her husband, his father and mother, and several neighbours, including a spokesman (*budauli*), arrived at the home of Chandra Bahadur's headman or subba, where they were soon joined by Chandra Bahadur and several of his agnates and neighbours. The subba, assuming the role of spokesman for the Indreni side, began the discussion by asking where the visitors had come from and on what business. The husband's spokesman answered: 'we have come in search of a lost thing'. The subba replied that 'when the panther roars, the goat runs away', implying that they must not assume that their daughter-in-law had been stolen. Chandra Bahadur had sent several kinsmen to search for her, he added, and they would soon know where she had gone. If it was discovered that she had indeeed fled with another man in an adulterous marriage (*jari*) they would be entitled to claim compensation (*jarikal*).

After a further exchange of local aphorisms the conversation turned to the fact that Harka Moti had been left at her natal home for too long. The subba remarked: 'As is the custom in *Das Limbuan, Satra Thum* (a ritual formula for speaking of the traditional Limbu homeland) you came to ask for our daughter. Then we made a marriage between them and we hoped for their love and happiness. But for many months you didn't come to ask for her. When did you marry her, do you remember? Long ago! And you still didn't come to get her.' The husband's spokesman obliquely accused Chandra Bahadur of not sending her to her husband soon after the wedding, while the Indreni side insisted that the husband should have come to fetch his wife. Then, hinting that Harka Moti had not been too happy with her new in-laws during the short time she had spent in their house, the subba added:

> You have to know how to behave to a daughter-in-law: give her food and clothes. Or she won't want to stay in her husband's home. But if she stays too long in her natal house, who knows what will happen? We are men, we have only one mouth and we want to eat regularly, but women have two mouths, so how can they not be hungry all the time? When a girl becomes a woman she notices everything. She doesn't care what her parents say. To go *poila* (i.e. away with a man) is natural. They go themselves, and it is our custom, so they are not blemished when they do so.

In response, the husband's father replied 'it is our nature to change old things for new. So she has gone with a new husband, and you want a new son-in-law.' Chandra Bahadur's supporters protested vigorously that this was not so, that they valued and liked their affines too much to want to change them. 'She was naughty (*badmas*) and went away, but we don't want to break relations between us,' insisted one. Another added, 'If I had a daughter I would now give her to you. But unfortunately I don't have a daughter.' (At that point one of the women in the house shouted 'then give him your wife', which brought universal laughter, and numerous ribald comments on how difficult it was for old men to make children.)

After two days of inconclusive discussions, during which the husband's side sought an admission that the girl had in reality formed a new marriage bond – so that they could claim compensation – and the representatives of Chandra Bahadur played for time so that they could delay payment, it was agreed that if within three months the girl was either not found or found to have entered an 'adulterous marriage', the cuckolded husband (*sadhu*) and his supporters would come to take compensation. A bottle of spirits was then given to the husband's spokesman, who in turn presented Chandra Bahadur's subba with a bottle. These were drunk and the visitors were presented with another bottle 'for the road'.

Several months later the aggrieved husband returned with his representatives to claim compensation. It was clear by this time that the woman had left him for another, and that since the adulterous union had been formed while she was at her parents' home, and nominally under their charge, the initial responsibility for meeting the payment was that of her natal family, although it was understood that in time they would seek reimbursement from Harka Moti's new husband. Discussions this time concerned mainly the sum to be paid, since it was always a negotiable amount, based in part on the initial wedding and bridewealth costs (borne by the bridegroom's side), and also on the mandatory fines fixed by the courts should the matter enter their jurisdiction (a threat nowadays open to the aggrieved party). A third factor to consider was of course the ability of the girl's father to afford the compensation, since while he could expect some assistance from agnates and neighbours, basically it was a cost for which his household alone was responsible.

It was recognized that Chandra Bahadur could not meet the amount finally agreed, and discussions then proceeded to consider the possibility that the aggrieved husband would accept marrying Chandra Bahadur's youngest daughter, Harka Moti's sister. This was referred to as *doli bharauni* – filling the bride's palanquin, and acknowledged as an old Limbu custom, most often following the death of a wife. For all sides it seemed to provide the ideal solution to the whole problem. It was agreed that women from the Indreni settlements would accompany the girl to her new husband's village as her bridal party, and the wedding would be made, but the usual bridewealth payments would be waived by Chandra Bahadur. In the meanwhile affinal relations between the two families would be preserved. Everyone seemed satisfied with the outcome of negotiations until it was discovered that Harka Moti's younger sister, on hearing that she had been promised as a bride to her former brother-in-law, had fled to a neighbouring village, and refused to agree to this arrangement.

At that point, all those taking part in the talks turned in exasperation and anger on Chandra Bahadur, who it was felt was responsible for the whole mess, since he clearly had no authority over his daughters. The matter was then taken to the Village Council, whose mainly high-caste members lost no opportunity to comment adversely on those Limbu habits (drinking and dancing) which led to these 'unorthodox' liaisons in the first place. In the presence and with the agreement of the original negotiators they proposed that Chandra Bahadur leave immediately for Panchthar district with a spokesman and a few agnates to seek compensation from the 'seducer' (*jar*), i.e. Harka Moti's new husband, for his adultery. Indeed, why this had not been done already was a question which a number of Indreni residents were asking. Alternatively (and this was the solution the Council members seemed to prefer) they urged Chandra Bahadur to persuade Harka Moti to return to her original husband. Several instances were recalled of Indreni women who had left their marriages to form new unions, but subsequently decided to resume their earlier relationship. Although it was rumoured that Harka Moti herself favoured the latter course of action, the cuckolded husband was firmly opposed, saying that the girl was now 'spoiled'.

Discussion: Disputes and the Assertion of Identity

I left the field soon after, and never did discover the outcome of this case, but it raises several issues as regards the nature of 'internal' disputes among the Limbus. For one thing, marriage relationships are easily formed and severed, largely at the behest of the partners themselves. They are therefore active participants in decisions affecting their own marriages, decisions which can, as we have seen, generate disputes which involve not only individuals but wider groupings. On numerous occasions I was told by men and women of the senior generation – many of whom had themselves made their own marriages (i.e. by 'theft' or adultery) – that the youth get up to all sorts of 'mischief', and it is the elders who must try to sort it out. The latter are especially concerned that affinal ties carefully nurtured over many years are threatened by the wilful behaviour of the young people. Thus in the case of Harka Moti, Indreni residents were very anxious to preserve the links which had been formed with the settlements from which their current adversaries had come, since these ties had been built up through multiple unions in both directions over many years. The threat constituted by the dissolution of or disturbance to a single marriage is therefore something to be avoided, or at the very least managed with great delicacy. There is thus an inherent contradiction in Limbu marital usages between on the one hand the fluidity of individual relationships (in the early years of the marriage) and on the other the desire to preserve affinal links.

Secondly, despite the influence of high-caste Hindu values in many areas of their lives, which has for one thing led to an increasing tendency to arrange the marriages of children, this has not affected the largely egalitarian nature of either affinal links or gender relations. Whereas the high-caste emphasis is on the sudden and dramatic incorporation of the young wife into and subordination within her married home, the new Limbu wife only gradually relinquishes (but never severs) her ties to her natal family, and retains a large measure of autonomy in her married residence.

A Limbu household is beholden for its ritual well-being to its women, since its personal gods are those of in-married wives, who in effect are thought to bring their own mothers' deities with them to their married homes. Their relationship with the latter also provides a contrast with that of high-caste women. The Limbu husband's family have to transfer large amounts of money and property, in the form of bridewealth and special gifts, over a three-year period, to acquire rights to her children, but there is no sense in which, like their high-caste counterparts, in-marrying women are absorbed into the lineages of their husbands after marriage (see Gluckman 1950; Leach 1961). A woman's natal household even retains the right to perform her obsequies on her death unless a special payment, called *saimondri*, is made by her husband's household.

Such on-going links with natal families give women a certain independence of movement both before and during the early years of marriage. It is only after the birth of children that her 'centre of gravity' shifts towards the married home, her commitment to her husband's kin is strengthened, and the likelihood of an adulterous liaison is reduced. Even then, Limbu women retain strong links with their birth families throughout their lives, and are always made welcome there. The high regard in which they are held in both of the households to which they are linked gives them a strong sense of their own value, and this becomes evident during disputes, where they play an active though informal role. Once the formalities have been dealt with by the male elders, the women are free to comment, interject, even abuse the other side. In one case, which occurred because a young man took a second wife while his first was visiting her natal home, the latter, her younger sister, and their mother accompanied the negotiating party to the Indreni settlements, and for a time were the most vociferous participants in the talks (see below). The point, then, is that the position and comparative autonomy of Limbu women do not simply provide a contrast to those of women among the high castes, but also both serve to define the contours of Limbu identity and constitute a challenge to the dominant culture in eastern Nepalese society.

Finally, turning to the management of disputes, it is widely acknowledged that only the elders can manage the disagreements occasioned by the disruptive flirtations and sexual liaisons of the young. To do this requires a knowledge of Limbu tradition (*mundhum*) and custom (*rithi thithi*), a wealth of local folklore and moral tales, a gift of oratory, and an ability to persuade alongside a readiness to compromise. Alas, only a few elders actually possess such a combination of qualities, and they are regularly called upon to act as spokesmen (*budauli*) whenever a potentially conflictual situation arises. Thus, no man who has 'stolen' an unwed girl, or 'seduced' a woman already wed, would think of approaching her father directly to convey the news, introduce himself to his new affines and pay his first instalment of bridewealth or compensation without a spokesman in tow; and frequently these matters are left entirely to representatives.[9]

The risks of allowing the young to speak for themselves were starkly demonstrated on one occasion during discussions to resolve the disturbance caused by the precipitous decision of an Indreni man – taken while he was attending an annual fair at which a great deal of dancing and drinking usually takes place – to marry a second wife while the first was at her natal home in Panchthar district (see above). When news reached there of what had occurred, a party – which included various relatives led by the woman's father's brother, acting as spokesman – set out for the Indreni settlements, and descended on the compound of the erring husband's father. The latter quickly gathered together a group of representatives, including several subbas, who sought to calm the anger of the visitors with soothing words and gestures of appeasement: 'To bring more than one wife is not against the customs of the Limbus. Many of us have more than one wife. Still, if you think we are at fault we beg your pardon. You are our affines, as you were before, and your daughter is our first daughter-in-law, just as she was before.' At that point the young man who had caused the upset was instructed to approach the visitors and bow in the appropriate manner to his in-laws. But instead of doing so in silence, he commented that they had obviously come here to quarrel, a remark which shocked the entire gathering, raised the temperature of the visiting delegation, and required his rapid retreat from the scene. There was general agreement that the young do not know how to behave in these matters, and there were offers of apologies and further placatory formulae from the Indreni representatives.

Both individuals or groups directly involved in a dispute thus require to be represented by spokesmen, and supported by close relatives and/or neighbours. One or both delegations usually include(s) a subba, who will almost invariably – as in the Harka Moti case – act as spokesman, or otherwise play a leading part in negotiations. In Limbuan there is a long tradition of subbas as judicial figures. Their role in dispute settlement was formally acknowledged by the Nepalese government, which granted them the right to hear most cases (with the exception of capital and other grave (*panchkhat*) offences) thoughout the extent of their kipat domains, including the lands granted to non-Limbu immigrants. The 'court' – composed of a subba and his appointed assistants and officials, or of several subbas sitting in concert – was labelled *amal*, and had the authority to impose settlements, fine and mete out limited punishments to those who came before it.

The powers of the amal have long since been removed, but the subba's active participation in managing quarrels within the Limbu community has not abated. While people still refer to the arena within which negotiations involve the subbas as an amal, the latter no longer have the power or authority to impose solutions. Yet, as we have seen, their role in composing and mediating disputes is crucial. For one thing, they are deemed the ideal vehicles for articulating Limbu norms, and providing the necessary authority to both secure and guarantee an agreed settlement. For another, as repositories of Limbu custom and continuity, subbas are (or should be) adept at articulating the appropriate formulaic statements – usually in the Limbu language – regarding Limbu custom which serve to reduce tension and identify an area of common interest between the contending parties. In this sense their 'formalized' speech sets the scene for more pragmatic negotiations to proceed (Parkin 1975). Sometimes this pragmatic talk, I should note, includes uninhibited exchanges between aggrieved husbands and wives, as happened in the case of the Indreni man who took a second wife. As regards the appropriate forum for dealing with disputes resulting from marital practices, for the most part these are composed within a Limbu context. A constant need to assert their identity – seen as threatened, marginalized and downgraded by the dominant sectors within society and the institutions of the state – has led to a self-conscious reiteration of what are regarded as distinctive Limbu traditions. Among these are the right of the young to make their own marital decisions, and the corresponding duty of the elders, led by subbas and budaulis or spokesmen to help compose the disturbances arising from such choices. Despite the occasional annoyance, even anger voiced by the elders at the apparent irresponsibility of the younger generation, the assumption is that the latter are acting in accord with long-standing Limbu practice, and so attract no moral opprobrium. As Jones and Jones point out, both the 'theft' of single girls and other men's wives are 'common and acceptable forms of marriage ... neither is viewed as illegitimate' (1976: 66). Neither they, nor their families, are 'blemished' by it. The frequent references to such behaviour as in some sense 'mischievous' mimics, I suspect, the judgements of high-castes and increasingly of those Limbus who prefer to arrange the marriages of their offspring.

At the same time, the informal subbas' court or amal can claim no monopoly on their management. Limbus are aware of the laws on adulterous unions and the readiness of the courts to deal severely with offenders. They are also ready – as happened in the case of Harka Moti – to turn to the Village Council to seek an external, mediated solution where preferred negotiation procedures seem to fail.

Conclusion

In this paper I have focused on the politico-historical context of east Nepal in order better to make sense of the character and management of disputes in a small cluster of settlements in the region. While it would be clearly inappropriate to suggest that the political milieu determines typical forms of contestation, there is a sense in which it can serve to generate certain 'trouble cases' and inhibit others (see, for example, Starr 1978). In the district of Ilam, two prominent kinds of disputation were identified and considered, although others might have been highlighted as well. One, resulting from a historic confrontation over the attempt by earlier-settled Limbus to defend and preserve their 'tribal' land and, as they see it, their identity as a distinctive group, from the predations of mainly high-caste immigrant settlers in the area, involved members of the community, and especially their subbas, in litigation over the better part of a century. This unequal struggle between largely illiterate and increasingly marginalized people on the one side, and members of a highly literate, ritually dominant, and economically as well as politically expanding sector within east Nepal society on the other, could have only one outcome. The legal institutions of the state were in no sense impartial arbiters in the contest.[10] They were seen (accurately) by both sides as instruments of state policy, which was, in effect, to abolish all forms of 'tribal' tenure and reduce the power of hitherto autonomous communities like the Limbus occupying remote areas of the country, and satisfy the demands for land of mainly high-caste immigrants settling in these territories. It is perhaps worth noting that the collective experience of legal action by Limbus to defend ancestral lands helped to create awareness of a common cause, and led ultimately to alternative forms of political resistance (see Caplan 1970: 181–9).

The other kind of 'trouble case' examined arises out of the vagaries of 'mate selection' among the Limbus, which threaten existing affinal relationships, and create the potential for serious intra-community quarrels. At the same time these quarrels draw attention to Limbu gender relations, which may be seen to constitute one form of resistance to high-caste ideological hegemony. To understand how these disputes are composed therefore requires us to attend, as Rosen suggests is a pre-requisite for any analysis of legal process, to the 'categories of meaning by which participants themselves comprehend their experience and orient themselves toward one another in their everyday lives' (1989: xiv). As we saw, in the context of the amal subbas, spokesmen and other elders, through their formulaic utterances, underline anew valued ways of knowing and behaving, thereby reaffirming a sense of stability and identity in an everyday world of flux.

Yet it would be inaccurate to assert that particular disputes enter only one kind of settlement arena. While most kipat cases found their way to the courts (although historical documentation tends only to record decisions of adjudicatory bodies), forms of mediation and negotiation were also tried, as the case of Dul Prasad Limbu attests. Moreover, without awareness of what Gulliver calls the 'pre-history' of a dispute (1979: 268) the issue of whether it enters an adjudicatory or mediatory arena may be largely irrelevant. Where it becomes part of a 'pervasive factional' divide, as did the case of Dul Prasad, the precise procedural mode is a tactical and not necessarily a substantive question. Alternatively, while disputes generated by Limbu marital practices are resolved principally through community negotiating structures, other more prescriptive possibilities are available and, on occasion, utilized. More significantly, perhaps, these alternatives have now become part of the wider discourse surrounding the prosecution and settlement of disputes, and as such provide ever-wider choices for disputants.

Notes

1. Gell notes that 'Hindus' who entered Muria Gond territories last century continued to acknowledge the Muria as the 'true owners of the land' and participated in the Muria ritual system because it was the Muria gods who 'ensured its fertility' (1986: 117).

2. For a time following the conquest the state strictly controlled the sale and purchase of raikar land in many parts of the country, so that individual rights in such lands were limited to its cultivation and enjoyment of the harvest. But the government was gradually compelled to acquiesce in a variety of 'extralegal' practices engaged in by peasants to secure greater autonomy in their lands, and towards the latter part of the nineteenth century raikar lands had in effect become private property (see Regmi 1976: 171–8).

3. For similar reasons, the colonial Government of India from time to time took steps to ban the alienation of tribal land to non-tribal people. Gell notes that Muria land was legally prevented from being sold to non-adivasis (Gell 1986: 124). According to Singh, this policy can be traced to the Wilkinson Rules of 1833 (Singh 1985: 12).

4. There has been a district court in Ilam since the last decade of the nineteenth century. Before this cases were heard in a regional court situated in an adjacent district, or referred to a peripatetic juridical body (*dodaha*) appointed by the government that operated as a court of inspection with powers over lower courts.

5. This practice of providing periodic incremental loans (*bard*) was very common, since with growing land shortages (and rising prices for raikar land) another creditor could easily be found to provide an amount greater than the original loan, which would allow the kipat-holder to repay the debt, recover the land and transfer it to the new creditor, in return for this additional loan.

6. The 'Village' over which the Council or panchayat exercises jurisdiction is much wider than the Indreni settlements, which constitute approximately one-third of its population and area.

7. Jones and Jones found that about 40 per cent of first marriages in the Terhathum area of Limbuan were not arranged by parents (1976: 66). Nor is it only Limbus who practise such forms of marriage. The first Nepalese Legal Code, promulgated in 1853, contained a lengthy section dealing with adulterous marriages, and the ways in which redress could be sought (see Fezas 1993).

8. Among Limbus, wife-givers are, if anything, superior to wife-takers. On one occasion, watching the arrival of a new Limbu son-in-law at his wife's natal home with quantities of bridewealth goods, my Brahmin companion was shocked to hear the young man's father-in-law abuse him for the paucity of his offerings. No high-caste wife-giver would dream of addressing the son-in-law with anything but respect.

9. Even arranged marriages require the delicacy of approach which only the spokesman can manage. One Indreni man, who was in constant demand to act as a representative for others involved in such potentially conflictual encounters, put it this way: 'The boy can't go by himself, someone else has to go. The speaking work is the budauli's. If an incompetent person goes to speak for the boy's household the other side might be angry and send them away. So the budauli has to be sincere and clever. He needn't be old ('budauli' comes from the word for old/elder – *budo*). But he must know how to speak.'

10. Starr and Collier (1989: 7) note that all the contributors to their edited volume on legal anthropology share the assumptions that the law is never neutral nor are the courts an impartial arena.

References

Allen, N. J. (1987). 'Thulung weddings: the Hinduisation of a ritual cycle in east Nepal', *L'Ethnographie* 83: 15–33

Bista, D. B. (1991). *Fatalism and Development: Nepal's Struggle for Modernization*. Calcutta: Orient Longman

Burghart, R. (1984). 'The formation of the concept of the nation-state in Nepal', *Journal of Asian Studies* 44: 101–25

Caplan, L. (1970). *Land and Social Change in East Nepal: A Study of Hindu–Tribal relations*. London: Routledge

Caplan, L. (1990). '"Tribes" in the ethnography of Nepal: some comments on a debate', *Contributions to Nepalese Studies* 17: 129–45

Caplan, L. (1991). 'From tribe to peasant? The Limbus and the Nepalese state', *The Journal of Peasant Studies* 18: 305–21.

Chemjong, I. S. (1958). Introduction to *Limbu–Nepali–English Dictionary*. Kathmandu: Nepal Academy

Chemjong, I. S. (1966). *History and Culture of the Kirat People*. Phidim, Nepal: Tumeng Hang.

Fezas, J. (1993). 'Custom and written law in Nepal: the regulations concerning private revenge for adultery according to the Code of 1853', in *Nepal, Past and Present*, ed. G. Toffin. Paris: Editions du CNRS

Gell, A. (1986). 'Newcomers to the world of goods: the Muria Gonds, in *The Social Life of Things*', ed. A. Appadurai. Cambridge: Cambridge University Press

Gluckman, M. (1950). 'Kinship and marriage among the Lozi of Northern Rhodesia and the Zulu of Natal', in *African Systems of Kinship and Marriage*, eds A. R. Radcliffe-Brown and M. Fortes. London: Oxford University Press

Gregory, C. A. (1982). *Gifts and Commodities*. London: Academic Press

Gulliver, P. H. (1979). *Disputes and Negotiations: A Cross-cultural Perspective*. New York: Academic Press

Jones, R. L. and Jones, S. K. (1976). *The Himalayan Woman: A Study of Limbu Women in Marriage and Divorce*. Palo Alto: Mayfield

Leach, E. R. (1961). 'Aspects of bridewealth and marriage stability among the Kachin and Lakher', in *Rethinking Anthropology*. London: Athlone

McDougal, C. (1979). *The Kulunge Rai: A Study in Kinship and Marriage Exchange*. Kathmandu: Ratna Pustak Bhandar

Melford, J. B. (1966). 'Kipat tenure and land reform'. Unpublished report for FAO/OPEX, Kathmandu

Parkin, D. J. (1975). 'The rhetoric of responsibility: bureaucratic communications in a Kenya farming centre', in *Political Language and Oratory in Traditional Society*, ed. M. Bloch. London: Academic Press

Regmi, M. C. (1971). *A Study in Nepali Economic History 1768–1846*. New Delhi: Manjusri

Regmi, M. C. (1976). *Landownership in Nepal*. Berkeley: University of California Press

Rosen, L. (1989). *The Anthropology of Justice: Law as Culture in Islamic Society*. Cambridge: Cambridge University Press

Sagant, P. (1970). 'Mariage "par enlèvement" chez les Limbu (Nepal)', *Cahiers internationaux de sociologie* 48: 71–98

Sagant, P. (1981). 'La Tête Haute: maison, rituel et politique au Nepal oriental', in *L'Homme et la Maison en Himalaya: écologie du Nepal*, ed. G. Toffin. Paris: Editions du CNRS

Singh, K. S. (1985). *Tribal Society in India*. Delhi: Manohar

Starr, J. (1978). 'Turkish Village Disputing Behavior', in *The Disputing Process – Law in Ten Societies*, ed. L. Nader and H. F. Todd. New York: Columbia University Press

Starr, J. and Collier, J. F. (1989). 'Introduction: Dialogues in Legal Anthropology', in *History and Power in the Study of Law: New Directions in Legal Anthropology*. Ithaca: Cornell University Press

Chapter 8

Disputing Human Passion: The Negotiation of the Meaning of Love among the Giriama of Kenya

David Parkin

One of Gulliver's most important theoretical distinctions is that between negotiated settlement and political judgement (1979). In the first, litigants agree to reach a decision through debate and the display of persuasive argument. In the second, a decision becomes acceptable to litigants because it emanates from a person or position of recognized superior power. One could always argue, as does Gluckman (1965), that all forms of litigation involve power contests, even when decisions are socially presented as reached through negotiation. Yet it is difficult to ignore the cultural implications of Gulliver's distinction: negotiation may be regarded as an activity in its own right, which is not expected necessarily to lead to a mutually acceptable decision. In this article, I refer to the way in which people in a community discuss, for instance, a dispute as involving not only a question of rights, wrongs and culpability, but an existential predicament: how else in those circumstances could that person have acted and what are the wider social directives and constraints that make sense, or non-sense, of the event?

The so-called *crime passionelle* is popularly alleged to have special cultural significance in certain parts of southern Europe, sometimes to the extent of absolving perpetrators of their crimes, usually men murdering lovers or spouses in fits of jealousy or revenge, or out of pride and shame. Whether or not the concept of *crime passionelle* may be regarded as of at least some social significance in all societies, the focus on jealousy, revenge and linked emotions does lie at the heart of much African ethnography, including that of Eastern Africa (see especially Harris

1978 and Heald 1989). What is clear from this material is that the cultural expression of such emotions provokes the questions of choice, interpretation and personal identity that I mentioned at the outset, and at the same time challenges the anthropological claim to engage in cross-cultural translation: for example, is an individual's 'passion' recognized as a single, motivating force in human affairs, or is it inseparably cast as the essence of all social interaction and not as the specific if temporary property of any one individual? Analysis of disputes and of attempts to understand and settle them offers one way of asking such questions.

A Story of Passion?

I begin with a dispute having tragic consequences. It happened during August of 1989. The rains had just about finished, and the seasonally gentle sun was drying out the land in eastern Kenya between the fertile coast and the dry Tsavo game park. An unprecedently good year for the maize crop was promised. People were in unusually good spirits in an area otherwise known for repeated drought and famines. A mother in her mid or late twenties went into a forest glade a few kilometres from her father's homestead, accompanied by her three children, aged four, two, and four months, and there hanged them and herself from a tree.

She had been living at her father's home for just over a year, having finally left her husband after ten years of marriage and much violent quarrelling. She had during that time moved constantly between her father's and her husband's home. She had wanted to finish with her husband, but her father had been unable to return the very high bridewealth payments which had been made for her, and so she had had to return each time to her husband. Without exception people say that the quarrels arose from the husband's accusations that she slept with other men. It was in fact only during the last four years that she had produced children, and, thinking that the husband had been infertile, some people suggested that, quite reasonably, she may indeed have sought lovers to make her pregnant. The woman had always denied any adulterous relationships during the nine years that she had lived with her husband.

The third child, of four months, however, was conceived and born during the last year of her life, which had been spent away from the husband. Although it is quite possible that occasional sexual relations may have occurred between her and her husband during this year, the unanimous view was that the woman must have produced this third child by a lover. The husband accused his wife of as much, and demanded to know the name of her alleged lover with a view to extracting from him the compensatory payment of *malu*, to which he would have a right by law, and which amounts to the not inconsiderable sum of about Shs 1,200/-, plus expenses for the elders who preside over the case.

The woman consistently denied any knowledge of the matter. The husband insisted that, if his wife refused to divulge her lover's identity, she herself would have to pay the compensation and costs. After continued pressure from her husband, the woman finally 'confessed', without naming him, to the existence of a lover living far away. It is customary for elders rather than the cuckolded man to approach an adulterer for compensation. The alleged distance from the area of the adulterer made this impracticable, and so the husband demanded that the woman herself secure the compensation from her lover or bring the man to the area for the case. It was at this point that the woman killed herself and her children.

Two interpretations were made of this tragedy. There is that of the woman's father and family. They claimed that the husband himself had murdered all four people. Even those who did not agree with this interpretation said that a person who is angry enough can indeed do anything, even kill their own children. The second interpretation came from people outside the woman's family. This was that the woman was trying to protect the identity of her lover, who was in fact a man who lived locally.

A third possible interpretation – that the woman regarded herself as innocent but was unable to cope with the colossal stress imposed on her, given her husband's threats and the public nature of the quarrel – was not made. In other words, the preferred interpretations located the cause of the death squarely in the triangular relationship between woman, husband, and alleged lover, an obvious case for the people in the area of what one might call a *crime passionelle*.

The motivating emotions were the husband's excessive anger and the woman's excessive despair. The husband's jealousy was not mentioned here, but might have been in other contexts. The implications of the deaths will continue. The woman's family, and the husband and his family, will be judged to suffer from the contamination of bad blood, called *kilatso*, which will spread throughout the two families, making them infertile and causing deaths among them, unless completely eradicated through purification. In other words, at stake is the survival and continued social perpetuation of families and their descent groups.

I asked people precisely what might be the nature of and personal feelings behind the love a woman would feel for a lover she was trying to protect, or that of a man, perhaps jealous, for a woman who had rejected him. The questions which I posed are, of course, loaded with Western assumptions, and I was not surprised that they went unanswered. Westerners may write novels on and speak about love as a self-contained field emotionally affecting only the two or three people involved, but they have no right to assume that this is the case elsewhere.

Among this people, the Giriama of Kenya, to speak openly of love, or to hear others speak of love between men and women, is often to speak of the socially destructive effects of passion and of its role in the perpetuation of disaster. And yet it is evident that the Giriama love not only passionately but compassionately as well: they care for each other as individuals, as well as as members of groups. Why is love publicly presented only, or at least mainly, in the former way? Is this view, which we may call social love, in some sense the definition of love among the Giriama?

The Love of Western Essentialism

I shall return to the Giriama. But let me for the moment raise some questions about the way, as a Westerner, I have given attention to these interpretations. While it is true that Westerners normally define love in unacceptably essentialist terms, with only Barthes's study as a disarmingly disturbing attempt to do otherwise (Barthes 1978), it is nevertheless instructive to examine *how* it has sometimes been defined in the western tradition. One kind of view, exemplified by Rollo May, an American psychotherapist (1969: 37–8), is to break love down into four components: first, lust, libido, or plain sex; second, eros, 'the drive of love to procreate or create – the urge, as the Greeks put it, towards higher forms of being and relationship'; third, *philia*, or friendship and brotherly love; and fourth, *agape*, the love of God for humanity, expressed by humans as devotion to the welfare of each other. Note that, in this description, eros is represented as aiming for 'higher forms of relationship'.

A more popular version of Western love is from the book, *Women Who Love Too Much*, by Robin Norwood, another psychotherapist, who simply takes the dualism of eros and agape, and translates eros as passionate love and agape as compassion (1985: 242–4). But, according to Norwood, eros or passionate love does not in this description aim for higher forms of relationship. On the contrary it is presented as in direct contradiction with agape or compassion. More than this, Norwood implies that we are misguided in believing that passion can lead to compassion, when in fact the conversion of passion into compassion is precisely what destroys the passion and, for many, the main reason for continuing the relationship.

This contrast between, on the one hand, love as an ideal whole that can be attained, and, on the other, as more likely to be split into the irreconcilable opposites of passion and compassion, exists today in various forms. Therapy presupposes the attainment of the harmonious ideal, while much drama, literature, song, poetry, and the media-reported crises of everyday life take the sceptical view, as well as the idealist. Of course, neither is right nor wrong, but they are a means by which we divide neatly into two parts that domain of experience which Westerners call love, desire, sexuality, care, concern, and tenderness, but also destructiveness, suffering, and the exercise of power.

Another way of saying all this is that modern Western discourse sets up the opposition between passion and compassion and then allows some people, let us call them idealists, to argue for their harmonious resolution, and others, the sceptics, for their permanent separation. Yet, whichever the perspective, the problem of passion and compassion is seen primarily to be a matter of the two or three people involved, both as arising from them and as having consequences for them alone. Wider social consequences are considered secondarily, if at all.

Western Views of African Love

Let me raise two questions here. First, how far is this debate between the sceptics and the idealists found in Africa and elsewhere? Second, is love in Africa so cast in terms of its wider social consequences that the debate is in fact rendered in quite other terms? Full answers would require extensive comparison, and I will confine myself much more humbly to the Giriama.

At this point I would like to disentangle some of the existing confusion on the subject of love in Africa. Anthropologists, more even than voyagers, have often started from the assumption that no such debate exists in Africa, and have, on the whole, clinically refrained from such matters, even and perhaps especially in describing courtship and marriage, which are represented as rule-governed behaviour.

Almost as a sop, however, we do find, scattered in the anthropological literature on marriage in Africa, references to the recent introduction from the West of the so-called concept of romantic love (Little 1973; Obbo 1980). This notion of romantic love seems to encapsulate the idealist and sceptical aspects, while suspending judgement as to which triumphs over the other. And certainly, in modern African magazines, newspapers and television, and in locally produced novels, especially in towns, there are reports of agonies of passion and pleasure similar to those found in Euro-America. In fact they are not identical, but show sufficient overlap to qualify as yet another Western import shaped by specifically African local conditions. They enjoy the same ambivalence of being treated seriously by some and dismissed as nonsense by others. Read any Nairobi newspaper and you are struck by the same antinomy: of love as a painful affliction needing some cure, sometimes attached to threats of suicide by the aggrieved, and of love as something patiently to be understood and nurtured, and to be tenderly rather than passionately pursued, without undue dependence on sex, because that way it is likely to last longer, or to seem as if it would.

This generous bestowal of a mixture of Erika Jong and Barbara Cartland on the rather better-off urban elements of Africa does raise the question of what Africa is supposed to have had beforehand. Is the implication that there was no equivalent of romantic love, however we define this, and, if so, what kind of love might be said to have existed? More than this, we must recognize that it is still only a minority of people in Africa who live in large towns, and a still smaller minority who have access to Western-influenced literature and media.

Digging more deeply, it is a little disturbing to sense the hidden suggestion that 'they' in Africa simply did not in the past have those elevated emotions that peoples in the West allegedly have. One doubts that the Middle East, Southern Asia, and the Far East, with their textual traditions depicting love as an art form, have been characterized in quite this way, whatever other prejudices there might have been.

In fact, Schapera's *Married Life in an African Tribe*, published in 1940, describes the process of growing up and of courtship and sexual and erotic overtures in terms familiar to Westerners, as do the few other ethnographic accounts that touch on the subject of love between men and women. How much this is an unconscious imposition of similarity is difficult to say. I would say, in any event, that the ethnographic claim that the Western concept of romantic love has only recently been introduced into Africa presupposes differences of essence which are not then borne out by the reports.

Thus, in the work of Schapera and others and in the African societies in which I have worked, I see men and women coming to desire and cherish each other, and to range backwards and forwards over the classical gamut of lust and eros, as well as, later with their children and kin, of agape and philia. That is to say, I see them as wanting each other sexually, yet apparently converting this desire into on-going relationships of compassion, hedged around admittedly by social constraints inhibiting separation and divorce. Such compassion seems sometimes to incorporate and sometimes to contradict the sexual, at the same time as in other relationships it comprises parental, filial, and brotherly love. This may be a description of the obvious, useful in refuting any racist implications, but it does not go far enough, for we still need to know how such concepts and relationships are talked about, or not talked about, and so give value to the experience we call love.

Idealists and Sceptics among the Giriama

Among the African people I describe, the Giriama of coastal Kenya, the concept of love as a tension between passion and compassion is not marked, that is to say, is not a recognizable area of conversation. Yet, at the same time, the Giriama have a wide and sophisticated vocabulary of emotions and an indigenous medical system heavily concerned to cope with emotional stress and disorder.

In talking about the love of a parent for a child, it is clear that the Giriama are describing what we call compassion. The term *hendzo* is used for the abstract noun, and there is a verb, *kuhendza*, which means to love. The same term is used to describe love between a man and woman. It includes both compassion and passion, as far as I can judge from observation, and always has a paramount reference to the fact that the couple have sexual relations. It does not, however, presuppose a tension between compassion and passion. More than this, it seems most often to occur in conversations about the tragedy and disastrous consequences of such sexual relations as I described in my opening example, or, as in other examples, in relations in which a sexual prohibition has been broken, with the result that the couple may become infertile, lose their children if they have any, and cause the same affliction to spread to their co-resident kin and affines.

This social marking of love in terms of its wider tragic consequences privileges the negative aspects of passion and sexuality over and above considerations of quieter compassion. Much as one has to investigate evil in order to understand morality, or misery as the window on to happiness, so love among the Giriama seems to be most accessible at the point at which it is at its most socially destructive.

I think that a clue as to why this is so is not just the tautological explanation of society's needing to perpetuate itself, and so publicly curbing the breach of sexual prohibitions and their harmful consequences. Rather, we can understand this emphasis on tragic love as part of a debate in Giriama society focused on differences of power, and hence of discourse, between young and old and between men and women. It echoes the debate between idealists and sceptics which I introduced earlier, except that the idealists are vociferous and the sceptics muted. I will try and explain this.

First, there are the idealists among the Giriama. Mainly these are elders who denounce improper sexual love, which is the only love that they are likely to talk about, as socially harmful. For them, emotional conflicts can be reconciled. There is no question of an irresolvable tension between passion and compassion.

Emotions which control individuals are illnesses to be cured, though this is done through customary medical expertise and not by the individual alone. Proper sexual love is sexuality harnessed in the interests of acceptable courtship and life-long marriage producing many children. Most such elders who have influence are men but they do include some senior women whose own sons are becoming important. They are joined by men who are not elders but whose personal circumstances ally them to the elders' view, an example being the husband described in the initial case who sought compensation for his wife's alleged adultery.

Second are what we might call the muted sceptics. These are most women and some young men, who, by their actions and sometimes in song, dance, and spirit possession, challenge the view that emotions that control persons are sickness. For the sceptics, there is indeed a tension. This is that individuals may sometimes be controlled by emotions, including that of passionate love, but may also struggle to control emotions for their own ends rather than in the interests of social others, whose motives are questioned. While not apparently a tension between passion and compassion, I suggest that this draws paradigmatically upon similar notions. The debate is therefore about the social legitimacy of expressing particular kinds of emotions: who can express what to whom and under what circumstances.

Here, there is a parallel between the struggles that make up Giriama society and their guarded displays of lust, love, and affection. It is destructive forces which seem to take up most peoples' attention, such as witchcraft and the hatred and revenge that follows it. Similarly, they mostly refer to the negative consequences of passion and not to the possibilities of compassion. Individuals seem to be made up of both these latter, but we cannot tell which is being valued at any point in time: quiet love and concern may be taken for granted but, occasionally, the tendernesses and lusts of love break through as of greater importance for some. But is this how the Giriama see it?

The Social Context of the Idealist Position

Let me now describe those aspects of Giriama society which permit the emergence of an authoritarian idealist position which talks only of socially relevant love and a contrary position which is sceptically individualist and by implication revolutionary.

Three institutions constrain women's sexuality, and the choice of partners made by young men and women, and create the conditions for dissatisfaction and sometimes protest among them. These are polygyny, child marriage, and widow inheritance. From the authoritarian viewpoint of elders, these are the basis of known Giriama society.

The Giriama are or were politically uncentralized. They had central capital towns, one of which is still a symbolic focus, but organize themselves for marriage, settlement, and much ritual through a system of exogamous patri-clans. They once had a generation- and age-set system, and remain strongly gerontocratic, with most men above the age of forty likely to become polygynous, having on average two or three wives. Men marry between the ages of twenty-six and twenty-eight, while girls are married at on average fifteen years of age. Child marriage is illegal, but still is practised occasionally in outlying areas. It happens when a man needs bridewealth for a son or for some contingency and approaches a wealthier man, offering him his young daughter for the immediate payment of cash or cattle. At an agreed time some years later, the betrothed girl will leave her natal homestead to join her husband.

As in many African societies, a widow can be inherited by her former husband's brother, and so becomes this man's wife. The rationale for this practice is that it is the family comprising the brothers that made the marriage payment for the wife. The wife has the right to choose which of her husband's brothers, including his paternal cousins, will inherit her. But she cannot refuse to be inherited. Marriage generally is not normally arranged in the strict sense of the term. But fathers and mothers exert strong pressure on particular couples to marry and discourage what they regard as unsuitable unions. Most marriages are between local people, whose families are already well known to each other and probably related. Marriage into the father's clan is not permitted, but is encouraged in the mother's or father's mother's clan. More generally, marriages of sons and daughters are aimed at securing mutually beneficial personal alliances.

The three practices of polygyny, child marriage, and widow inheritance mean that many young women are married to older men not of their choosing. Parents exercise remarkable influence over their children, backed up by the power of the much-feared parental curse. A parent may curse a child of any age if the latter disobeys or is disrespectful to the parent. The curse is believed to make the man or woman infertile, and can only be removed after admission of culpability and special pleading to the parent. Generally, then, young women and to a lesser extent men are rarely able to reverse decisions or refuse a marriage choice made on their behalf.

Resistance to Absolutism

But attempts are made. This may be done under cover of a traditional form of marriage by capture (*wa kuhala*). This form of marriage is sometimes no more than a fiction, the desirability of the union having been worked out beforehand by the couple's parents. But at other times it genuinely involves elopement by the couple, who are always young people, often marrying for the first time. It is seen by both young and old as a countervailing measure taken by young men and women to usurp elders' control. In most cases, the parents of one of the pair will have had no objection to the union, and eventually the marriage will be acceptable to both families. But sometimes both parents disapprove, and the couple are refused the marriage blessing, which is regarded as essential to the fertility of the union and its happiness. These are the kinds of cases which may end in the suicide of one or both of the pair. It was put to me as follows:

> Love (*hendzo*) under these circumstances is always uncontrollable. It is, and always was, the cause of suicide when young men and women are forced to marry other than their lovers. They normally kill themselves by hanging. This is called *walogwa na shulamoyo*, literally 'they are bewitched by despair'. The elders say that such a person was sent the despair by an evil witch, but we young people say it is the elders themselves who cause the death.

In this remark we see both a questioning of elders' power and the hint of a struggle between public definitions and personal experiences of love.

Young men and women are most likely to court each other at dances, especially those which are held at funerals lasting up to seven days and nights (Parkin 1991: 125). Dances are competitive displays. A youth tells a girl beforehand, or indicates through eye-talk and gestures, that he is interested in her, and she in turn chooses by dancing up to him, or not, as the case may be. That more or less settles the issue.

Male suitors will also press their advances on such other occasions as are available for instance 'chance' meetings on paths to water-holes, or while on visits to relatives. Older boys teach younger ones the skills of how to sweet-talk a girl, which consists of delicately expressed admiration for her beauty and character.

Premarital sex is nowadays usual, but normally only with the man whom the girl will eventually marry. Many men seem unaware of the full and precise nature of female sexual response, recognizing on the one hand women's liking for the physical act and sometimes even accusing them of seeking too much of it, yet unaware of women's orgasm which, as far as I can judge, is not therefore a common feature of women's sexual life. A Giriama colleague at Nairobi University, who gives me permission to quote him, said that when he was young he would be frightened by the ecstatic response of a girl which occasionally occurred, and which he now recognizes as orgasmic.

This is not ethnographic voyeurism. It gives the background to the condition of women's sexuality in a society where their choice of spouse is already limited and constrained. It is a situation not dissimilar to that in Western society a few decades back. Young couples meet, fall in love, are physically attracted to each other, and then are either diverted into another relationship, or themselves do marry but settle into a routine which may become unsatisfactory to either the man or woman, perhaps compounded if the husband later takes and favours a younger wife or mistress.

It is important to emphasize here that Giriama men and women are aware of the possibility of personal choice in marriage. This is not a society in which arranged marriages are so much the exclusive expectation that choice is unthinkable. Yet it is the frustration of choice by elders that seems to crush the possibility of talking about love as a complex of human emotions which are both positive and negative, and both passionate and compassionate. It is as if, by permitting open discussion of the right of individual men and women to choose each other, elders fear that this untidy complex of unpredictable emotions would take priority over such considerations as marriage alliance, material exchange, and the reproduction of children. Sexual love without thought for marriage may well occur both before, during, and outside marriage, but it is another thing for elders to acknowledge and legitimize it. As supporters of an essentialist ideal bordering on moral absolutism, they crush those who work at these margins between individual and society. The result is that, when what Westerners perceive to be loving relationships are talked about, they are described by such elders as illicitly sexual and no more.

This is given substance by the common allegation by men, young as well as old, and sometimes by women, that young women who are forced to marry older men, and women in unsatisfactory relationships, are inevitably drawn into adulterous relationships with lovers. The term *musena* means either friend or lover, and its ambiguity is used cleverly to great effect. *Muzembe* means only lover, and has the connotation of secrecy, wantonness, and adultery. *Zembe* means worthless or idle, while the phrase *manahendza uzembe* used by men means that women love in an indiscriminate way, i.e. promiscuously. Older polygynists commonly complain that their younger wives commit adultery with lovers 'in the bush' on their way to and from collecting water or some other errand. They complain but know that any ensuing children will be theirs, and appear often to think that this is a job best left to more capable others provided it is undiscovered. Discovery, nevertheless, absolutely requires the cuckolded husband, however old, to seek compensation (*malu*) from the adulterer, which is profitable as well as restoring honour and social relations.

The frequent talk by men of women's adultery and sexual insatiability seems to me over-optimistic. The female workload is colossal, even by African standards, and has been noted as such by many travellers. It is difficult to know when during the day a married woman actually has time for her liaisons. Even during the much-cited walks to and from a water-source, a woman has to carry a heavy bucket on her head, a child on her back, some firewood and wild spinach collected on the way, and perhaps a hoe or other article collected from a relative or friend on route. Other burdensome chores await her at the homestead, to which she must return as soon as possible. While it is likely that would-be lovers do arrange to meet on such occasions, it is clear that prolonged and intensive meetings are unlikely. Trysts arranged by sympathetic others are impossible given the efficiency of gossip networks linking homesteads with each other. In so far as men and women do meet each other in this way, it appears that they do so for a variety of motives, which are as likely to include mutual personal attraction as much as lust, and may, perforce, have little to do with sex at all. In some cases at least, we may imagine a version of our own medieval courtly love in which the couple do meet, but so fleetingly that amorous expectations remain largely suspended. In any event, the liaisons are an unclassifiable mixture of such qualities.

Indeed, what is interesting here is the way in which both men and women characterize such illicit liaisons as being for the purpose of sexual intercourse when, as seems to be the case, they are as much exchanges of affectionate and loving companionship as they are of passionate embrace, whether or not sex takes place. In other words, in this already sequestered area of secrecy the negative innuendoes of illicit sexuality take priority over what are evidently much more complex emotions.

The Illicit as Disease

This is the point at which we may note that, not only is the possibility of compassion quashed in favour of that of sexuality, but illicit sexuality is often, perhaps usually, characterized by the idealists – usually male elders – as leading to the woman's infertility, the death of her own or her lover's children, his own wife's infertility, and the affliction of their respective homesteads with these misfortunes. In fact, these problems are supposed only to arise if a woman has sexual intercourse with a brother of her husband or with a fellow clansman. But re-interpretations of alleged cases often occur, and other reasons can be found by a diviner for giving adultery as the reason for the occurrence of death, sickness, and infertility in a home.

In other words, the complexity of passionate and compassionate love outside marriage becomes interpreted by elders as sexual excess, which is further divined as comprising and causing illness, death and misfortune. The link with medical pathology is here clear. It makes sense of the way in which, in conversation, and in the diagnoses of diviners, love (*hendzo*) is grouped together with a number of different harmful emotions and conditions as all being forms of externally imposed illness (*ukongo*): these emotions include desire, lust (as in *vitunusi* or *tamaa*) bitterness (*utsungu*), grief (*sumazi* and *zingizi*), envy (*kidzitso*), hatred (*hamene*), self-hatred (*dzimene*), despair (*shulamoyo*), fear (*woga*), loneliness (*uvumvu*) and others. As sicknesses they are regarded as beyond the victim's control, since things beyond human control are viewed as sickness. Such states are sent by witches or take the form of spirits troubling the body or mind, which may themselves have been sent by witches. Only reversal of the witchcraft by a doctor or exorcism or pacification of the spirits by a diviner will enable the victim to control these passions, and to tolerate such conditions as poverty and the death of loved ones.

It is not surprising that under the welter of such passions and conditions defined as illness, a concept of compassion is buried, and that the sexual love of eros becomes rendered as destructive rather than positive and transcendental. More than this, it is the negative associations of love that receive the greatest attention as forms of uncontrollable illness such as jealousy, hatred, despair, grief, incest, adultery, and the variously named afflictions leading to death and infertility.

The Expression of Emotions

This view of emotions, including love, as illnesses requiring cure supports the position of the moral absolutists, that is the elders, who act as social guardians. Yet in their diagnoses diviners do touch on the problems of passion and compassion in a way we can identify. It is the work of diviners to account for the causes of illness and misfortune and to suggest cures. They reach their diagnoses by invoking the power of special spirits, who are able to explore and discover reasons for the patient's unhappiness. Through the voice of these spirits the diviners talk, for instance, of the despair and loneliness of the patient's heart as well as the lust and longing for someone. But the divinations are closed sessions and never involve named individuals; patients and the objects of their desire, and in some cases those who have caused their unhappiness, are identified through allusion rather than directly.

It is as if the closed divinatory session allows for some private expression of people's desire for the unattainable. It allows them to speak of their inability to reconcile their rapid and perhaps violent changes of care and lust for the same person, or of men's inexplicable impotence and, among women, of the possession spirits which make love to them every night yet frighten them, to take just a few examples. The talk at the sessions, and at spirit possession dances mainly affecting women, implicitly questions the idealist or absolutist view of love and sex as being uncomplicated phenomena provided people observe social rules.

At spirit possession dances, for instance, the spirit-speech that goes on between the possessed and the spirit-medium refers to the spirit, i.e. the woman, being neglected by her husband, his lack of care and concern, his favouritism towards another, and his meanness. The spirit asks for compensatory gifts. But it also refers allusively to sexuality: one common phase of possession has the spirit, i.e. the woman, demanding her *mshindo*, which can roughly be translated as a sudden blow, violence, sensation, excitement, or treat, and is taken also to mean sexual orgasm.

Spirits are often taken to embody human emotions. While spirits/emotions do control women, and so rank as illness, they can themselves be controlled by the possessed woman herself provided she knows their wants, often by herself becoming a spirit medium or diviner. In other words, women in these sessions counter the dominant view that they are always subject to the control of their emotions and act instead as their own agents. It is difficult to resist the conclusion that women here are demanding from their husbands sexual satisfaction as well as care, concern, and material well-being. But the spirit-medium in charge of a session never goes beyond passing on the demand to husbands that they provide their wives with gifts. He leaves unanswered the women's questions seeking a satisfactory joining of sexuality and compassion. Moreover, this talk of the women sceptics does not replace the public pronouncements of elders at moots deciding marriage choices, adultery compensation, and questions of the inheritance of widows and property. It remains subdued.

At funerals, also, there is what we may call revolutionary song and protest, particularly by women, but this gives way in due course to an emphasis on the need for fertility and reproduction, for which only legitimate sexuality is thinkable. For instance, aggressively sexual taunts interwoven with the subject of death are the themes at funerals in special songs and dances performed as the corpse is carried from its house to the grave and as it is buried and for some time thereafter on the same day. Women begin the songs (called, first, *Kihome*, and later *Kifudu*), which are expected to be abusive both of the corpse, whether male or female, and of men in the neighbourhood. The body used to be beaten aggressively as well, but this is no longer the case.

The singers angrily accuse the deceased person of having inconsiderately left the living with unresolved problems. There is the sense of: 'how dare they walk out of this impossibly difficult existence that we call life?' They obliquely refer to the deceased and his or her former relationships, often that with their spouse, telling a tale of jealousy, witchcraft, revenge, death, and implying adultery, mentioning specific clans and groups as being especially avaricious. They sing also of some clans, by which they indirectly mean particular husbands and wives from these clans, as being jealous of their spouses, and of husbands who do not sleep with their wives or favour one wife over another. Men's abuse songs may accuse wives of drunkenness, laziness, and promiscuous adultery. Both men and women make fun of the others' genitals, in each case mocking their size and uselessness, sometimes linking this tauntingly to the sexual uselessness of the deceased man or woman. In these exchanges, sexuality is linked to private passions and resentments, but not to rules of social reproduction.

As the day wears on, however, and as days succeed each other in the funeral, the abusive songs give way to praise songs, and then to songs of sympathy for the bereaved. The sexually aggressive, and its links with lust, anger, hatred, and witchcraft, thus yields to the compassionate during the course of the ceremony. At the same time, people attending the funeral divert their attention from the reviled but now buried body of the deceased subject of the ceremony to the living bereaved, who are shown pity. This switch from abuse to sympathy preserves a sense of social continuity. It allows a hostile emotion to give way to a gentler one, much as passion may yield to compassion. Ignored in this process is the idea discussed earlier in this paper that passion may contain the emotional intensity that destroys compassion, or that the hatred a person feels may in fact be their love.

What do I mean by this latter remark? The position of the absolutists, namely the elders, is that of persons in authority who wish to hide the complexities and randomness of love behind duties of marriage and sexuality and to define extreme shows of emotion as illness. In effect they hide such potentially uncontrollable love by warning of the anger and hatred that excess of it may cause.

Perhaps talking only of the tragedy of love, as do the Giriama social guardians, is an aspect of a blocking-off process: it keeps expectations constantly low by telling the lovers that their love can never be more than short-lived or at best uncertain, either because the passion must spend itself quickly or because they are likely to experience the untimely death of, or separation from, a lover, spouse, child, parent or sibling.

Here, we begin to understand the absolutist position of the elders. It is true that their control of marriage provides them with profitable alliances. But, as homestead heads, ancestral spirit guardians, and political spokesmen of the land, they have a number of difficult roles. It is they who are expected to ensure that rain falls, crops grow, women and livestock are fruitful and multiply, taxes are paid, and central government officers kept at bay. And yet they are supposed to do so in a harsh and unpredictable physical environment, in an area governed by demanding officials and politicians senior to them.

Their distrust of the individualistic and usurpatory qualities of discussable love merges with that of their physical and political environments. They control how people speak of love and of their environment through the same warnings and metaphors. They warn that the fertilities of land and of women are equally vulnerable to the same abuses of relationship rules. In other words, the elders' concealment of love's complexities behind an emphasis on tragedy, hatred, and illness is part of a wider distrust of personal, social, and physical uncertainty.

Conclusion: Sceptical and Idealist Positions

I have suggested that the Giriama elders, in privileging the need to preserve social harmony, hide not just the problems of individual love but, by extension, other existential uncertainties. The young men and women who do raise questions about such uncertainties and want to talk about the disjunctions between marriage, sex, and love, eventually become the elders or the oppressed who fall into line. In this way the dominant view in society continually re-defines sex and love as legitimately aimed at reproduction.

Gulliver's analytical distinction, to which I drew attention earlier in this chapter, is critical. While the absolutist position of the elders reflects the idea of control through political judgement, the questioning attitude and uncertainties of young men and women mirrors that of settlement through negotiation. Yet there is also a paradox. On the one hand, the young themselves eventually assume the authority of political figures making unambiguous judgements. On the other hand, in so far as compassion presupposes that a couple will negotiate their respective emotional needs rather than make the often asymmetrical demands of each other that are characteristic of passion, we find the defenders of compassion, namely the elders, in effect giving support to a negotiable rather than an authoritarian understanding of conjugal amity.

This suggests that even under the guise of their authoritarianism, the elders are really working within a negotiable framework: they want compassion to be the blueprint for couples in love as well as marriage, and try to act against what they see as the threats of untrammelled passion through political judgements which are really more performative than they are punitive. They can never in practice stem the lusts and socially unacceptable loves for each other of persons standing in socially prohibited categories: it is sometimes the very attractiveness of the socially unacceptable, including certain forms of adulterous incest, that make illicit passion irremovable from generation to generation. Each generation slightly alters the line between the prohibited and acceptable: intra-clan sexual and marriage prohibitions may become redefined in a later generation as legitimate liaisons between separate clans or similar units.

Political judgement is therefore never a finite category. It may instil fear in one case, but have little or no effect on those that follow. It is to that extent a performative exercise by elders that does little more than demonstrate the temporality of their own power in contrast to the more persistent social changes occurring over the generations. To that extent, the law legitimating political judgements is not only out of date with practice, it also provides the contrary model against which the youthful and innovative invent new styles. In the *longue durée* it is only settlement through a kind of implicit negotiation, thence leading to change, that perdures. What is centrally at issue is the play of power in human relationships at the levels both of intimacy and formal authority, which is not just the existential dilemma of how to keep power while giving some of it away, but more importantly the fact that persons in authority are not permanently empowered but act as though they are. It is the different cultural idioms in which these dilemmas are expressed that ethnographic study uncovers.

References

Barthes, R. (1978). *A Lover's Discourse: Fragments*. London: Penguin
Gluckman, Max (1965). *Politics, Law and Ritual in Tribal Society*. London: Oxford University Press
Gulliver, P. H. (1979). *Disputes and Negotiations: A Cross-cultural Perspective*. New York: Academic Press
Harris, G. (1978). *Casting Out Anger: Religion among the Taita of Kenya*. Cambridge: Cambridge University Press
Heald, S. (1989). *Controlling Anger: The Sociology of Gisu Violence*. Manchester: Manchester University Press
Little, K. (1973). *African Woman in Towns*. Cambridge: Cambridge University Press
May, Rollo (1969). *Love and Will*. New York: Dell Publishing
Norwood, Robin (1985). *Women Who Love Too Much*. London: Arrow Books
Obbo, Christine (1980). *African Women: Their Struggle for Economic Independence*. London: Zed Press
Parkin, D. J. (1991). *Sacred Void: Spatial Images of Work and Ritual among the Giriama of Kenya*. Cambridge: Cambridge University Press
Schapera, Isaac (1940). *Married Life in an African Tribe*. London: Faber and Faber

Chapter 9

'Youth-Development' – Conflict and Negotiations in an Urban Irish Youth Club

Stephen Gaetz

Philip Gulliver's unique contribution to the literature on dispute settlement has been to provide a model of negotiations with a wide range of applications. He argues that negotiations 'comprise a set of social processes leading to interdependent, joint decision-making by negotiators through their dynamic interaction with one another' (Gulliver 1979: xvii). Gulliver's model of negotiations provides a powerful tool for the analysis of the dispute-settlement process where disputing parties do not have access to mediators or adjudicators, yet must continue a complex and conflict-ridden relationship. In fact, what separates Gulliver's work on dispute settlement from those concerned with adjudication in court contexts (Gluckman 1965; Hoebel 1954) and councils (Kuper 1971) is his attempt to make sense of negotiations that occur outside such structured contexts. Through his historico-ethnographic approach, Gulliver endeavours to examine negotiations in 'real-world' contexts (Gulliver 1979: 60), where the eventual resolution of disputes is by no means certain.

In this paper, I examine the antagonistic relationship between the staff of a youth-development centre in the city of Cork, Ireland, and the young people who frequented it. This relationship was characterized by frequent disagreements and conflict, in which a variety of strategies – including avoidance, self-help and negotiation – were utilized to achieve outcomes. Yet in a case such as this, it is necessary to avoid treating specific disagreements as analytically discrete phenomena. As Starr and Yngvesson have argued, 'many disputes are only one event in a series of events which make up a relationship' (1975: 560). This is the perspective to be taken here, and one that is well-suited to Gulliver's processual approach to dispute settlement, which involves an articulation of cyclical and developmental processes.

The three disagreements to be discussed, then, are best analysed as cyclical events in a much larger dispute (still unresolved by the time I completed my fieldwork),[1] centring around contested interpretations of the purpose of the youth centre. A 'Youth-Development' strategy was to be employed by the staff to encourage the active participation of young people in decision-making. However, as will be seen, rather than systematically encouraging strategies of empowerment, the staff by and large treated the young people in a paternalistic manner. They were typically quick to use their power and authority to rein in what they perceived to be unacceptable behaviour by the users of the centre. The young users of the centre of course resisted attempts by the staff to 'control' them, and pressed for more input into how the centre was run. Their resistance often took the form of disruptive and sometimes destructive forms of behaviour. There was in a sense, then, a battle between staff and users over who should control the agenda of the centre.

The inability of the staff and the users to reach a suitable compromise through negotiations may seem puzzling, given the obvious advantages to both parties of an absence (or reduction) of conflict. The central dispute between the staff and the users can best be made sense of if, as Gulliver has argued, one takes account of the wider social context in which specific disagreements take place. In particular, it is necessary to examine, on the one hand, the significance of power, and on the other, the role played by rules, norms, values and beliefs in affecting the actions and strategies of the various political actors (Gulliver 1979: 51). The interplay between both features is significant in a context such as this, where the relationship between the disputants is clearly asymmetrical. While the young people who frequented the centre were working-class, early school-leavers from the local neighbourhood, the staff (who were given the authority to run the centre) were from skilled working-class and middle-class backgrounds, were educated and came from outside the area. Both had different understandings of their own and each other's roles, and hence developed divergent approaches to negotiations that reflected their class backgrounds and their perceptions of what strategies would best influence the others. There was no single discourse within the centre.

This case raises some important questions about youth-development as a practice. For instance, can and should the empowerment of working-class youth be encouraged according to middle-class notions of participation and leadership? If, as I argue, the operationalization of youth-development becomes problematic in practice, does its perceived 'failure' in fact exacerbate tension, entrench antagonistic positions and lead to conflict?

By examining such factors, insight will be gained into the persistence of conflict within the centre, and into the enduring relationship between staff and users. While continuous episodes of conflict seemed to indicate the failure of the negotiation process to reconcile divergent visions of the purpose of the centre (and power divisions within it), relations between staff and users did not rupture to the point where the centre could no longer operate. On the other hand, the lack of an adjudication process and/or of a successful negotiation strategy seemed to dictate that the cycle of unresolved (and occasionally violent) disputes would continue.

The Setting

The parish of Ballinaclasha can be found on the south side of the city of Cork, in the Republic of Ireland. The approximately 7500 residents live in a mix of public and private housing estates. In the 1980s Ballinaclasha had acquired a reputation throughout the city as an area with substantial youth problems, most notably high unemployment (particularly amongst working-class youth from the public housing estates), inadequate education (many young people were early school leavers), substance abuse and crimes such as vandalism, assault and joy-riding. From the perspective of most young people in Ballinaclasha perhaps the biggest 'youth problem' was that they felt that there was nothing to do, particularly at night.

In response to local concerns, the Irish government and Ogra Chorcai (a prominent voluntary youth-work organization) established the Ballinaclasha Youth Development Centre in 1985. Operating out of a community building in the south end of the parish, the 'centre' (as the users called it) was set up for unemployed young people, and in particular, early school-leavers.

Open weekday afternoons, the centre daily attracted from ten to thirty young people (mostly male), providing recreation, social and life-skills development, and a place to 'hang out'. The facility consisted of an office (which dispensed information on government and volunteer youth services) and two large rooms with a coffee bar, two billiards tables, several games tables and chairs. Most of the activities in the centre focused around the billiards table and the dartboard. People waiting their turn would listen to music, play cards, pass around cigarettes and talk.

Since the day the centre opened it had been an arena of conflict between the staff and the users. Disagreements were played out and resolved without the involvement of outsiders, either as adjudicators or mediators. There was an agreement by the staff and the users to settle all disputes 'in house', and not to involve parents, other youth workers, the police, the parish priest or local community leaders in any capacity.[2]

Throughout 1987, the centre was staffed by four paid youth workers (both male and female), all between the ages of eighteen and twenty-five. In charge of the centre was the Youth Development Officer, Sinead O'Leary, a 23-year-old from a small town in the central part of Ireland. An equally dominant figure was James Sharkey, the Activity Organizer, who lived in a middle-class suburb in the east end of Cork. Both had several years of youth-work experience, but little formal training. Two 'teamworkers', considered junior members of the staff, were assigned to the centre for six-month periods. The fact that the teamworkers were hired temporarily, and that their youth-work training and experience was minimal, meant that they often had difficulty in establishing a clear role for themselves within the centre. Other than myself, the centre had no volunteers.[3] All the staff were hired by Ogra Chorcai (rather than by local residents), and they all lived outside the parish. Most significantly, all came from middle-class or skilled working-class backgrounds, all had a secondary school education (some third-level) and for the most part they all came in to the youth-work profession having to 'unlearn' many of the prejudices they had built up about working-class teenagers.

The vast majority of the users of the centre were males between the ages of fourteen and twenty, from unskilled working-class backgrounds. Throughout this paper, I refer to them as 'the boys' or 'the lads', not only because of the relative absence of female teens (on a typical day there might be thirty males present, but never more than three females), but because of the degree to which their lifestyle valorized an aggressive, working-class masculinity and refusal to submit blindly to authority. In a sense, they were not unlike Willis's 'rebels' (1978) and Jenkins's 'lads' (1983).

The boys were in most cases early school-leavers, and because they lacked adequate education, skills or resources, faced a high risk of unemployment. They were thus placed in a situation where they had plenty of free time, but limited resources with which to engage in leisure. While female teens were equally likely to find themselves in a similar situation, their 'youth culture' was less likely to emphasize the type of 'street corner' behaviour characteristic of the boys (Gaetz 1992).

Because of the boys' highly visible street youth culture and postured masculinity, many Ballinaclasha residents identified them with area youth problems, including glue-sniffing, vandalism, joy-riding and assault. One result was that in many ways the boys felt themselves to be outsiders in their own parish. They were not likely to be members of local clubs, not only because such places might lack interest for them, but also because they were excluded by those who participated in, and operated, youth clubs in Ballinaclasha. Many of the boys felt their reputation as the area's troublemakers was largely unjustified. Said one youth, lamenting the lack of say that the boys had in local affairs: 'We haven't any say. We can't scratch our hole and we get blamed for something. All the snobs get treated differently. They're all well looked after by the priest, boy!'

The centre was thus to play an important role in the lives of many of the lads, because it was the one community-based service where they were made to feel welcome. The centre provided them not only a range of activities during the day and a sheltered location in which to meet friends, but also an opportunity to develop skills and participate in decision-making, ideally in an environment of mutual respect. The lads were clearly enthusiastic about having a greater say in the running of the centre; there was a strong desire on their part to make the centre 'their own'.

Yet, while the boys clearly valued the centre, it did not escape becoming a locale for conflict, aggressive confrontation and vandalism. It was not uncommon to find broken windows and furniture, writing on the wall and damaged equipment (the continual smashing of billiard cues meant that quite often a mop-handle was all that was available for playing billiards), or the theft of billiard balls, cups or the dartboard. While vandalism and disruptions occurred for a wide range of reasons, such acts cannot and should not be explained simply in terms of delinquency. Rather, in many cases they represented the most outwardly visible manifestations of conflict between the staff and the boys.

The various disagreements can be analysed in their own right as evidence of the intensity of the antagonism between the staff and the boys. However, they can also be interpreted as cyclical events in a much larger dispute, that is, over decision-making and control within the centre. The youth-work practice of 'youth-development' figures centrally here. Youth-development, a mandate of this centre, is a youth-work concept that entails encouraging young people to develop skills, strategies and the confidence that would allow them to take greater control of their lives as they grow into adulthood. For example, the centre was to provide a locus both for the learning of such skills and, in assuming assertive participatory and leadership roles within the centre, to put such skills into practice. Central to this practice is the devolution of power downwards, so that young people are invited to play an influential role in decision-making. Power within the centre, then, was to be negotiated between staff and the young people who attended.

However, there is often a contradiction between the 'rhetoric' of youth-development and actual practice in youth-work settings. The youth-work staff at the centre, for instance, operated with poorly defined strategies of how to encourage youth-development, and in actual fact, allowed youth input and assertion of power to proceed only to a very limited point. Minor disagreements often developed into full-blown disputes when young people saw their efforts at asserting power and influence within the centre thwarted. Aggressive displays became a means by which the boys could signal their displeasure with the way things were being run (in most cases incited by a particular event or conflict between the staff and the boys) and their desire to bring about what they felt was a resolution to the dispute.

Disagreements within the centre were typically resolved in one of three ways. First, the staff used their power and authority in order to impose a solution to a disagreement. This tended to work best when the users of the centre were divided, being unwilling and perhaps unable to rally behind a single negotiating position. Second, the boys often used strategies of 'self-help' when it appeared that the staff were unwilling to negotiate. This could lead to a situation where the staff were forced to negotiate, or to accept the solution imposed by the users of the centre. Third, in some cases there were negotiated settlements which followed a process of give and take, usually involving a cyclical process of threats and intimidation by both sides. The result was that eventually each side agreed to a solution which, while perhaps not entirely suitable to either party, at least brought the disagreement to an end.

Case No. 1: Jugs and the Cup

Jugs, a 15-year-old, walked into the centre one early Friday afternoon and headed straight for the second room to play a game of billiards. James, a youth-worker, anticipated potential trouble, since Jugs, who had been known to cause disturbances in the past, was 'mad at him' (annoyed with him). This was because of a conflict the two had had several days earlier, when James publicly asked Jugs to 'quit acting like a langer' (a derogatory term to which the lads took great offence) and to be careful with the billiard cues, which Jugs had been swinging recklessly. Jugs was offended because he was reprimanded in public, in the presence of several of his friends.

Things went smoothly for about 10 minutes until Jugs went to fetch a cup of water. When he returned and sat down, he 'accidentally' dropped the cup, spilling the water and breaking its handle. He and two of the other lads – his friends – were smirking over what had happened. James perceived the dropping of the cup to be no accident, and he confronted Jugs, saying that the whole intention of getting the cup of water was to drop it. Jugs did not respond, but simply smirked and prepared for a game of billiards.

About half an hour later when James was out of Room 2, a loud crash was heard; the cup had been thrown against the wall. James went into the room and angrily told Jugs and the other two lads present that they should leave the premises and not come back for the rest of the day. Two of the lads left, but Jugs refused, still smirking. James again asked Jugs to leave, and after what seemed like a long wait, Jugs left the second room and entered the main room, but he had no intention of leaving. Instead, he went and stood beside Masa, a nominal leader of the lads. Jugs gambled that Masa would back him up and would either challenge James, or that Masa's support would be a signal for the other lads to escalate the vandalism. Masa, himself busy with a game of billiards, completely ignored Jugs, signalling clearly to all that in this case he did not support Jugs or his claim, and that he was not willing to risk his own prestige by participating in any new disturbance or by challenging James. If Masa did not support Jugs, it was highly unlikely that any other lads would do so, as Jugs had very little prestige amongst them. When it was clear to Jugs that he stood alone and that there was no possibility of the lads coalescing into a group in order to defend his honour, he chose the path of avoidance – that is, he stormed out of the centre, and did not return for over a week.

In this case, James exercised his authority as a member of the staff to bring an end to his conflict with Jugs. In challenging James's authority, Jugs miscalculated his support. He was unable to turn his personal dispute with James into a public dispute between the staff and the lads, because his personal prestige amongst the lads was low. Furthermore, because he was known to cause trouble in the centre regularly, his attempt to use vandalism (and encourage its escalation) as a threat was interpreted by the lads as 'messing' rather than as a rebellious act.

Case No. 2: Masa and the Billiards Table

The centre had acquired a second billiards table in March 1987. It was placed in Room 2 along with the other table, because the staff felt that one room should be for billiards and the other for general activities (drinking coffee, card-playing, darts, listening to music). The boys did not like this arrangement, and eventually Masa, who acted as their spokesman, went to two of the staff members and made the suggestion that one of the tables should be moved out of Room 2 and into the main room. He gave a number of reasons: first, the three young women who frequented the centre didn't like to go into that room to play billiards because all the lads were in there. As a result, they weren't keen on coming to the centre at all. Second, the close quarters in the billiards room exacerbated tensions between the lads. Masa argued that, 'Pauly and Jugs don't get along with the Western Star fellows,[4] and so they don't like to play billiards in that room either'. Third, given the level of deterioration of the centre (the radio was broken and the dartboard had been stolen), the placing of two tables in one room led to a situation where most people congregated only in Room 2 and the first (and larger) room went virtually unused. According to Masa: 'All the messing that goes on in there is because there are so many of the fellows in there, like. There's too much action and not enough room. The main room is a boring place to be – no darts, no billiards to watch.'

Masa was told by the staff that his suggestion would be discussed at the next staff meeting, after which they would then get back to him and the boys. When the staff finally did meet, the decision was made to change nothing. One of the senior youth-workers (who was not present when Masa made his argument) said: 'I think it works better with the two tables in one room. I suppose the table could be moved, but I don't like the lads coming in and making demands on the staff like that. They have to go through the proper channels.' The team of youth-workers agreed, in spite of the fact that the staff had never established 'proper channels' for requests of this nature. The underlying motive behind their decision appeared to be that they were wary of giving in easily to the demands of the boys, lest the latter should start pushing for more power in the centre. Their strategy was to exert their authority rather than to negotiate.

When the staff announced their decision the next day, the boys made it clear that they were not pleased. They became restless and the level of tension in the centre began to rise. Still, there was no immediate response from the boys. Things continued as they had for the next several days, with growing support being voiced for Masa's plan. An opportunity was created for the boys several weeks later when, one Friday, the three staff members present decided to go outside and work on installing the new volleyball posts in the courtyard in front of the centre. After forty-five minutes one member of the staff re-entered the centre to see what was going on, as the centre was only very rarely left in the hands of the lads (the staff had left Masa in charge). When inside, it was discovered that on their own, the lads had quietly moved one of the tables to the main room (a difficult feat, given how heavy and awkward slate tables are). There was no messing going on, and things were much calmer than they had been for a while – all this without the supervision of the staff.

The lads chose to use a 'self-help' approach to bring an end to their dispute with the staff when it became apparent that the staff were unwilling to negotiate. The staff had chosen to use their authority to block the request of the lads. Given the opportunity, however, Masa and his friends were able to move the table and bring about a suitable outcome. Though James later revealed that some staff members were very unhappy about what had happened (seeing it as a threat to their authority), moving the table back was out of the question. It would have been a difficult task for the staff and it is unlikely they could have solicited any help from the lads.

Case No. 3: Sparky and the Core Group

In the summer of 1987 the 'core group' became a focus for conflict between the staff and the users. The core group consisted of a group of 10 young people, selected by the staff, who one day a week participated in a more intensive youth-work programme. This included seminars, life skills training, special activities and field trips. The staff felt that by concentrating their efforts on a smaller, select group, they could achieve more effective results. Both the boys and the staff recognized that there were problems with the core group. The boys felt it could be improved if they had more say in setting its agenda and in organizing activities. The staff felt that things were getting 'a bit stale', and decided that several new young people should be added to inject some new blood into the group.

The conflict over the destiny of the core group came to a head with the return of Sparky, a 17-year-old. A former 'regular' at the centre, he was now unemployed again after several months of work. Having been part of the core group prior to his employment, he and his friends assumed that he would be immediately reinstated as a member. However, he and the lads were told by one of the youth-workers that this was not the case – that he would have to apply along with the others, and go through an interview.

Many of the boys felt that the position taken by the staff was unfair, and one afternoon three of them – Duckser, Sparky and

Rocky – confronted several of the staff members and expressed their dissatisfaction with the decision and the process. Said Duckser: 'This is not on. You can't penalize Sparky for getting a job. I'll tell you this much ... I'll be after thinking twice about getting a job in the future if it means losing a place in the core group.' Rocky added, 'It'll be a fucking disgrace if you let that langer Jugs in but not Sparky. Jugs is a messer and he's always after wrecking the place, and Sparky doesn't do that.'

Staff members James and Caitriona listened, and responded with 'We understand what you're saying, but nevertheless, the procedure that we've laid out will be followed.' After a heated exchange, it became clear that the staff were unwilling to give ground, so the boys stormed out, with Duckser shouting, 'If you let Jugs in and not Sparky, we're quitting.'

At a staff meeting the next day, there was some disagreement on how to interpret the actions of the lads. One of the teamworkers discounted the activities of the boys, suggesting that they had just come in with a bad attitude that day and were complaining about everything. Another agreed, saying that the boys had already enough say in what was happening within the core group and that they were just trying to be difficult. On the other hand, James agreed with the lads' view that Sparky should be allowed in the core group and was happy to see them stand up for themselves. However, he still felt that it was necessary that the lads follow the procedure as laid out by the staff. Sinead O'Leary, who had not been present during the confrontation, agreed with James's point of view.

During the next several days, the level of tension in the centre was high. There was more 'messing' than usual, with small acts of vandalism such as the tearing down of posters, and aggressive posturing between the lads (suggesting the possibility of a violent outburst). On occasion, several of the lads would mention within earshot of the staff that 'there will be war' if Sparky did not get back into the core group.

Interviews for the core group began on the following Wednesday. This was not a particularly easy process for most of the boys, as they were uncomfortable in such contexts, having little experience with formal interviews. Sparky arrived for his interview, having relented and agreeing to follow the staff's procedure. However, the interview became an opportunity to subvert the process, by giving minimal (and often sarcastic) answers to the questions posed by the staff, refusing to co-operate fully and making clear his displeasure at having to go through the process. His lack of co-operation (his was the only interview that followed this pattern) became a rebellious challenge to the staff: having followed their procedure, would they (or could they) now reject him?

After the four who had applied were given interviews, the staff had a meeting and it was decided to let them all in, even though there were officially only two spots open. The decision to accept them all, including Sparky, was based on several factors. First, the staff were indeed swayed by the validity of his argument that obtaining employment should not be penalized. Second, Sparky did show up to his interview, even though he was not entirely co-operative. Finally, and perhaps most importantly, the staff were concerned about the very real possibility of chaos if Sparky's application was rejected. Said James, 'I think we should let Sparky in because there will be war out there if we don't.'

A settlement was thus negotiated that was suitable to both the staff and the boys. By letting Sparky in, then, the staff defused a potentially explosive situation and at the same time reinforced the view that they, not the boys, set the agenda for the centre, and that the process that they had established for selecting the core group was legitimate. The boys, on the other hand, got what they wanted. Sparky was allowed into the core group, and though he did have to submit to an interview, he did it decidedly on his own terms.

Power and Negotiations

Gulliver has argued that power is an essential feature of negotiations, yet, ironically, it is one that few models of negotiations take into account (Gulliver 1979: 51). In the case discussed in this chapter, what is significant is not just the unequal distribution of power between disputing parties, but the fact that the types of power wielded by the staff and the lads were different. The power exerted by the staff was rooted in the fact that they had been given, by the government and Ogra Chorcai, the responsibility of running the facility (indeed, for insurance purposes, at least one of the staff was required to be present on the premises while it was open), for working out the budget for the centre and for making purchases of equipment and supplies. They were mandated to deliver a range of youth-work services, including life and job-finding skills, to plan and organize activities and trips, to maintain order within the centre and to encourage youth-development. Yet while there were some responsibilities (dealing with insurance and the budget) that the staff could not delegate to the boys, virtually all other tasks and responsibilities could have ideally been open to the participation of the young people who frequented the centre.

Coming from skilled working-class and middle-class backgrounds and being more educated than the lads enabled the staff to exercise a form of power rooted in their ability to use language and skills to entrench their authority. They were, for instance, able arbitrarily to invoke notions of an acceptable process for dispute settlement, indicating that the lads must 'go through the proper channels', and use deference when addressing the staff concerning changes to the centre, as was seen in Case 2. As a last resort, the staff could invoke the privileges (hence power) granted to them by their employers to determine when, and indeed if, the centre was to open. It was they who, both literally and figuratively, 'held the keys'.

Unlike the staff, the boys had no formal power in the organizational structure of the centre. Their level of participation (and the form it took) was determined basically by what the staff would allow. The root of the power of the lads lay in their ability to make life difficult for the staff. With limited formal power to wield, they exerted power and control through the only tactics that they perceived to be effective in this situation: aggressive acts such as vandalism, disruption and lack of co-operation.

This situation should not seem unusual. Gulliver has argued that where other channels of influence are unavailable, the use of strategies of self-help becomes 'a regular means not only to express the strength of dissatisfaction and determination, but also to precipitate a crisis so that other procedures can be initiated or resumed' (Gulliver 1979: 1). In Case 2, for example, the boys used strategies of self-help when it became clear that the staff were unwilling to negotiate the rearrangement of the billiards tables. In addition, the mere threat of self-help strategies in Case 3 arguably had an effect on the staff's decision to let Sparky return to the closed group, in spite of his less than satisfactory interview.

However, as Case 1 demonstrates, strategies of self-help did not always work, revealing an inherent weakness in the position of the lads. For while the staff presented a united front on virtually every issue within the centre (in spite of the private differences they may have held), the boys could not count on such displays of unity among themselves. The boys, it is important to note, were not a group. Rather, they can be characterized as a loose association which could, at times, coalesce into an action set. The boys regularly distinguished between disruptive acts they referred to as 'messing' (that is, seemingly purposeless acts, or ones related to individual and personal disputes) and more 'rebellious' actions that were seen to reflect the wider interests of the users of the centre. The former actions were seen in an unfavourable light and were negatively sanctioned through threats, public condemnation and ostracism by the rest of the boys. The latter, however, could become calls to action. In Case No. 1, Jugs was unable to turn his personal dispute with James into a broader dispute over the rights of the lads in the centre, and so his smashing of the cup was seen by the other lads as 'messing'. The dispute came to a conclusion without an escalation in conflict because, in the end, Jugs stood alone.

Negotiations and Asymmetrical Power Relationships

Gulliver's approach to negotiations involves the articulation of two interconnected models: one that is cyclical, the other developmental. Disputes such as those I described above must be interpreted as cyclical events in a much broader developmental process of negotiations, in which the wider issue at the centre of disputes between the staff and the boys was the contested interpretation of 'youth-development' and the role of the boys within the centre. That is, were the boys merely to be consumers of a service, subservient to the authoritarian directives of the staff, or rather, were they to play a greater role in decision-making in the centre?

The three cases presented above also demonstrate several contexts in which it is clear that power within the centre was contested. It should be noted that the outcomes of the first two cases were more typical than the third. That is, most conflicts within the centre ended without a negotiated settlement; rather, either the staff or the users prevailed in exerting their power to force a resolution. The significance of this is that in most cases, negotiations within the centre ended at the bargaining stage. The outcome of each dispute meant that the opposing parties were forced continually to reassess their own strategies and make adjustments in future conflicts. More importantly, the lack of a routinized process of dispute settlement meant that antagonisms were not resolved, but were often carried over into later disagreements and disputes.

As a result, disputes within the centre became cyclical events in a larger process of negotiation that, ironically, did not appear to be heading towards a clear resolution. It is here that Gulliver's developmental model provides insights that cannot be garnered from other processual approaches such as phase development models (Swartz, Turner and Tuden 1966). Gulliver doesn't assume the inevitability of a linear progression of events or of the necessity of a tidy resolution to conflict in the form of a return to equilibrium. In his developmental model, phases can overlap, negotiations can break down, procedures can be truncated. Disagreements persist through successive cycles of dispute settlement. It is in fact contextual factors intrinsic to the ethnographic setting that make a straightforward process of dispute settlement problematic.

This of course raises the question as to why negotiated settlements to specific disputes in the centre were so infrequent, and why the larger dispute over the power of the boys within the centre had not been resolved. The staff, for instance, seemed entrenched in their authoritarian position, acting in many ways as the 'centre police' rather than as facilitators of youth-development. On the other hand, the lads were all too willing to use aggressive and sometimes violent tactics to achieve their ends. The lack of co-operation and destructive habits of the lads was often cited as evidence that they were not yet ready to take more responsibility in the running of the centre.

An effort to establish a process of negotiated settlement to disputes within the centre would probably have brought benefits to both the staff and the boys, yet this was not the path sought by either party at the time. While one can look to the inadequate training of the staff, or the 'lack of maturity' of the boys to explain this impasse, a more fruitful approach is to examine some fundamental and underlying differences between the staff and the users: the structural and cultural features that define their asymmetrical roles.

Norms, Values, Beliefs and Conflict

Of course, the use of power in dispute settlement is contextualized by another significant feature of negotiations: the divergent norms, values and beliefs that underlie the behaviour, strategies and interpretation of 'rules' of the disputing parties. The fact that the staff and the lads came from different class backgrounds meant not only that they had prejudiced opinions about the capabilities and competencies of one another, but that they operated with dissimilar ideas about how to resolve disputes. Furthermore, their strategies for negotiations were based on different sets of assumptions. For instance, the main strategy of the staff to incorporate the lads into the decision-making process was to set up official committees that were to meet on a regular basis. These tended to be short-lived and were not always productive, as the lads did not always show up, and when they did, they were often silent and reluctant to participate. The staff often expressed their frustration with the seemingly contradictory position adopted by the lads, where they claimed to want more say in the running of the centre, but were unwilling to participate on committees in a way that the staff wanted them to. This was seen by the staff as evidence that the lads were 'not ready' to assume more responsibility.

Further frustrating the staff was the fact that when activities were organized that the boys seemingly expressed interest in, few lads actually participated when the time came; there was thus little guarantee that the efforts of the staff were to be rewarded. Uncertainty over whether the boys would actually participate in what the staff had arranged, as well as the failure of the staff-initiated 'committee-style' decision-making process and the destructive behaviour of many of the lads within the centre, in fact served to undermine the staff's faith in 'youth-development'. The response of some staff members was then to assert their authority.

This authoritarian response is also indicative of the degree to which external factors did indeed play a role in shaping the relationship between staff and users. In youth work, it is not uncommon for staff to feel frustrated by the lack of co-operation from their clients. Without extensive and proper training, a clearly defined agenda (and well-understood measures of programme success), and an adequate level of supervisory support, youth-workers often resort to a 'policing' function in institutional contexts such as this. It gives them a clear sense of purpose within the centre, and is reinforced by middle-class notions of 'service' on the one hand and 'control' on the other, in dealing with people from working-class backgrounds.

The actions of the boys – both in terms of how they asserted power and how they responded to the authoritarianism of the staff – must also be interpreted in terms of the norms, values and beliefs identified with their class location. For instance, the reluctance of the lads to participate in committees in the way the staff had intended was not necessarily due to their 'lack of responsibility', but rather was a reflection of their lack of experience of committees and their feeling of discomfort working in structured and organized environments. From the standpoint of working-class youth used to being on the outside of most local institutions (even working-class ones), such committees were often interpreted as being simply another institutional setting with (middle-class) authority figures determining the agenda. Considering the fact that the staff seemed always to have the final say in committee decisions, the lads believed that this set-up was not very different from other institutional contexts that they were used to and alienated from, such as school, work or other clubs in the area. Their own youth culture stressed rebellion against authority and the valorization of masculinist working-class values, that is, the refusal to submit to rules and structures that they felt challenged their sense of autonomy. So, while the boys did want to participate in decision-making, they were uncomfortable in committee-like contexts and preferred one-on-one consultations, a method that the staff did not like or agree with, as in Case 2, in which Masa's attempt to put forward his case about the billiards table failed because he 'didn't go through the proper channels'.

The reluctance of the lads to submit to authority was also seen in their occasional refusal to co-operate with the plans of the staff. During periods of conflict, it was not uncommon for the lads to stay away *en masse* from organized events. Like strategies of self-help, such lack of co-operation became a powerful expression of resistance, demonstrating that the boys could, on their own terms, sometime control events in the centre. In fact, it often succeeded in undermining the confidence of the staff, especially considering the amount of work that often goes into organizing activities.

The boys were, then, able to take action in a variety of ways as a means of asserting their interests, expressing their desire for more power and forcing the staff to retreat from entrenched authoritarian positions. The strategies they employed cannot be simply derided as the inconsequential and delinquent acts of teenagers. Action was taken by the lads in contexts where they felt they had no other means by which to bring about change, resist unpopular decisions, contribute to decision-making or exert power. Their actions did have results, for the staff had to accommodate their interests or risk losing control.

The acts of resistance of the boys, through strategies of self-help, can be seen as a form of ritualized rebellion, an attempt to undermine the authority of the staff according to their own rules, values and models of behaviour. However, this form of resistance, not unusual for working-class youth cultures of 'the lads' (Downes 1966; Willis 1978; Hall and Jefferson 1976), has inherent limitations. The failure of their efforts to provide negotiated settlements to their disputes with the staff lies in the fact that they did not control this arena of conflict, any more than they would a school or the workplace. This facility was provided for them, the roles of staff and users were defined for them and, in the final analysis, the Youth Development Centre could be taken away from them.

Conclusion

In this paper, I have used Gulliver's model of negotiations to analyse the conflict between the boys and the staff at the Ballinaclasha Youth Development Centre. The unique contribution of his model is that it provides a means of making sense of dispute-settlement processes where the path to a negotiated settlement is uncertain and certainly not linear. By emphasizing features of negotiations such as power, norms and values Gulliver draws attention to the significance of contextual factors in shaping how conflicts are (or are not) resolved.

The three cases presented here are intended to explore the nature of conflict in the youth-development centre. Significantly, few disagreements end in negotiated settlement, and antagonisms tend to be carried from one conflict to the next. The failure of the staff and the boys to resolve their dispute over power and authority in the centre must be understood in terms of contextual features that define their asymmetrical relationship. In the final analysis, the conflict between the staff and the boys is best understood in terms of the antagonisms built into class relations, and how these are (or can be) manifest in the delivery of youth services. The attitude of the staff, their 'role' in the centre – indeed the *raison d'être* of the centre itself – reflected a paradox inherent in the middle-class notion of 'youth-development'. That is, there was a desire, on the one hand, to empower the boys to assume leadership roles and to take part in decision-making. On the other hand, such power was to be exercised according to rules, values and models of behaviour determined by the staff in an arena created not by the lads (or the people of Ballinaclasha for that matter) but by dominant institutions (the government and Ogra) which were not representative of the working class.

Notes

1. The research for this project was conducted in 1987–8 in the urban parish of Ballinaclasha, in the city of Cork, Ireland. A wide range of methods was used, including participant observation, interviews with young people and those involved in youth services, and an examination of community association records. I participated as a youth-worker at the Youth Development Centre and worked with the community association in their efforts to respond to the need for improved youth services. Pseudonyms have been used for the names of people, places and organizations.

2. This does not mean that in an extreme case – such as serious physical assault, the burning down of the centre or a flagrant abuse of power by the staff – outside forces would not be called in. However, no such incident had occurred in the short history of the centre. It should be noted that breaches of certain laws by the users (possession of drugs, minor assault, vandalism, theft) were not deemed by the staff to be serious enough events to war-

rant police intervention. This does not mean that such behaviour was tolerated by the staff, but rather that they used their own sanctions.

3. As a volunteer youth-worker and as a researcher, I was in a unique position to observe the conflict between staff and users. I came to know all members of the staff quite well, and was treated as an 'equal' during meetings. On the other hand, I knew the boys very well also, and many I considered friends. I saw them not only in the context of the centre, but also on their turf as well – at the Western Star, in their homes, at pubs, sporting events, etc. While I did at times play a role as a 'broker' between the staff and the users, in each of the three cases described above, my involvement (aside from being an observer) was minimal.

4. The Western Star was a local shopping plaza (with few shops still operating) that was a well-known hang-out for a group of the boys from the northernmost end of the parish. While they became associated with this location, they were not a 'gang' by any conventional definition of the term. Most young people of their class background – wherever they were from in the parish – were able to hang around together, without conflict based on territory or group allegiance.

References

Downes, D. (1966). *The Delinquent Solution*. London: Routledge and Kegan Paul

Gaetz, S. (1992). 'The Provision of Community-Based Youth Services in Cork, Ireland: The Relevance of the Concepts of "Community" and "Youth"', *Urban Anthropology* 21: 1

Gluckman, M. (1965). *Politics, Law and Ritual in Tribal Society*. London: Oxford University Press

Gulliver, P. H. (1979). *Disputes and Negotiations*. New York: Academic Press

Hall, S. and Jefferson, T. (1976). *Resistance through Rituals*. London: Hutchinson

Hoebel, E. A. (1954). *The Law of Primitive Man*. Cambridge: Cambridge University Press

Jenkins, R. (1983). *Lads, Citizens and Ordinary Kids*. London: Routledge and Kegan Paul

Kuper, A. (1971). 'Council Structures and Decision-Making', in *Councils in Action*, ed. A. Richards and A. Kuper. Cambridge: Cambridge University Press

Starr, J. and Yngvesson, B. (1975). 'Scarcity and disputing: zeroing in on compromise decisions', *American Ethnologist* 2: 553–66

Swartz, M., Turner, V. and Tuden, D. (1966). *Political Anthropology*. Chicago: Aldine Press

Willis, P. (1978). *Learning to Labour*. Farnborough: Saxon House

Chapter 10

'Law' and 'Custom': Marital Disputes on Northern Mafia Island, Tanzania

Pat Caplan

Introduction

Gulliver (1963) conceived the political and judicial modes of understanding dispute settlement as two ideal, polar types of process, but later he went on to criticize such an approach as inadequate, recognizing that everywhere both norms and power are pervasive elements in all dispute processes (1979). In this chapter, I consider a society in which there is a variety of norms, which are manipulated and used selectively by disputants.

The people of Mafia Island, Tanzania,[1] are Sunni Muslims and utilize the Shafei canon of personal law (*sheria*). They are also Tanzanian citizens, subject to the laws of the secular state, which are also usually termed sheria in Swahili, sometimes amplified by the term *za serikali* (of the government) and also known as *kanuni*. But there exists in addition a wide variety of local custom and practice (*mila* or *ada*) which is not codified, but which is often recognized by the courts.[2] Although Islamic law itself recognizes the existence of mila, the prescriptions of each sometimes vary, or even conflict, as will be seen below.

As a young postgraduate student carrying out fieldwork on Mafia Island, Tanzania, in the mid-1960s, I found this situation very confusing, and wrote despairingly to my supervisor, P. H. Gulliver, that there did not seem to be any clear ideal norms of conduct in this society of the kind that I had expected to find. He wrote back telling me firmly that I must not oversimplify. In retrospect, I realize that part of my problem was that of the anthropology of the time. Every society was supposed to have a set of ideal norms, and it was the job of the anthropologist to record these, although it was generally recognized there was often a big gap between what people said and what they did; thus the second task of the anthropologist was to collect 'statistical norms'. Today we are more likely to see cultural norms as areas of contestation, an approach which is adopted in this chapter.

In earlier work (Caplan 1982, 1983) I considered the significance of sheria and mila in terms of their relative implications for gender relations:

> in effect, there are two sets of ideologies and two sets of practices – sheria/sunna and mila – in use on Mafia, each of which presents a rather different picture of gender relations ...
>
> ... the distinction exists in most other areas [of the coast] for which we have information and indeed, it is precisely the blend of sheria and mila which constitutes Swahili culture. However, the 'mix' is not always the same ... where mila is unimportant, women tend to have a very subordinate status, whereas gender relations are much more egalitarian in areas where it is important (1982: 30).

In his recent book on the Swahili (1992), Middleton has taken issue with the idea that Swahili culture is divided by gender into two separate sub-cultures – that of Islam and the sheria, which is the domain of men, and that of custom or mila, which is that of women, a view suggested by Eastman (1984, 1988). Middleton asserts that 'Interesting though these suggestions are, it is a simplification to assume that male and female areas in Swahili society are separate from each other: they are complementary and neither has ideological or religious existence or meaning apart from the other' (ibid.: 119).

In more recent work, I have considered gender relations on Mafia Island, Tanzania, in relation to food, health and fertility, and shown that in these areas women are often considerably disadvantaged (Caplan 1989). An examination of the sheria might appear also to suggest that women labour under great disadvantage in legal terms, particularly in relation to divorce, property and inheritance, and their husbands' authority. Yet as the cases which follow demonstrate, women are not lacking in agency – they utilize a variety of resources with which to pursue their interests, including both sheria and mila. So too do men, and one of the questions raised at the outset is the extent to which women are more likely to appeal to mila, and men to sheria, given the way in which each of these ideologies appears to advantage one sex rather than the other.

In this chapter, then, I want to consider further the distinction between mila and sheria in terms of the way in which they are used in disputes, especially marital disputes. I will attempt to show that neither mila nor sheria are fixed entities; rather they are subject to interpretation by disputants who invoke them in their disputes. Consequently, disputes and legal cases, as Rosen (1989) has recently observed, are as good a place as any to study a people's world view, including their views on gender relations.

Marriage and Divorce

Marriage is virtually universal, and takes place for women after puberty, and for men some years later. In recent years, the age of marriage for both has risen somewhat, since girls do not marry until after the completion of primary schooling at around the age of sixteen, while young men often spend several years living and working on the mainland before marrying. First marriages for both are arranged by parents, but, according to mila, grandparents must also give their consent.

Marriage in Islam is a contract, not a sacrament, and at the marriage ceremony mention is made before witnesses of the sum of money which the groom agrees to pay to the bride (*mahari*). In fact, the mahari is rarely paid until the death of the husband or the divorce of the wife, but technically a wife has the right to claim it at any time. If she does so, it is usually because relations have become strained and she hopes to precipitate a divorce, as in Case 5 below.

A newly married couple live in a separate house and cook separately from their parents from the inception of the marriage. Husband and wife generally cultivate land together and grow subsistence crops, although women do a good deal more agricultural work than do men. Husbands are responsible under Islamic law for providing their wives with shelter, food and clothes, although in practice house-building, like subsistence agriculture, is a joint activity. Husbands generally do provide the bought food, which includes the *kitoweo* (usually fish, more rarely meat) for the curry, as well as sugar, milk and tea, and kerosene for the lamps. Since few households grow enough staples to last for a year, husbands also have to purchase additional food in the lean months. The money for such purchases comes mainly from the sale of cash crops – coconuts – although some men also earn money from fishing, trading, and doing odd labouring jobs for others in the village or migrating for work to the mainland. Women also own coconut trees, but in much smaller numbers than men; they also earn money by plaiting and selling raffia mats. Women not infrequently contribute to their own maintenance and even that of their children. However, any money earned by a woman, like the property which she brings to the marriage, should, under the sheria, remain hers to do with as she wishes (cf. Caplan 1983).

Under Islamic law, men have the right to divorce their wives simply by pronouncing the formula (*talaka*), although it is not complete until this has been done three times. Husbands do not have to give a reason for this action.[3] A husband who wishes to divorce his wife is supposed to take or send her back to her male kin – her father if he is alive, or a brother. In actuality many divorced women go to live with their mothers, who may be themselves widowed, divorced or remarried; such women build a separate small house, and cultivate and cook for themselves. A wife who has been divorced has to observe a period of *edda* for three months before she can remarry. It is not infrequent for a husband to divorce his wife, but then to recall her before her period of edda is ended and most husbands delay until then in pronouncing the third and final talaka. Indeed, many go through the first stage of divorce, but refuse to give their wives their final talaka, thus leaving them in a state of being neither properly married nor properly divorced. Many husbands even ask their wives to 'buy' their talaka, which women may do by countering with a claim to their mahari, although the husband usually asks more for the talaka than the agreed mahari. Islamic law does not recognize the legality of 'buying' a divorce in this way; but many women prefer to pay up, or forfeit their mahari, rather than have the trouble of seeking a divorce at the court in the District Capital, Kilindoni.

It is much more difficult for a woman to initiate a divorce.[4] She may seek to persuade her husband to divorce her by asking for her talaka, and if he proves reluctant, utilize a variety of methods to change his mind: withdrawal of sexual services, demanding her mahari, insisting on a division of the jointly cultivated crops and proceeding to use her share outside the household (e.g. for contributing to the rituals of her kin), taking a lover, leaving her husband or threatening to do so. She may also enlist the help of her kin in persuading the husband either to mend his ways or give her a divorce. On the whole, relatives will seek to bring about a reconciliation if at all possible, but if a woman is determined enough, they will generally support her in seeking a divorce through the District Court. This she can only do by invoking the sheria on grounds which Islamic law recognizes: primarily, failure to maintain her properly.

In the next section, I consider the way in which marital disputes are handled, and the extent to which appeal is made to law and/or custom by both women and men.

Forums for Settling Marital Disputes Within the Village

There are three different forums which can be used for the settlement of marital disputes. The first is that of kin, particularly elders, who may attend a *baraza* (meeting, lit. veranda), perhaps best translated as a moot. The aim of kin is usually to achieve a reconciliation through a process of negotiation.

The second kind of forum is that of the Village Council, which acts as a court of first instance. The Village Council may hear cases in a formal or an informal way. In the latter instance, the Chairman and perhaps one or two other members meet privately with disputants. Usually, the Council tries to mediate rather than adjudicate, as in the following case:

Case 1. A Marital Dispute Leads to Accusations of Poisoning

> In 1966, Juma and his wife Saidia quarrelled and she asked for a divorce. He refused to give it to her. She threatened to poison him if he did not do so. Later, Juma saw a little bottle under the mat, and took it to his ten-house cell leader,[5] accusing his wife of poisoning him. He also took it to the dresser at the clinic, asking him if it contained poison, and the dresser said it did not. Juma then took his wife's sanitary cloth, wet it and squeezed it out into the bottle. [This was to provide the 'poison'.] His wife caught sight of him doing this and shouted out at such an incredible breach of customary taboos (*miko*);[6] she went immediately to accuse him before the Chairman of the Village Council.

The Council called all the parties, including the dresser, and decided that the wife's version of events was correct, particularly as the husband had also taken her sanitary cloth and thrown it away. The Council sought to resolve the dispute by finding out why the couple had quarrelled in the first place. It turned out to be largely because of the wife's bad relations with her husband's mother, who lived next door. It was decided they should move house to live next door to the husband's father instead.

Here the Council sought the root cause of the problem and suggested a way of resolving it, to which all parties agreed. But the Council also has the power to invoke sanctions, including physical punishment, as in the following case:

Case 2. A Husband is Punished for Unjustly Suspecting his Wife

In 1966, Waziri went to a wedding in a neighbouring village without his wife, Mwasiti. When he got back, he saw that she had put on make-up and plaited her hair. He was angry, saying 'If I'm not here, for whose benefit have you done this?' He took hold of her, threatening to punish her by shaving off her hair. She hit him. His mother, who lived next door, heard the commotion and came in and Mwasiti hit her too. Then Waziri's brother arrived and said 'Take her back to her place' (i.e. to her parents), so he took her to her father's brother's house (her father was deceased), and she stayed there for a few days. Then her husband came with his brother to take her back.

The wife's relatives had heard that they were coming, and themselves turned up in force. The father's brother's wife said loudly 'Aren't there any people left in the world?' (meaning that the husband had come only with his brother, not with other kin). Another of the wife's kin answered her: 'Oh, they never bore many children there, and there aren't any elders there either.' However a woman who was related to Waziri but married to one of the wife's kin took offence at this, accusing her of 'taking the pus from our rotting wound to conceal it'. She in turn was accused of insulting the second woman, and the two women began to fight each other physically.

The Village Council was meeting to decide the case when they saw the women starting to fight. The women were separated and taken off home, and the case proceeded. Waziri was told that he had done wrong to accuse his wife of infidelity and threaten her and that he could not get his wife back until he had been punished by 5 strokes of a stick. His sister told him to refuse the punishment and divorce his wife, promising to provide the clothes (*kanga*) for a new wife herself. But Waziri really did want his wife back, and so he submitted to the beating.

This case illustrates a number of significant points: firstly, women rarely submit meekly in marital disagreements – Mwasiti in fact ended up hitting not only her husband but also his mother. Secondly, women can usually count on the support of their kin in such disputes, and may well be able to count on that of the Village Council as well if husbands are deemed to have behaved unreasonably.

Another point is that women have other means of prosecuting quarrels than taking them to a forum. The singing of songs at rites of passage (circumcisions, girls' puberty ceremonies and weddings) or at the preparations for them is a customary way of scoring points off opponents. The songs never mention people by name, but everyone present, including very often members of the 'other side', know to whom they refer. Furthermore, although they are sung in the courtyard where the women are gathered, the men who sit in front of the house can hear them too, often to their great embarassment. For example, the foregoing case did not end with Waziri's punishment, as the women pursued the quarrel through song.

Case 2 Continued: The Song Duel

> At a wedding, one of Mwasiti's sisters sang a song about Waziri's mother and her daughter. Shortly afterwards, the daughter sang songs in reply about Mwasiti's relatives.
> *Mume wangu ananitaka, lakini dada kamshika kwa mitalasimu.*
> My husband loves me, but [it is only because] my elder sister has got him through love magic.
> [This suggests that the only reason why Waziri loved his wife was because her elder sister had used love magic on him – why else would he have put up with a beating?]
> The second was a song about the physical appearance of Mwasiti's father's sister:
> *Miguu ya fagio, kaja kuudhi wenzio.*
> 'Broomstick legs' has come to bother her co-wife.
> [Mwasiti's father's sister, an exceptionally skinny woman, was often called by this rather insulting nickname.]
> The third song was one which also insulted Mwasiti's older sister:
> *Tom alikuja arusi, kaja kuchuma umbea.*
> 'Tom'(the nickname of Mwasiti's elder sister) has come to the wedding, she has [only] come to pick up gossip.

As is pointed out elsewhere in this volume (see Colson's Chapter 4), disputes are not always resolved to the satisfaction of all parties, and may be pursued over long periods of time by a variety of means. Furthermore, not all disputes are resolved at the village level. If the Council is unable to deal with the matter, a dispute may be taken to the District Court in the island capital, Kilindoni.

Going to Court

Recourse to the court is particularly likely if a wife wants a divorce which a husband refuses to give her.

Case 3. Mwabora Seeks a Divorce

> Mwabora was married by her parents to a young man from her village who took her to live in Zanzibar. The marriage was very unhappy and her husband was often violent. After a particularly bad quarrel, relatives of Mwabora eventually intervened, pointing out to the husband that he had no right to treat his wife that way as she remained 'someone's daughter' (*mtoto ya watu*). They said that he had to take her back to her natal home.
>
> When she returned to Mafia, Mwabora sought a divorce, but her husband refused to give it to her. Her parents supported her and went with her to Kilindoni to present a case to the court.

There was no question of her being able to use her husband's violence as a reason for divorce; under Islamic law, the complaint had to be one of failure to maintain. The court record reads as follows:

Kilindoni Court Records

> *The plaintiff states*: 'The defendant is my husband and he has been married to me for a period which is not less than nine years, but in all of this time, I have just had to put up with things. However, I have now had enough (*nimeshindwa*, lit. I am defeated), I do not get clothes unless I see to it myself, or my relatives help me. Finally I went to the elders of our village to complain. My husband was called [to them] and obliged to pay what I was owed, but even then, my husband did not give it to me. For this reason, I went again to the elders, and they gave me a letter with which I have come to court today.

Judge: Mwabora has accused her husband Mohammed of owing her 100/- mahari and food and clothes for nine years. The defendant agrees about the debt of 100/- but he denies any lack of food and clothes. The plaintiff [on the other hand] has explained that for the nine years in which she has lived with her husband, he has given her neither food nor clothes. Such things have not been obtainable from her husband. She lives by helping herself, or [with help from] her parents. Furthermore, he has already appeared before the elders' baraza charged with owing [maintenance]. The elders obliged him to pay these things to the plaintfiff, but the defendant did not do so. The testimony of the defendant is called into question [lit. defeated] because he is talking nonsense.

After hearing this case, I agree with the testimony of the plaintiff that it is true that the defendant is not supporting his wife with food or clothes because the plaintiff said that even the clothes in which she went to the baraza she got [herself]. Again there is the testimony of the letter which I got from the elders. This letter bears witness to the fact that the defendant was given the option of paying his wife's mahari and giving her food and clothes. But in front of the elders he replied that he had no means [with which to do so]. Thus it appears that the truth lies with the plaintiff.

Decision. Although the defendant wants his wife, he is extremely poor. But in spite of that fact, if he wants to be with his wife, he has to follow the law [sheria] and give her the necessities of life. The plaintiff should give four kanga together with 20/- as the first instalment of her mahari. He must give these within a period of 10 days and the remainder of the mahari must be paid in 5/- instalments each month until he has paid it off.

Directive. If the defendant fails to pay these things, the plaintiff has the right to get a divorce paper [talaka] according to the obligations [laid down by] the law of Islam. If the defendant is unable to return to live with his wife, costs of 10/- are to be paid by the defendant to the plaintiff, who is awarded the case.

The husband was either unable or unwilling to pay for the clothes and mahari in the time stipulated, and so Mwabora finally got her divorce. A number of similar court cases in Kilindoni were brought by women against their husbands on the grounds of lack of maintenance, a breach of the sheria, since no other grounds for a divorce initiated by women were admitted.

Case 4: Using All Resources: The Story of Mwajuma

Women thus use a variety of strategies, and a mixture of mila and sheria in their marital disputes. In the case which follows, a determined woman does precisely this to prosecute a series of disputes arising from the ending of her marriage.

Part 1: Mwajuma's Divorce

> Mwajuma had been married to Ali for a number of years, and they had three sons, who in 1965, when I first met them, were aged between eight and twelve. Ali had made a trading trip to Dar es Salaam, and on his return, some of his relatives claimed that his wife had committed adultery in his absence. She denied this, but he divorced her anyway.
>
> The alleged lover also divorced his wife because, so the latter told me, she had been very angry with him for having this affair with Mwajuma. Another informant told me that Mwajuma had twice gone to her lover's house after Ali had divorced her. On the first occasion, the lover's wife had slapped her face and pulled her clothes. The second time, she had again threatened her but other people had intervened. As a result of this, her husband had sent her away and she had spent a month at her parents' house before her husband recalled her, and so the divorce was not finalized.

In the case of her adultery, a husband might well divorce his wife, although in many instances I came across in the village, a husband would pronounce the first talaka, take his wife back to her father's house and leave her there for a while before recalling her, often after elders from both sides had acted as mediators, which is what happened in the case of the lover and his wife. In the case of Ali and Mwajuma, Ali not only sent his wife away, but refused to recall her, even though he was under considerable pressure from public opinion to do so. Elders did attempt mediation, but Ali was adamant that he did not want his wife back, and so he finalized her talaka.

Case 4, Part 2. Disputes over Property

> Mwajuma did not take her divorce quietly, but immediately accused her ex-husband before the Village Council of not having given her a fair share of the property.

Her initial complaint concerned their bed, which she maintained had been bought for her by her parents, who had had it specially ordered from Dar es Salaam. Her father and brother supported her in these claims. Her husband could not deny her ownership of the bed, since it is customary for this item to be bought by the woman's parents, but he claimed that he had paid the carriage charges and therefore should retain it; he had receipts to prove his story. Finally, Mwajuma agreed to pay the carriage charges and she got back her bed.

There was then a further dispute about ownership of coconut trees. Mwajuma claimed that they had planted the trees together, and that therefore she should receive half of them. Ali, on the other hand, claimed that she had scarcely ever worked on the coconut land, but she brought witnesses to say that she had. The Village Council went out to inspect the land and told Ali that the three trees there which he had inherited from his father were his, but that the remaining trees should be equally divided. Ali refused to accept this judgement, so the Council wrote a letter to the Court in Kilindoni. Mwajuma took the letter and set off for Kilindoni, but on the way there, she met a government official who told her that it was her ex-husband's job to pursue the case, since he was the one who had not accepted the Village Council's judgement. The government official then went to Ali asking him to recall his wife, and make up the quarrel. Failing that, he suggested that they divide the trees equally. Ali did not agree to either suggestion, so the government official went to inspect the trees.

He found it difficult to make a decision, partly because one piece of land actually had no trees on it. Ali still claimed ownership of it because he said he had previously owned trees on it which had since died. The government official referred the case to a newly-established sub-court in Kirongwe in the centre of the island, which awarded Mwajuma one-third of the trees, and two-thirds to Ali.

Mwajuma did not pursue this case by appealing to the Kilindoni court, but she did continue cultivating on the land next to the trees, which Ali claimed as his, and which they had cultivated together the year before the divorce. Mwajuma sent her sister to Ali to inform him of her intention to cultivate there. Ali tried to persuade the Village Council to turn Mwajuma off the land, but was persuaded to drop this case, since she had already done the work and therefore, under customary law, owned usufructuary rights until the harvest.

Under Islamic law, women retain ownership of their property after marriage; thus anything that Mwajuma brought with her into the marriage, such as the bed, remained hers. However, the question of property acquired after marriage is more complex. At the time of this case, in the 1960s, it was common for men and women jointly to plant coconut trees, although not infrequently men did this work without the help of their wives. If they were jointly planted, then they were also jointly owned and had to be divided. Although under Islamic law women inherit property at the rate of one-third to a man's two-thirds share, in cases of divorce or separation it was more usual, certainly at the village level, to invoke mila and for women to be awarded equal shares with their ex-husbands. This indeed had been the judgement of the Village Council, which was upheld by the government official; but the Sub-Court in Kirongwe used the Islamic formula, possibly because there was a better chance of Ali's accepting it, possibly because there was some doubt about exactly how much work Mwajuma had done in planting the trees, but also probably because such a court was more likely to utilize Islamic law than custom.

In the case of the land, Ali was in a weaker position. Since there were no trees on it, technically he could not claim ownership, since at that period in Tanzania all land was the property of the state, and anyone could use a piece of unused land. According to village custom most land was allocated through membership of descent groups; but land close to trees that were individually owned was often also claimed by the individuals who owned the trees, as in this case. However, again according to custom, once someone has done the work of 'cutting' a field and planting a crop, they cannot be asked to leave until after the harvest.

What was interesting about people's comments on this case was that it was often said that the disputes were less about property than about their relationship and emotions. It was noted that both parties were relatively well off by village standards, and therefore the issue of the property was relatively unimportant – rather, the common interpretation of this series of disputes was that each was bitter and angry and thus determined to punish the other, although some also added that Mwajuma's behaviour was a way of sending messages to her ex-husband that she wanted him back.

Once it became clear that Ali was unlikely to recall her, Mwajuma set about finding another husband, since although single women can manage on their own, economically they are usually worse off than married ones. Although first marriages are invariably arranged by parents and elders, women who have been divorced or widowed are usually free to choose their own partners in subsequent marriages.

Case 4, Part 3. Mwajuma's First Attempt to Remarry

> It was reported that Mwajuma had tried to persuade her lover to marry her, but he had refused. She then arranged a marriage with a man in Kilindoni who was said to have a government job. When her relatives discovered that his job was very menial they put pressure on her to break off the engagement.

This was only one of several instances I came across in which women, particularly those from groups in the village claiming higher socio-religious status, were pressurized not to marry men considered of lower status, as in this case (Caplan 1975: 137–41). Mwajuma then decided to seek a husband of high status:

Case 4, Part 4. Mwajuma's Second Attempt to Remarry

> One of the people who had been instrumental in stopping Mwajuma's proposed marriage was her cross-cousin Abdallah, one of the most respected men in the village, who occupied important political and religious posts. Mwajuma told him that since he had prevented the marriage she had arranged, he should marry her himself, and indeed, cross-cousin marriage is a preferred form according to Swahili custom. She was able to take the initiative in this because a further customary aspect of cross-cousin relations is that they are joking relations (*watani*). Her attempts to persuade him to marry her were carried on through the medium of this licensed joking. When he refused either to marry her, or to pay her the compensation she claimed under custom, she snatched his hat (*kofia*) and refused to give it back.

> Abdallah was extremely embarrassed and afraid that his wife would hear about what had happened and suspect that he was having an affair with Mwajuma, so he went to her house to get the hat back. She refused to hand it over, whereupon he became angry and hit her several times. She immediately went to the Council Chairman and accused Abdallah of assault. A Village Council meeting was called to discuss the case and Abdallah claimed that his behaviour had also been part of *utani* (joking). The Council disagreed and decided to fine

Abdallah 10/-, to be paid to Mwajuma. She however refused this solution and also refused the mediation of elders from both sides. She insisted upon having a letter from the Village Council to take to the Kilindoni court, as a result of which Abdallah was arrested and charged with the criminal offence of affray and grievous bodily harm. The case appears in the Kilindoni court records, and here I give only the judge's summary:

Kilindoni Court Records

I have followed the evidence which has been given by the accused ... And I agree with the evidence of the plaintiff, together with her remark that the accused has done wrong. The reason for saying this is that the accused himself says that Mwajuma is his cousin ... If this is indeed the case, it shows that the accused and Mwajuma are cross-cousins, and that according to the mila of cross-cousinhood (*ubinamu*) there is the law (sheria) of joking. The deed which Mwajuma did to the accused in jest is not a serious case, it was only to take his hat. Now if Mwajuma is his *binamu* she had the right (*haki*) to take his hat. Furthermore, that which was said to the accused by the plaintiff Mwajuma – that he should marry her – was not wrong. Because there is a law (sheria) [which allows it], and it is not a bad thing for a person to marry their cross-cousin. Here however, the accused entered into wrong-doing by hitting Mwajuma and injuring her (contrary to section 241 of the Penal Code). But after seeing the report of the doctor and receiving evidence that the accused only hit her in an ordinary way (*kwa kawaida tu*), for this reason I am not going to put him in gaol. The punishment of the accused is for a first offence. Furthermore, the accused, after committing the offence, did not try to deny (?) it. Because this is a first offence of the accused, I give him a sentence of a fine of 10/- or else 14 days in prison. The period for payment of the fine is only 2 days. There is no appeal, since the accused confessed his guilt, and because it is a sentence of under 30/- (which does not have a right of appeal).

Utani is unquestionably part of the mila complex, as the judge recognized in his summing up; but he also noted that mila has its own rules (sheria), which set reasonable limits on 'joking'. The judge also stated that there is a law (sheria) which allows binamu to marry, and therefore Mwajuma had the right to invoke it to Abdallah.

The defendant tried to defend his beating of Mwajuma in terms of utani, but the judge was clear that he had surpassed customary limits, and that joking relations did not include beating.

For this reason, he acceded to Mwajuma's invocation of the penal code (state law) and punished Abdallah, although the punishment was very light. It is probable that he recognized that Abdallah had been totally humiliated by the whole process.

In all the cases discussed so far, women are seen to be agents, utilizing a variety of strategies and invoking mila, sheria and state law to achieve their ends, often highly successfully. Law, however, is always a double-edged weapon, and in the next section, I give a case in which a woman is totally unsuccessful in her endeavours, and, paradoxically, this is because of the invocation of mila.

The Power of Mila

Men invoke the sheria to divorce their wives, but women may also invoke the sheria to obtain divorces from reluctant husbands. Women invoke mila to seek land and other property rights, and to seek the support of kin in prosecuting their cases, but mila, as in the following case, also demands that elders have more power than juniors. This aspect of mila meant that a woman failed in her attempts to end her marriage:

Case 5. Fatuma Tries to Leave the Village and her Husband Saidi

> In the summer of 1985, Fatuma, who was married to Saidi and already had two children by him, was expecting another. Saidi had two other wives – one had seven children and was pregnant again, the other had two children. The second wife had gone home to her mother's house for her delivery, which in this case, unusually, meant travelling to Zanzibar, taking all seven of her children with her.
>
> As she was not only in an advanced stage of pregnancy, but also very unwell with severe anaemia and oedema, I was surprised to find that Fatuma did not intend to return to her parents' house for the three months prior to the birth, as is customary, in order to be looked after. Eventually she told me that her parents were angry with her for having got pregnant and borne a child while still an unmarried girl. Matters were made worse because her father is an important religious official in the village.
>
> Saidi received news that his second wife had given birth at the house of her mother's brother in Zanzibar, her mother meanwhile having

moved to Mombasa. Rumours reached him that she did not intend to return to him but to go on to Mombasa to her mother's house. He realized that he was in danger of losing her and wanted to go and fetch her back, but knew that he could not leave Fatuma in her present state.

Fatuma meanwhile had asked if I would take her with me to Dar es Salaam when I left the village a few weeks later at the end of my stay. She had a sister living there who would look after her. She told me that she wanted to stay on in Dar after the birth and would support herself by making mats, selling cooked food or maybe 'finding someone else'. She felt that she could no longer stay with her husband, who had no means to support her or his other wives properly, but was only good at making them pregnant (*mzazi kweli*).

Her husband agreed to the idea of her going to Dar (obviously she had said nothing to him about her plans for remaining there), and on a visit to the District Capital I booked tickets for her and the children as well as myself. On my return, Saidi told me that he would have to have the permission of her parents. Fatuma disagreed: 'Isn't it just a matter of informing them?'

Fatuma's mother came to see them and said that she and Fatuma's father were not willing for her to go to Dar, but they didn't offer to have her stay with them either. When she left, Fatuma threatened to go to Dar without their blessing. Saidi was alarmed and said that they would be angry and blame him. He said he must have their permission, adding 'It's not legally necessary (*si sheria*) but it's customary (*mila*). But in this place, it's often better to break sheria than to break mila.'

In this case, husband and wife were ostensibly in agreement with the idea of the wife going to Dar es Salaam, although for different reasons. For Saidi it would mean freedom to go and patch things up with his second wife. For Fatuma, it would not only mean immediate help with the pregnancy and birth, but also the possibility of escaping her unsatisfactory marriage. The parents, however, were not in agreement with the couple, being unwilling for it to be made so obvious that they were not helping their daughter themselves, and perhaps also concerned that she might find very undesirable ways of supporting herself in Dar es Salaam.

Under the sheria a husband has the right to determine his wife's movements, so Saidi could have sent her to Dar. But mila dictates that parents should be consulted and give their consent. Even after marriage, a woman remains 'someone's child', which can be highly advantageous to her in most instances, giving her rights in her natal group(s) and support in the case of marital disputes, as with Mwabora in Case 5. But Fatuma's parents did not support her, and used mila to control her movements. It is particularly paradoxical that in this case, Fatuma's father, one of the main upholders and interpreters of sheria in the village, utilized not its precepts, but those of mila to prevent his daughter's departure.

Conclusion: What Then Is The Law?

It is thus obviously not possible to say that mila usually advantages women, while sheria disadvantages them. It is true that mila is associated with a kinship and descent system that gives women equal land and residence rights throughout their lives, and ensures that they normally have the material and moral support of their kin even after marriage. It is also part of a complex of ideas that gives women a good deal of sexual autonomy (cf. Caplan 1976). Sheria on the other hand allocates many advantages to men in marriage, including the right to determine a wife's movements, and, not least, the right to divorce her. However, the fact that the sheria also gives women rights to their own property is not insignificant. Furthermore, women can generally use the provisions of sheria to end unhappy marriages by claiming lack of maintenance. Nor, as has been seen, is it the case that in disputes, women are necessarily more likely to invoke or be advantaged by mila and men by the sheria; either sex may invoke either code. This is important, for it suggests that both are part of Swahili culture, utilized by both women and men, as Middleton suggests (1992: 119).

Now I do not want to give the impression that sheria and mila are fixed sets of norms; it is true that the former is written and the latter unwritten, but the interpretation of both is continually renegotiated in the disputing process (cf. Moore 1989). In everyday speech, clear distinctions are not always made between the laws of the state, Islamic law, and local custom. People often use the term sheria for all three, condemning behaviour of which they do not approve by labelling it as 'si sheria', a phrase whose meaning can range from 'unlawful' to 'out of order'. As Starr and Collier have recently pointed out, law may be viewed 'as a contested metaphor that represents and reproduces a social and symbolic ordering system and that changes as groups of human agents seek new social forms ... or even a new society' (1989: 25).

A recognition of both the power of norms, and of their fluidity, enables us to move beyond a sterile concept of 'legal pluralism' to a realization that legal systems are better viewed as 'indeterminant orders' (Moore 1989) and 'contested metaphors' (Starr and Collier 1989). Such a move also enables us, as Comaroff and Roberts have pointed out, to dissolve the apparent discrepancy between rules and behaviour (1981: 243), and to seek in dispute settlement 'an essential key to the disclosure of the socioculture order' (ibid.). People thus use mila and sheria selectively in different contexts, generally calling upon whichever is most useful to them in their disputes and negotiations with others. Both are a part of the Swahili world-view, utilized by both women and men. Norms, then, not only may be counterposed to power, but are themselves also contested and therefore changing.

Notes

1. Fieldwork was carried out on Mafia Island, Tanzania in 1965–7 (funded by the University of London and the Worshipful Company of Goldsmiths), in 1976 (funded by the BBC), and in 1985 (funded by the Nuffield Foundation).

2. Since the encactment of the Magistrates' Courts Act in 1963, there has been a unified court system in Tanzania consisting of three tiers – Ordinary Courts, District Courts and the High Court, with the addition of a Court of Appeal of Tanzania in 1979. Customary law, Islamic law and state law are recognized at all levels, and have been so since 1961 (Wanitzek 1988: 5).

3. The rate of divorce in the village is high – when I carried out a census in the village in the mid-1960s, men over 60 had had an average of 2.5 partners each, and women of the same age two each.

4. Most of the cases in this paper relate to my first period of fieldwork in the 1960s. In 1971, a new Law of Marriage Act was passed which gave women more rights. However, I did not find this being invoked during my fieldwork in 1976 and 1985.

5. During the 1960s and 1970s, all houses were grouped into ten-house cells, each of which had a leader. This was the lowest officially-recognized unit of social and political organization.

6. Men are supposed to avoid women's menstrual blood, and should not touch, or indeed even see, their sanitary cloths.

References

Caplan, A. P. (1975). *Choice and Constraint in a Swahili Community: Property, Hierarchy and Cognatic Descent on the East African Coast.* London, New York, Nairobi: International African Institute/ Oxford University Press

Caplan, A. P. (1976). 'Boys' circumcision and girls' puberty rites among the Swahili of Mafia Island, Tanzania'. *Africa* 46, 1: 21–33

Caplan, A. P. (1982). 'Gender, Ideology and Modes of Production on the East African Coast', in *From Zinj to Zanzibar: History, Trade and Society on the Coast of East Africa*, ed. J. de Vere Allen, pp. 29–43. Wiesbaden: Franz Steiner Verlag

Caplan A. P. (1983). 'Women's Property, Islamic Law and Cognatic Descent', in *Women and Property, Women as Property*, ed. R. Hirschon, pp. 23–43. Beckenham: Croom Helm

Caplan A. P. (1989). 'Perceptions of gender stratification', *Africa* 59, 2: 196–208

Comaroff, J. and Roberts, S. (1981). *Rules and Processes: The Cultural Logic of Dispute in an African Context.* Chicago: Chicago University Press

Eastman, C. (1984). 'Waungwana na Wanawake: Muslim ethnicity and sexual segregation in coastal Kenya', *Journal of Multilingual and Multicultural Development*, 5: 97–112

Eastman, C. (1988). 'Women, Slaves and Foreigners: African Cultural Influences and Group Processes in the Formation of Northern Swahili Coastal Society', *International Journal of African Historical Studies*, 21: 1–28

Gulliver, P. H. (1963). *Social Control in an African Society*, London: Routledge and Kegan Paul; Boston: Boston University Press

Gulliver, P. H. (1979). *Disputes and Negotiations: A Cross-cultural Perspective.* New York: Academic Press

Middleton, J. (1992). *The World of the Swahili: an African Mercantile Civilization.* New Haven, London: Yale University Press

Moore, S. F. (1989). 'History and the Redefinition of Custom on Kilimanjaro', in *History and Power in the Study of Law*, ed. J. Starr and J. F. Collier. Ithaca and London: Cornell University Press

Rosen, L. (1989). *The Anthropology of Justice: Law as Culture in Islamic Society.* Cambridge: Cambridge University Press

Wanitzek, U. (1988). 'Legally Unrepresented Women Petitioners in the Lower Courts of Tanzania: A Case of Justice Denied?' Paper presented at the International Congress of Anthropological and Ethnological Sciences, Zagreb

Chapter 11

Courts of Death among the Alur of Uganda

Aidan Southall

Introduction

So much jural activity in African societies conveys to outsiders the sense that offences are seen more often as an infringement of status and property rights rather than infringements of a moral or ethical code. In this paper, I discuss the Courts of Death, an open tribunal held by the Alur of Uganda on the occasion of the second funeral to establish the cause of the death which has occurred. These indicate that a strongly-held system of moral evaluations of social behaviour is in fact present, although not formally codified. It is a dynamic system, which has evolved and adjusted to the changing sequence of conditions under colonial and independent rule.

In principle, death cannot occur from natural causes, but only through the ill–will of other human beings, living or dead. There is thus a constant accumulation of diverse accusations and charges in relation to every death. The details of past cases will ultimately be forgotten with the passage of time, as those of the most recent deaths are added to the corpus. Such tribunals arise mainly from the deaths of elders, or at their instigation. The accusations inevitably give expression to the tensions and disputes in the community, revealing the hatreds, enmities, quarrels and wrongdoings which festoon the network of interpersonal relations. One death and its associated accusations is not isolated from another, but rather, all deaths tend to become intertwined in the fabric of emotions that not only sets kin and neighbours at one another's throats through mutual suspicions and accusations, but also binds them together in mutual dependence for support against others. Being at the same time articulated in a web of kinship that is regarded as eternal and unchanging in its structure and presence, although the individual components gradually change, the public debate by the local leaders on the accumulation of charges and countercharges, as they are rehearsed and re-rehearsed at each important second funeral, constitutes a negotiated and bargained collective moral judgement on the community by itself. The outside observer, accustomed to written codes of moral behaviour, tends to be struck by the absence of systematic or explicit moral rules, but they are essentially expressed in practice, and it is at second funerals that they receive their most authoritative and consensual expression, not in abstract statement but in concrete judgement, implemented not by specific institutions but by the force of public opinion.

News of death and death rituals spreads like wildfire, because the attendance of kin is the ultimate moral obligation, sanctioned by the fear not only of supernatural retribution, but also of losing one's rights in the distribution of property. The senior elders of the group assemble the day before and spend the night in the house of a kinsman near the site of the ritual, mulling over the labyrinth of accumulated issues which will be, once again, brought into focus upon a specific death. Beer should be provided, without which the elders say they can neither think nor speak clearly. Everyone knows in general terms which category of people is supposed to fulfil each part of the action, and while some are found wanting others carry on with the task. There is open criticism and fierce argument, with serious accusations flying about, but there is a kind of subliminal consensus which clearly rejects the wilder accusations and charges. The next day the crowd gathers and some of the principals in the matter eventually make their speeches. Suggestions of who should or should not speak are shouted out, and those who ramble on too long are tactfully told by some respected peer to step aside. The speeches are couched in a common stock of local idiom, symbol and metaphor, allowing everything to be conveyed by oblique allusion and proverb, so that actual phrases uttered have no specific meaning for anyone outside the community. They cannot therefore be reproduced in their entirety, yet something of their flavour must be presented.

In this article, I discuss a second funeral held for a young girl, daughter of Celestino Abala, in Palei Paruda during May 1972, and begin with two of the speeches made on that occasion. The main events referred to go back forty years or more; any beginning is an arbitrary point in the stream of events, and no conclusion is clear-cut. In the next section I attempt a straightforward account of the alleged events that led not only to the death of Celestino's daughter, but also to those of two men called Anderea and Ucungi, whose second funerals were tacked on to hers. The genealogy on the following page shows the interrelationships of the main characters.

The Speeches of Cesario and Celestino Abala at the Funeral of Celestino's Daughter

The first speech was made by Cesario, who was the classificatory cross-cousin (FFBDS) of Celestino, father of the dead girl. Cesario acted by common consent as master of ceremonies and introduced the proceedings. He began by referring to a set of quarrels only indirectly linked to the deaths.

Cesario's Speech

> Then there is another matter, as far as this child is concerned. It happened when he went and encountered a problem over there. It was like a problem of grasshoppers; then so-and-so began saying 'When they came from here they spoilt my sweet potato leaves for planting. My Padea grandfather said "Are there really people who are prepared to quarrel with me face to face?"' This is the concern of that child, this is his involvement with the death, all of which you were told one day, and you heard.

[He then turned to Celestino's daughter's death and its possible causes.]

> Then there is this other matter, that of this brother [Celestino] of ours. Matters which are brought together can be dealt with more quickly. Now, what he has to say is that on that day, over there, he dragged the matter out until it became a dispute. He dragged it out and it became a quarrel, so he will deal with that death question [as well], because we have joined together that funeral question to ours. Here he is, Celesti꜀ ꜀. As to what I have to say, in the way that one speaks in the house, I have explained it to you, and that is it. For that brother of ours, it is as if *athupa* (evil destiny) was present – just now I found him

226   Aidan Southall

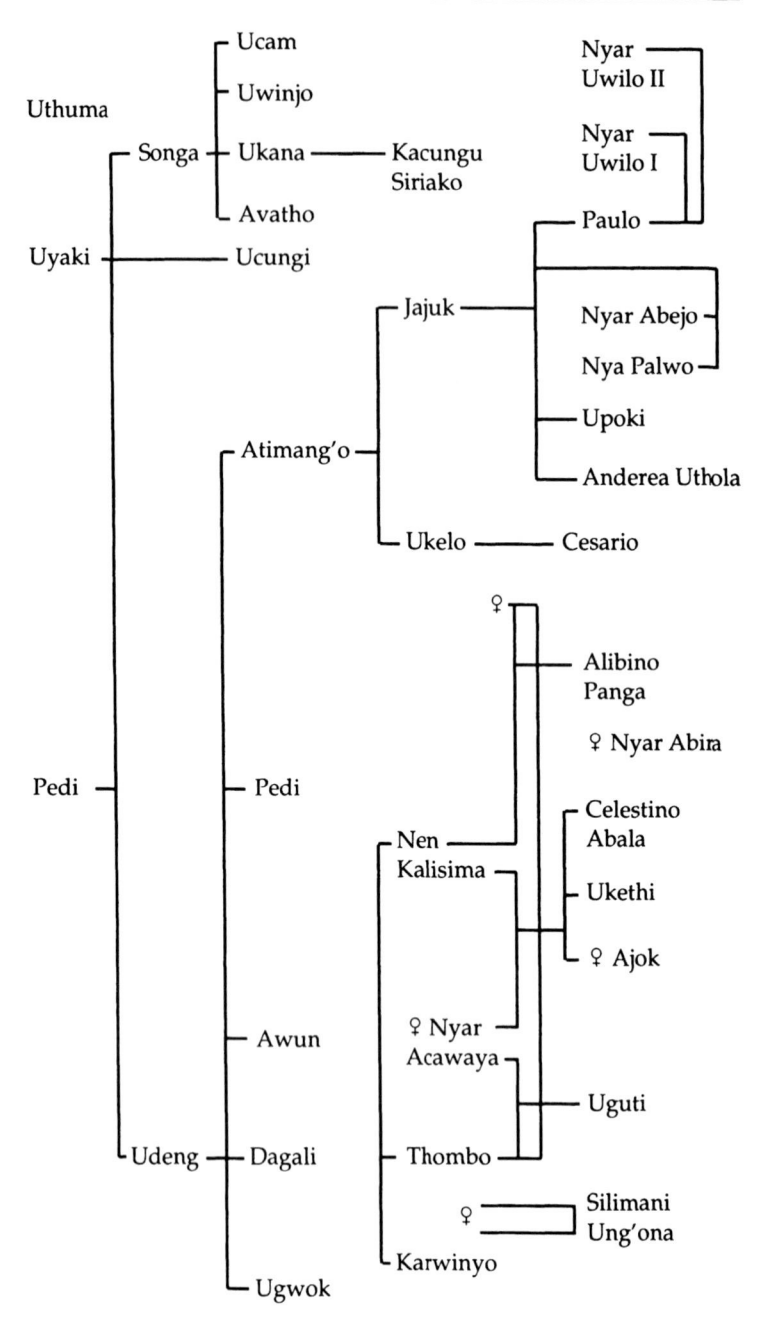

```
Uthuma ─┬─ Songa ─┬─ Ucam
        │         ├─ Uwinjo
        │         ├─ Ukana ── Kacungu Siriako ─┬─ Nyar Uwilo II
        │         └─ Avatho                    ├─ Nyar Uwilo I
Uyaki ──┼── Ucungi                             └─ Paulo
        │
        ├─ Atimang'o ─┬─ Jajuk ─┬─ Nyar Abejo
        │             │         ├─ Nya Palwo
        │             │         ├─ Upoki
        │             │         └─ Anderea Uthola
        │             └─ Ukelo ── Cesario
Pedi ───┤
        ├─ Pedi ─┬─ Nen Kalisima ─ ♀ ─┬─ Alibino Panga
        │        │                    │   ♀ Nyar Abira
        │        │                    ├─ Celestino Abala
        │        │                    ├─ Ukethi
        │        │                    └─ ♀ Ajok
        ├─ Awun  │
        │        ├─ ♀ Nyar Acawaya ─┬─ Uguti
        └─ Udeng ┤                  │
                 ├─ Dagali ─ Thombo ─┘
                 │          ─ ♀ ── Silimani Ung'ona
                 │          Karwinyo
                 └─ Ugwok
```

Part of Pa Pedi Lineage of Palei Clan

coming here limping. He was coming as if athupa had struck him. And that is something that you have not seen amongst you. It was as if when he started off with it from there to come here, then he turned back, just as though today the pain had become acute and the wound incapacitated him, he is in agony with it there. So, as to what he has to say, I have explained it, it is finished. As to Celestino, as I have explained the nature of his involvement, it is he who will expound the whole thing to you fully, since it was he who that day blew it up into a dispute. That is all I have to say.

Celestino then made his speech, in which it should be noted that he refers to himself largely in the third person:

Celestino Abala's Speech

Celestino's beloved daughter went to school up to Primary VI, costing six cattle, and then death took her. I did not go for divination, I took her straight to hospital. Maybe her death came from Nen, my father (either because his unquiet spirit came and caused it, or maybe because those who hated him hated my daughter too), or maybe it came from Thombo [Celestino's father's brother], or Awun [father's father, that is the father of Nen and Thombo], or maybe from some anonymous distant ancestor. I don't know. The children of Nen, of Thombo, and of Songa's line are here. They were all cared for by Nen, who bought them clothes, gladly. If it had not been for my father Nen and my mother NyarAcwaya, they wouldn't have been alive. They should speak. They accuse me of spoiling my daughter's funeral. Yet when I took her to hospital none of them helped. When it becomes a matter of death they say it's for me to get up and explain it. I think I'm too young to speak, but if they think I'm old enough to do so, they might give me a stool to sit on. All this time they have neglected me. I buried my daughter alone.

[Thus Celestino claimed that Silimani was indebted to him because the latter had been brought up by the former's father, Nen. Silimani claimed on the contrary that Celestino was indebted to him because Silimani had brought Celestino up himself after the death of Celestino's father Nen.]

Death [actually] started over cultivation of the Aloda swamp. Until then nobody had cultivated Aloda. I planted maize for two seasons. Then I found the footprints of old women trespassing in my field to collect vegetables.

[He means that the wives of his father's brother's son, Silimani, were stealing his maize.]

> I did not prevent them, nor did my mother. I took my complaint to Silimani, but he refused to accept it, for fear that I would tell the elders of the Palei clan that his wives were stealing from me.

[Celestino was particularly riled because one of Silimani's wives had been passed on to Silimani by their brother Panga, and Celestino thought she should have been given to him. Celestino told Silimani that if he rejected the complaint about the maize, all the deaths in Celestino's family would be blamed upon his wives.]

> When a tree stubbed my foot they rejoiced [saying that] it would be good if I was buried. But I did not go for divination, I limped to hospital alone without anyone's help, as though I was not the son of Nen, to whom they were all beholden. They behaved as if I had no brothers. If I don't belong here they should tell me where I come from, so that I can pack up and go. And at that time I did go to Buganda for a year until I heard that a young puppy was being married [another daughter of his whom he had left behind]. My brother Ukethi sent me a report. When I came back I found everyone competing for my daughter's bridewealth. My brother Ukethi had refused them, saying, 'Celestino suffered alone taking his daughter to hospital, so I won't give them anything; they must wait until Celestino arrives from Buganda and he will kill a goat for them.' I came but I refused to do so. Then illness really began to take hold of me. Silimani and all of them were talking openly against me. I only had support from Uwilo, I was rejected by all Palei. So I returned to Buganda and used the sesame which I had planted to perform the twin rites for my sister.

> The quarrel grew. Silimani kept saying I had refused him cattle, and other things from the bridewealth. I went and accused him before the elders. He and Panga were fighting over NyarAbira, the wife whom Panga gave to Silimani. They accused her of acting like a man in supporting my brother Ukethi in his refusal to hand over my daughter's bridewealth to them. If my daughter had not died, NyarAbira would have been the one to do so, but her ancestral spirits must have been strong. Silimani wanted to use the bridewealth to make a marriage for his son. They had already used the bridewealth from my sister's marriage before, but this one that I begot I will use myself – this one for whom I dug the field [i.e. his daughter] killed me. My daughter was not killed by Jajuk's line [Anderea's witchcraft which was threatening to kill them all], her death was caused by the land, the swamp and Silimani's wives who stole from it.

Silimani's children raped Undiya's daughter, playing as children will. Undiya attacked all of them for their deed, but it was my child who suffered. I went to a wise diviner, who told me what to do, and my child was saved from barrenness. I am searching for the roots of the matter and when I find it I shall say. Anyhow it is in Papedi lineage not in the rest of the Palei clan. But they pretend it was I who ruined my daughter, yet they are responsible elders, why don't they speak out? I have no real brothers to help me, so I have joined my funeral with that of my distant brother Anderea, so that the little beer I have, with theirs, can suffice for the last funeral rites of my daughter.

The Events

Case 1: The Consequences of a Theft from a Kinsman

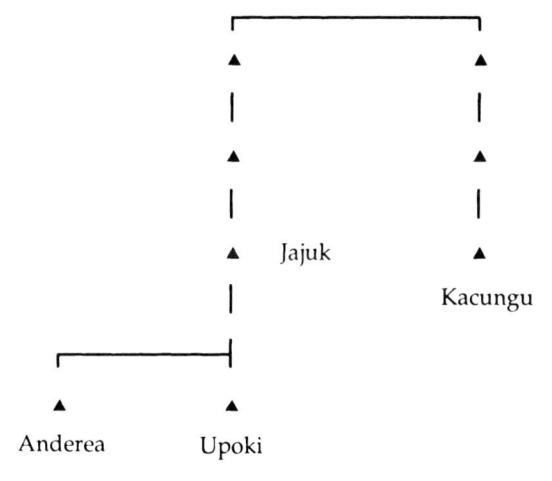

While all three were staying as migrant labourers in Buganda in 1934 Upoki-Jajuk of Palei Paruda clan and Ugera-Ufudha of Uwilo clan plotted and stole 70/- from Kacungu-Ukana. This was a heinous crime, as in Alur terms all were close kinsmen, Kacungu being Upoki's FFFBSS and thus termed both 'paternal uncle', and a lineage brother, while Upoki's brother, his brother's son and others in his immediate lineage were all married to women from Ugera's clan Uwilo, making Uwilo men mother's brothers or in-laws to Palei Paruda.

Upoki and Ugera denied the theft, so Kacungu planned witchcraft against them. Then they wrote him a letter confessing the theft and asking him not to bewitch them. Some Alur elders in that part of Buganda collected money to repay Kacungu, but then Upoki and Ugera refused to let them do this and withdrew their confession. At this point Upoki was locked up in gaol by an Alur policeman stationed in Buganda; he was also from the Palei clan, so that he saw his action as fulfilment of a kinship responsibility. Kacungu went to a nearby town and consulted a Muslim teacher and diviner. He was instructed to plant the metal butt of a spear into a grave, with a *riji* (amulet) attached to it. Upoki was released from gaol after two weeks for lack of evidence, but he fell ill and died within two days. None of the Alur concerned seemed to doubt that Upoki had committed the theft, nor that he was killed by Kacungu's witchcraft. Anderea, Upoki's brother, said 'Kacungu has killed my brother, so I am going to get witchcraft to kill Kacungu's sons.'

Case 2: Father and Son Quarrel over a Wife

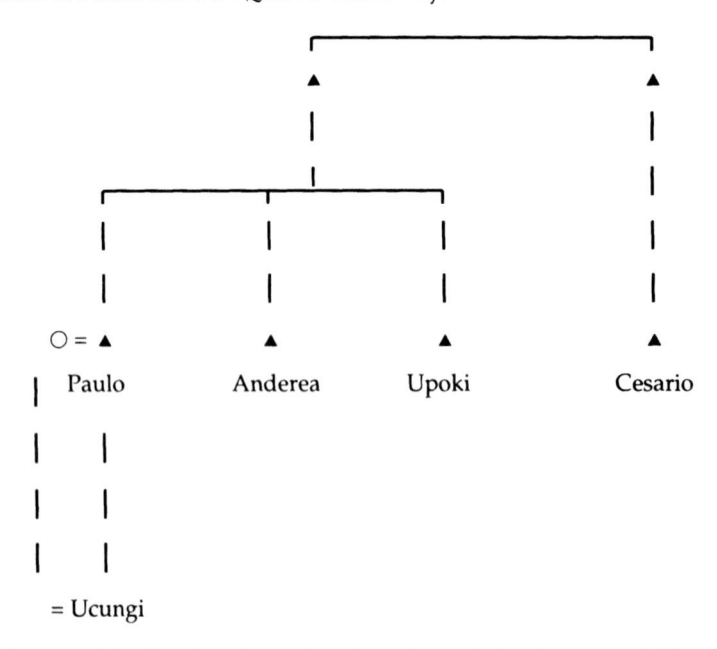

○ = ▲ Paulo	▲ Anderea	▲ Upoki	▲ Cesario

= Ucungi

Meanwhile Paulo, the other brother of Anderea and Upoki, became estranged from his son Ucungi. Paulo had some four wives, of whom two were from Uwilo and one from Okebo Palwo. The last was thought to be a witch who had killed one of the Uwilo wives, so Paulo drove her out. Driving a wife out of one's home is the usual sequel to deciding that she is a witch, though, of course, the latter may also be a pretext for the former, and is well recognized as such. Since wives are, in traditional principle, wives of the lineage and not just of the individual, it was a possible solution, when husband and wife could not get on with one another, for the wife to be transferred to another more compatible kinsman (agnate) of the husband, but not to his son, although the latter might inherit her at his father's death. Fathers were always touchy about sons interfering with their wives (stepmothers of the sons). Despite the fact that close agnates addressed one another's wives as 'my wife', demanding many services from them accordingly, and were addressed by them as 'my husband', much banter being included, no sharing of the sexual services of wives was permissible, and transgression of this generated very deep hatreds.

Thus when his son Ucungi later brought her back as his own second wife, Paulo angrily objected to this; furthermore, believing the woman to be a witch, he could not eat her food nor drink her beer. This meant refusing to share food with his son, who retorted: 'If you're trying to drive away my wife you can get out yourself otherwise my wife will bring you death, as you say she already has to one of your wives.' For the son to bring back the father's rejected wife was obviously provocative, but tempting, because probably Paulo had not yet got back the bridewealth he paid on her, so Ucungi got her with little or no payment.

In this case, the added issue of witchcraft meant an intolerable rift in the very heart of the family. It was not merely the witchcraft, but the break in commensality which was so abominable. This itself is seen as a state of sin, bringing almost inevitable supernatural retribution if not healed. There is a special term, *aro*, for misfortunes arising from this source, and a special procedure, *alika*, for curing them. The essence of the cure is, of course, the ritual reconciliation of the estranged kinsfolk, removing the potential curse and restoring the purity of the kin group. Ucungi did eventually ask his father Paulo to make beer for alika but he refused. Cesario, Ucungi's FFBS 'paternal uncle' tried to reconcile them and actually brought the beer and the medicine, but Paulo would still not agree, so Ucungi had to drink it alone.

Meanwhile, Anderea's witchcraft had been working against Kacungu and killed his sons, but his grandsons survived. However, in the end Kacungu's own witchcraft overcame

Anderea and he too died. Ucungi came back to Palei from Buganda to attend his father's brother's funeral. Why Anderea had not simply turned the death back (*alwokalwoka*) on to Kacungu, as Palei had begged him to do for years, is not clear. Or why did not Palei collect 30/- to go and pull the spear butt out of the grave? Potential mystical and physical action runs strangely parallel, the distinction not seeming significant to the Alur. People in Palei had also begged Kacungu to 'go and pull out that spear butt from the grave – you are finishing all of us'.

Although Ucungi had treated his father Paolo disrespectfully, his father had refused all efforts at reconciliation, thus seeming tragically to condemn himself and his family to an unending series of grievous misfortunes, or, cynically, providing explanations for inexplicable deaths. Kacungu himself seems to have been unassailable. It was said that, had he been living at home in Palei Paruda, instead of away in Buganda, he could not have got away with his behaviour. But in fact he stayed in Buganda and never came back. He became an *uvunio*, 'one who has left home for good'. He had nobody to represent him or speak for him at the funeral.

Case 3: A Quarrel Over the Building of a Shrine

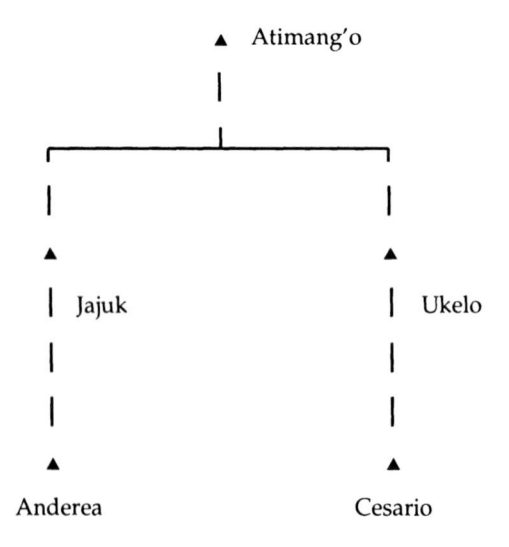

```
                   ▲ Atimang'o
                   |
         _____|_____
        |                   |
        ▲                   ▲
        | Jajuk             | Ukelo
        |                   |
        |                   |
        ▲                   ▲
      Anderea             Cesario
```

Before he died, Anderea had been possessed by the spirit of his father Jajuk. Cesario, Jajuk's elder brother's son, had wanted to build Jajuk's shrine for Anderea, to calm his spirit, but he was unable to do so because Paulo had taken away the sticks of the shrine and hidden them. A shrine cannot be built except by maintaining the physical continuity of shrine to shrine, by incorporating sticks from a senior shrine into every junior one.

While Jajuk was alive, he held the shrine of his father, Atimang'o. When Jajuk died, Cesario took sticks from his shrine to build the shrine of his own father Ukelo, Jajuk's elder brother. As head of a senior line, Cesario was also the proper person to build the shrine of Jajuk for Anderea. So Anderea was burdened with the problem of being unable to placate his father's spirit, as well as with the continuing threat of Kacungu's witchcraft. Paulo had wanted to build the shrine for his brother Anderea himself, but the elders refused, because Paulo was of a junior line. Anderea would have to pay some money and Cesario would have to give a goat for it. At first both refused and in any case, Cesario could not play his part because Paulo had hidden the remaining sticks from Jajuk's shrine to Atimang'o. This made the ancestral spirits angry, because their shrine had not been built. Divination actually showed Cesario to be a witch – simply meaning that he had failed to carry out his duties as an elder, however much he had tried to do so, thereby endangering the group. In the end a goat was taken from Anderea and given to Cesario for the shrine. Finally the shrine was built, permitting an ulcer, from which Cesario had been suffering on his foot, to heal.

Case 4: The Death of Ucungi (see genealogy for Case 2)

After Anderea's funeral, Ucungi returned to Buganda. He found that edible grasshoppers had alighted in his field there, and his sweet potatoes were all trampled down by someone who had come into the field to collect them. It was an Alur from Padea, whom he called *kwara* (classificatory-grandfather). When Ucungi accused him of trampling the sweet potato plant he said: 'Oh! Ho! Are there people who stand up to me? People who have done that have died before now!' (For he had already killed a man called Unega.) Next day Ucungi's wife found blood on his threshold and a message was sent back to Palei about it. Blood on the threshold is taken as an almost infallible indication that someone has been performing witchcraft. When it arrived Cesario again begged his 'brother' (FBS) Paulo to do something about it, in the way of reconciliation with his son Ucungi, before worse befell. But Paulo was adamant, saying that he was a Christian and could not perform those rites. Next day Ucungi went to hunt and was killed by a buffalo.

There is some ambiguity as to whether Ucungi was slain through the instrumentality of the charging buffalo by the malignancy of the Padea man who had trampled his field, or whether it was his own wife, the Okebo woman mentioned in Case 2, who was responsible for the blood on the threshold, thus confirming his father's view of her as a witch, or whether the buffalo attack was still the powerful witchcraft of Kacungu working its way through the family from long ago, or, finally, whether the cause was supernatural retribution for the sinful state of unreconciliation between Ucungi and his father. There seems to have been a cumulation of evil influences, and his death was thus monstrously overdetermined.

It was felt that an evil destiny *(athupa)* hung over Paulo, whereby he seemed to destroy himself as well as his agnates. He was going with Jerome to buy cement for the tomb of his son Ucungi (as if his son's death had finally brought him to his senses?). As the two of them were going down a hill with the cement on a bicycle, they both fell off and the bike tore Paulo's foot. He went to the sisters at the Catholic Mision, who poured iodine on it. But it developed into an ulcer and would not heal, making Paulo so lame that he could not walk. The elders were not sure exactly why this further misfortune befell Paulo, on top of the premature death of his son. But as we have seen, he had been pursuing a course of cantankerous, unforgiving behaviour quite well calculated, in Alur thought, to bring such a catastrophe upon him. He was thus unable to drag himself to the funeral we are describing, at which he would certainly have been expected to make a speech.

Case 5: The Death of Celestino's Daughter

The death of Celestino's daughter was not really intertwined in its antecedents with those of Anderea and Ucungi. But Celestino's minimal lineage, descended from Awun, is precisely co-ordinate with that of Anderea and Ucungi, descended from Atimang'o, Awun and Atimang'o having been brothers. There was a potential link between the two sequences, since Anderea's witchcraft directed against Kacungu was none the less dangerous and could have endangered them all by ricocheting. Celestino considered this possible cause of his daughter's death, but concluded that it was not due to Anderea, but to the quarrel in the field and the trespassing of Silimani's wives.

The public funeral treatment of the troubles in the two lineages of Awun and Atimang'o was also linked and unified by Cesario, who was the effective, though informal, master of ceremonies and owner of the dance which followed the funeral. Though belonging to the lineage of Atimang'o, Cesario was not himself directly involved in the sequence of quarrels, except in the incident of the building of the ancestor shrine, which was really to his credit rather than otherwise. He was therefore able to claim an impartial view, as a responsible elder acting for the good of Palei Paruda as a whole.

Case 6: The Quarrel between Celestino and Silimani

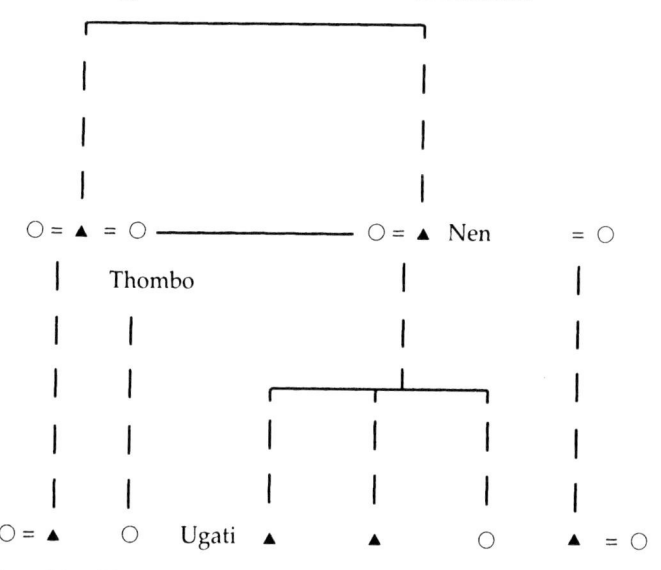

○ = ▲ = ○ ──────── ○ = ▲ Nen   = ○
    Thombo

○ = ▲   ○   Ugati ▲   ▲   ○   ▲ = ○
Nyarabira Silimani   Ukethi   Celestino   Ajok Panga Nyarabira

In his speech, Celestino claimed that Silimani and his other agnates had used up all the cattle paid for his sisters. Nobody seemed convinced by this, and Silimani's contrary version was accepted. This was to the effect that Celestino's father Nen died before Silimani's father Thombo, so that Thombo took over

Celestino's mother as well as Nen's other widow, begetting several more children by each of them. However the latter were all still young at Thombo's death, so that Silimani had to look after them all, including Celestino himself. These young children were the uterine siblings of Celestino and seminal siblings of Silimani, so that the obligation towards them was somewhat ambiguous, but lay clearly with Silimani by agnatic descent principles.

Silimani claimed to have arranged a marriage on behalf of Celestino, and explained what had happened to the other cattle. He claimed that he could have demanded four cows for looking after the young children and an ox for looking after Celestino, but in fact took nothing. When he came back from Buganda in 1935 he found a white calf which had been given by a man in bridewealth for Celestino's sister Ajok. Ajok must have left her husband, so Silimani had to pay him back his bridewealth. In order to do this he reared the white calf and its offspring with a lot of care and trouble. He managed to pay back Ajok's husband and only retained one of the calf's progeny to use in bridewealth to obtain his own wife. This was the only substance to Celestino's charge.

On the other hand, Celestino had used up many cattle from the bridewealth of his sisters (who were also Silimani's sisters). For example, Uguti was the daughter of Nen's widow by Thombo, that is, uterine sister of Celestino and seminal sister of Silimani. She first eloped with a man of Pakubi, and Celestino used the bridewealth. Then she eloped to the midlands ('Alur'), and again Celestino used the bridewealth. She then ran away a third time to Cypriano Uryem (my research assistant in 1949–51), but left him with two children and went to live with a man in Pei. Usually women who elope so often attract little bridewealth, yet the Pei man was said to have given five cows for Uguti, although he was at least her fourth mate. She may have been extremely attractive and was certainly very fertile. But by this time she was a pathetic creature, blind, being led about begging and generally despised. Silimani was angry when Celestino, after using up all the bridewealth that Uguti had brought on each occasion, sent her to Silimani for help when she became sick and blind. But the latter sent her back to Celestino to get 50/- to go to hospital. It was for this reason that Celestino accused Silimani of driving out the girls of the lineage for whom he was supposed to be responsible.

The sad case of Uguti again shows the cumulative effect of multiple causation. As sister of Celestino and Silimani she belonged to a family involved in bitter internal dispute and estrangement, recognized in Alur thought as likely to bring supernatural retribution upon the heads of any or all its members. But Uguti herself had behaved in a feckless manner, which contributed its own complement to the disputes in the family, and clearly transgressed the norms of proper wifely behaviour to the point of adding further reasons for misfortune to fall upon her.

All in all, Celestino left the impression of having tried on a number of occasions to do things on his own in a distinctly devious and therefore mystically dangerous manner, while using up nearly all the bridewealth cattle, many of which might have been claimed by Silimani, so that both Celestino's poverty and his almost pathological sense of isolation from brothers who hated him seemed to be the products of his own action and imagination, certainly not caused by Silimani.

Celestino claimed to have spent six cattle on his daughter's education, thus she reached the sixth (final) year of primary school, but then died suddenly. Celestino had not gone to the diviners, he had taken his daughter straight to the hospital, with no help from anyone. Because he was so angry Celestino actually prevented his kin from going in to the funeral in church. The elders said he ruined the funeral rites by not allowing anyone to speak, so in their view the matter of the girl's death was not cleared up properly.

Celestino attributed his daughter's death first of all to the old women, Silimani's wives, who had come to steal his maize. Silimani would not accept the accusation, Celestino said, because he was afraid of the Palei clan knowing that Silimani's wives were stealing from him. One of these wives had formerly been the wife of Panga who was transferred to Silimani because Panga accused her of being a witch. Celestino was angry because he thought she should have been transferred to him. He went to Panga and said 'Why did you give a wife to Silimani? You should have given her to me since we are the offspring of one father.'

Thus we see how brothers compete even for a wife whom one of them regards as a witch. This shows that one brother does not always take seriously the witchcraft accusations of another. There are so many levels of significance to witchcraft accusations. If one brother accuses his wife simply to get rid of her, another brother may take her over without regarding her as a dangerous witch, and without necessarily precipitating a rift in the family because of broken commensality, as occurred in the case of Paulo Uyaki and his son. In fact, Panga still came and ate freely with Silimani, including the food of the wife he had driven out as a witch, although Celestino refused to do so.

Celestino warned Silimani that he would blame Silimani's wives for all subsequent deaths occurring in his family. Later, when Celestino stubbed his foot on a tree, he said his kin rejoiced (presumably thinking it served him right). Again he did not go for divination, but limped to hospital alone without any help, 'as if he had no brothers', he said, and as if he was not the son of Nen who had actually brought up his brothers.

Celestino then went to Buganda for a year until he heard that one of the daughters he had left behind was getting married and all his kin were competing for her bridewealth. However, his full brother Ukethi guarded his property, saying that Celestino would kill a goat for them. But when he came, Celestino refused to do this. Then illness really began to take hold of him and members of the Palei clan began talking about him openly, including Silimani, who complained that Celestino had refused him cattle. So Celestino returned to Buganda for another year.

Case 7: Another Quarrel Between the Brothers Celestino and Silimani

Later on they were digging a field and a quarrel broke out between Celestino's wife and her husband's sister Uguti, which they brought to Silimani, as eldest brother, to settle. He refused, saying that Celestino should be there. Celestino came up at that moment, and hearing his name uttered by Silimani began to pick a quarrel with him at once. He threatened to stick a spear up Silimani's arse-hole and twist it round inside. Anderea then said to Silimani 'Let's go if he's talking like that.' So they moved off and Celestino began following, sharpening his spear. He called to Silimani to wait for him. Silimani retorted that he would not run away. Celestino began to insult Silimani further saying, 'Your father came from Madi long ago, I suppose he fucked with a piece of cloth?' (The Madi, like all foreign groups, were regarded as of lower status by the Alur.) 'No' said Silimani, 'he fucked and begot girls with whose bridewealth you have married.'

Silimani made a formal accusation against Celestino for this insult to his father, and the elders of Palei were really angry with Celestino for it. They began to murmur against Celestino. Such collective murmuring by elders is almost equivalent to a curse, and brings illness upon the victim of it. Celestino really became possessed by a kind of madness, and every morning at break of day he used to come round to Silimani's house blowing water from his mouth. Silimani went to consult a diviner and was told to construct a shrine of Jok Matar (the White Spirit) for his grandmother in his own village and then take sticks to construct one in Celestino's village. But instead of that Celestino brought the mediums of one of the newer spirit possession cults into his house. Silimani suggested that perhaps Celestino and his sister conspired to do this, because they were insulted by the idea of a grown man like Celestino having a shrine constructed for him by someone else. Given Celestino's feelings for Silimani, it was natural that he should react in this way, but in fact the construction of shrines has to follow agnatic seniority rules, irrespective of whether the possessed patient is adult or not.

So in effect Celestino was accusing Silimani of being a witch and trying to kill him. It was true that when Abala consulted a diviner, Silimani's name was given, but this was only in the sense that Silimani represented the Palei clan who were murmuring against Celestino. Here we see the fact that witchcraft and the legitimate moral sanctions of the group can be equated. Celestino broke his ties of commensality with Silimani, refusing to eat his food. Silimani claims that he did not reciprocate, actually taking food from Celestino to show that he was prepared to eat together. But if he gave food to Celestino, Celestino looked at it and threw it on the ground. Silimani claimed innocence and asked for himself and Celestino to take an oath on it before the elders.

Conclusion

Since all witchcraft accusations remained illegal in 1972 under unrepealed colonial ordinances, the official forces of law and order could be invoked. These Courts of Death were therefore a spontaneous manifestation of Alur culture, which in this respect was still an oral rather than a literate society. In pre-colonial times witches were controlled both by local opinion and action and by the mystical power of the kings, who were able to identify them. Those accused were subjected to trial by the chicken poison oracle. A person judged guilty several times thereby could only be put to death by his or her own people ransoming the witch from the king to compensate him for the loss of a subject. The courts of death may also have taken place at that time, during second funerals, but they were then part of a system which included more decisive mechanisms of ultimate action. As they were conducted twenty years ago, however, they provided an emphatic airing of moral evaluations.

Looking back now at these events of two decades ago, I see the obvious signs of weakening in mechanisms of reconciliation, which by the time of my last fieldwork in 1992 seemed to have broken down almost completely. Cesario could not persuade Paulo to be reconciled with his son, nor could he succeed in bringing Anderea into a state of grace before death overtook him. None of their kin could get Celestino to be reconciled with Silimani. My use of the concepts of 'state of sin' and 'state of grace' may seem anomalous, but it is well within the dictionary meaning of these terms.

The funerary Courts of Death provided an open, free and non-authoritarian forum, limited only by the rules of age and gender generally observed in the community at large. They cleared the air, offered a controlled safety valve and certainly exerted pressure towards reconciliation. They gave influential public expression to the uncoded moral and ethical principles towards which Alur communities aspired. They were set in a context which still displayed a communal and consensual (and hence in a sense unthinking) integration of basic life concerns, aiming at health and harmony, by transcending inter-group tensions, for the physical and social reproduction of Alur society.

Name Index

Abdullah (of Mafia) 215–17
Ajok (of Alur) 236
Ali (of Mafia) 212–15
Anderea (of Alur) 225, 228, 229, 230, 232–3, 234–5, 240
Anderson, W.T. 61
Atimang'o (of Alur) 233, 234–5
Attlee, Clement 87
Awun (of Alur) 227
Azikiwe, Dr Nnamdi 7, 83, 87, 88, 94–100, 103

Barthes, Roland 164
Berman, M.R. 47
Bianchi, Rinaldo L. 50–2, 59–60
Bicester, Lord 102
Birch, Nigel 92
Bishnu (of Indreni) 144–5
Bishop, Thomas 119
Bohannan, Paul 7, 19, 24
Bracken, Counsellor 120–1
Braithwaite, Sir John 93
Buber, Martin 68
Bujra, Janet Fitton viii
Bull, William 119
Burger, Chief Justice Warren 45

Calleros, J. Roman 56–7
Cantwell, Patrick 119, 124
Caplan, Lionel viii, 2, 3, 6, 9
Caplan, Pat viii, 4, 9
Carrick, Lord 114
Carter, Jimmy 46–7
Celestino Abala (of Alur) 224–8, 234–9
Cesario (of Alur) 225–7, 231–3, 235, 240
Chandra Bahadur Limbu (of Indreni) 147–50
Clifford, William 119, 120, 121, 122, 126–7
Collier, Jane F. 2, 6, 219–20
Colson, Elizabeth 4, 6, 67
Comaroff, John 1–2, 26, 220
Connally, Tom 52
Coolidge, Calvin 44
Cullen, L.M. 113

Davis, Sydenham 114–5, 117–22, 123–6, 126–30, 134–5
Dellapenna, Joseph 55, 57
Devine, James 118
Devine, Peter 119
Dilli Ram (of Indreni) 141
Dowling, Patrick 119
Duckser (of youth centre) 190–1
Dul Prasad (of Indreni) 142–5, 156
Dunphy, Michael 121, 124

Fallers, Lloyd 67, 69
Fatuma (of Mafia) 217–19
Fischer, Michael M.J. 21
Fish, Stanley 28
Foster-Sutton, Sir Hylton 83
Foster-Sutton, Sir Stafford 98
Franck, Thomas 43–4
Freud, Sigmund 19
Fuller, Lon 50, 51

Gaetz, Stephen 2, 3, 4, 5, 9
Geertz, Clifford 13
George IV 115
Gluckman, Max 3, 7, 23–4, 25, 31, 66, 67, 68–70, 161
Gong, Gerrit W. 40–1, 42
Grace, William 128
Gray, Robert viii
Gulliver, Philip vii–xi, x; *Disputes and Negotiations* x, 11–12, 27, 29, 32, 41; *The Family Estate in Africa* (with Gray) viii; *The Family Herds* vii; *Land Tenure and Social Change among the Nyakyusa* vii; *Merchants and Shopkeepers* (with Silverman) x; *Neighbours and Networks* vii, viii; *Social Control in an African Society* vii, viii; *Tradition and Transition in East Africa* viii; *In the Valley of the Nore* (with Silverman) x

Habermas, Jurgen 7–8, 12–15, 14, 17–18, 18–23, 27–9, 28, 30
Harka Moti (of Indreni) 147–50, 151, 155

241

Harlech, Lord 95, 96
Hayes, Douglas 56
Highet, Keith 60
Hoyne, Denis 119
Hutchinson, Edward 119, 126
Hyland, Michael 120, 128

Ifeka-Moller, Caroline viii
Innes, Henry 119, 122, 127

Jajuk (of Alur) 228, 229, 232–3
James (youth worker) 187–8, 190, 191
Jenkins, R. 185
Johnson, Christina 4, 5, 7, 9
Johnson, Walter viii
Johnston, Eric 57
Jones, R.L. 154–5, 157
Jones, S.K. 154–5, 157
Jugs (of youth centre) 187–8, 191, 194
Juma (of Mafia) 207–8

Kacungu (of Alur) 229–32, 234
Kelly, Edward 119
Keswick, William 91–2
Kindersley, Lord 88–9, 90–4, 102, 103
Kremenyuk, Victor 48
Krishne (of Indreni) 142–5

Laylin, John G. 50–2, 59–60
Lévi-Strauss, Claude 19
Linnerooth, Joanne 52–4, 57
Lister-Parker, Lord Justice Sir Hubert 83, 89
Loughlin, John 119, 121, 122
Lupton, T. 94

Macmillan, Harold 101
Malinowski, Bronislaw 25
Manningham-Buller, Sir Reginald 89–90
Marcus, George E. 21
Marx, Karl 19
Masa (of youth centre) 188–90, 197
Matson, R.C. 58
May, Rollo 164–5
McDougal, C. 140
McEnnery, Joseph 121, 124, 126
Middleton, J. 204, 218–19
Mohammed (of Mafia) 210–11
Moore, Sally Falk 4, 7–8, 65, 73
Morris, Joseph 128
Murphy, Fr F. 117, 119
Mwabora (of Mafia) 210–11
Mwajuma (of Mafia) 212–17
Mwasiti (of Mafia) 208–9

Nader, Laura 2, 4–5, 8, 9, 50–1, 68, 71
Neff, T. 58
Nen (of Alur) 227, 235–6
Norwood, Robin 165
Nugent, Anthony 119, 128
NyarAbira (of Alur) 228
NyarAcwaya (of Alur) 227

O'Connell, Daniel 130
O'Connor, William 119
O'Leary, Sinead 184, 191

Panga (of Alur) 228, 237–8
Parkin, David viii, 2, 4, 7, 9
Paulo (of Alur) 230–1, 233–4, 240
Pleass, Sir Clement 96
Power, Laurence 128

Quinn, James 126–7

Reagan, Ronald 44–5
Regmi, M.C. 140
Roberts, Simon L. 1–2, 26, 220
Rocky (of youth centre) 190–1
Ryan, Fr F. 120–2, 129
Ryan, James 118, 119, 126
Ryan, Thomas 119

Said, Edward 42
Saidi (of Mafia) 217–19
Saidia (of Mafia) 207–8
Schapera, Isaac 3, 167
Scudder, Thayer 71
Sharkey, James 184
Silimani (of Alur) 227–9, 235–9
Silverman, Marilyn x, 2, 3, 6
Songa (of Alur) 227
Southall, Aidan 3, 4, 6
Splint, Joshua 119, 124
Spruhan, John 118, 119, 124
Starr, June 2, 6, 181, 219–20
Sterling, Myles 119

Thombo (of Alur) 227, 235–6
Todd, Harry 71
Turner, Victor 68
Tylor, Edward 19

Ucungi (of Alur) 225
Ugera (of Alur) 229–30
Ugeti (of Alur) 238
Uguti (of Alur) 236–7
Ukethi (of Alur) 228, 238
Uncungi (of Alur) 230–2, 233–4
Undiya (of Alur) 229

Name Index

Unger, Roberto 22
Upoki (of Alur) 229–30
Ury, William L. 45–6

Walsh, Edward 121
Waziri (of Mafia) 208–9
Willis, P. 185

Wilson, Shirley 94
de Wolf, Jan viii

Yngvesson, B. 181

Zartman, I.W. 47

Subject Index

adjudication
  international disputes 39–42
  river rights 50–2
adultery 147–50
  difficulty of arranging 173–4
  Giriama code 162–4
  Mafia Island case 212
African Continental Bank 94–6, 99–100
Alternative Dispute Resolution (ADR) 5, 40, 41, 42
  attempt to stem rights movements 45
  privatization 49
  the professionals 45–7
  river disputes 50, 53
Alur people 3, 6
  Courts of Death 223–5, 238–9
  family disputes 227–39
anthropology
  actor-oriented 23
  archival method 115
  conceptual and empirical dualities ix
  ethnology versus grand theory 7–8
  notion of social evolution and civilization 39–42
  'Rules versus Power' debate 25–6
Anthropology as Cultural Critique (Marcus and Fischer) 21
Approaching the Past (Gulliver and Silverman) x
arbitration
  international disputes 39–41
archival method 115
Arusha people vii
  Gulliver's model of negotiation 27–30, 33–6
Australia 44
avoiding disputes 67, 70–1

Ballinaclasha Youth Development Centre 181–7
  Jugs and the Cup 187–8, 194
  Masa and the Billiards Table 188–90, 197

power and negotiations 192–9
Sparky and the Core Group 190–2
Bangladesh
  river dispute 58–60
Bank of England 83
  Bank Rate tribunal 5, 87–94, 101–3
Barclays DC and O 95
Britain *see also* Bank of England
  Dr Azikiwe accuses 95–7
  Empire 85–6
  public and private domains 87
  state and the public man 84–6
  tribunals 5, 7
British Bank of West Africa 95

Christianity
  law and justice 4
civil and human rights movements 5
  alternative dispute resolution 45
class
  making of the middle class in Thomastown 115–16, 123–6, 131–2
  working versus middle at youth club 182–3, 193, 196–8
colonialism 23
Colorado River dispute 52, 56–7
communication
  morals and truth 12–13
Communication and the Evolution of Society (Habermas) 12
conflict
  defining 133
corruption
  public men 84–7
courts 3–4
  Chief's/Local courts in Zambia 71–9
  of Death among Alur 223–40, 240
  District 206–7, 210–17
  public interest 67–9
  Village Council 143–4, 155, 157, 207–9, 212–13, 214, 215–16
Crime and Custom (Malinowski) 25
crime passionelle 161–4 *see also* love

244

Subject Index

cross-cultural negotiating behaviour 137
cyclical and developmental events 194–5

Danube River dispute 49, 52–4
death and funerals 3
  Alur Courts of Death 223–40, 227–9
  Giriama 176–7
'Dispute Resolution Notes from the Kalahari' (Ury) 45–6
disputes
  anthropology and 1–3
  assertion of identity 150–5
  crime passionelle 161–2
  cyclical versus developmental 194–5
  defining conflict 133
  differences in material interests 125–6
  Irish inhabitants versus George IV 117–22
  land 141–4, 155–6, 214
  marriage 145–50, 156, 205–19
  myth of restoring harmony 65–71
  pursuit of 3–4
  rituals 65–7
  rivers 128
  understanding 4–9
  youth centre 181–98
Disputes and Negotiations (Gulliver) x, 11–12, 27, 29, 32, 41
'Disputing without the Force of Law' (Nader) 50–1
diviners 175–6
dualities and theory 133

'The Emerging System of International Negotiations' (Kremenyuk) 48
emotions
  factor in negotiations 17–18
Ethiopia 43
ethnography 111
  dualities 133
  and grand theory 7–8
  versus grand theory 7–8
  Gulliver's belief in viii–ix
  problem of totalizing 32
  Thomastown 131–2
  the unquestionable 30–1
European Community 55

failure of negotiations 17–18
The Family Estate in Africa (Gulliver and Gray) viii

The Family Herds (Gulliver) vii
'The Forms and Limits of Adjudication' (Fuller) 50
Foster-Sutton Tribunal 5, 94–100
France 44
  Lake Lanoux dispute 50–1, 54–5

Ganges River dispute 58–60
Giriama people 7, 9, 164
  love 166, 167–9
  marriage practices 169–71
  sex and passion 171–80
Gorkha *see* Limbu people
'Governing the World without Governments' (Anderson) 61
Gulliver's model of negotiations 11–12, 15–18, 27–30, 32, 33–6, 198
Gwembe Tonga people 4, 6
  court case example 77–9
  dispute settlement 71–7, 79–80
  persistent anger 69–70

harmony 65–6, 69
  myth of 65–71
Hindus 2, 6
  land disputes 141–5
  marriage 145–6, 151–3
history ix
  contextualization 6
  honesty 7

ideal speech situation 12–15
Ilam 140–1, 155
In the Valley of the Nore (Gulliver and Silverman) x
India 52
  river dispute 58–60
Indreni people 140–5
  marriage 147–151
industrial societies
  money and power replace moral values 21
  moral consciousness 33
instrumental interpretation of norms 24–7
interest of disputants 12, 23
International Court of Justice 9, 43–5
  evolutionary social theorists 39
  Lake Lanoux dispute 51
  negotiation versus adjudication 42
  Third World nations 42, 43–5, 60
international disputes 5, 8, 61
  culture and nationality 47
  evolutionary social theory 39–42

non-governmental systems of
    negotiation 48
power over small nations 9
professionals 45–7, 49–50
rivers 49, 50–60
zero-sum outcomes 48–9, 53
Ireland ix–x, 2, 3, 112–17 see also
    Thomastown
    Irish inhabitants versus George IV
        117–22
    Municipal Reform Act 130, 132
    nationalist movement 130
    youth club disputes 181–98
Islam 203, 204
    marriage 205, 206, 210, 213–14
Israel
    Jordan Valley river dispute 57–8

joking 215–17
Jordan River Valley dispute 57–8
judges 3
The Judicial Process (Gluckman) 31

Kenya
    mother and children tragedy 162–4
Kilkenny 113
kinship
    as forum for settling disputes
        208–9
    sheria and mila 218–19

labour-management disputes
    negotiation process 16–17
Lake Lanoux case 50–1, 58
land disputes 214
    Hindus 141–5
    Limbu 141–4, 155–6
*Land Tenure and Social Change among
the Nyakyusa* (Gulliver) vii
law viii
    codes, discourse and language 6–7
    Habermas on evolution of 18–23
    instrumental interpretation of
        legal norms 24–7
Law of the Sea 60
Lazard Bros 88, 90–1, 92–3, 102–3
Lebanon
    Jordan Valley river dispute 57–8
Liberia 43
lifeworld/system problem 21–2, 28–9
Limbu people 2, 6, 137–40
    asserting identity 145–6, 150–5
    a case of adultery 145–50
    land disputes 141–4, 155–6
    marriage 151–5, 156, 157–8

love
    Giriama 166, 167–9
    sex and passion 171–80
    views of African 166–7
    Western essentialism 164–5
Lozi people 23–4, 31
    restoration of harmony 68–9
    'lumping it' 70–1

Mafia Island 9, 203–5
    marriage 205–6
    settling disputes 207–17
marriage 2–3
    Alur 230–1, 236
    assertion of identity 151–5
    divorce on Mafia Island 204–19
    Giriama 167–9, 169–71
    Islam and divorce 206–7
    Kenyan mother 162–4
    Limbu disputes 145–50
    mila and sheria 217–20
    political judgements 178–80
    power 9
    sex and passion 171–80
    western love 164–5
    western view of African love 166–7
Married Life in an African Tribe
    (Schapera) 167
Marxism 115–16
    and structural functionalism 24
material interest ix
mediation
    international disputes 39–41
men and women
    power 9
Merchants and Shopkeepers (Gulliver
    and Silverman) x
Mexico
    Colorado River dispute 52, 56–7
mila 217–20
morality
    cause of death among Alur 223–5
    gentlemen's code 83–7, 93–4,
        101–4
    Habermas 33
    industrial societies 21
    negotiations 12–13

Ndendeuli people vii, 4, 112
negotiation
    culture and nationality 47
    emotional content 17
    failure 17–18
    Gulliver's model 15–18
    international disputes 39–42

Subject Index 247

joint versus unilateral decision-making 41
self-help strategies 193–4
youth centre 192–9
Negotiation: The Alternative to Hostility (Carter) 46–7
Neighbours and Networks (Gulliver) vii, viii
Nepal 2, 6, 9, 155–6 *see also* Limbu people
river dispute 59
New Zealand 44
Ngoni people ix, vii
Nicaragua 44–5
Nigeria 3
Foster-Sutton Tribunal 5, 7, 94–100, 101–3
norms 203
gap between words and actions 205
Nyakyusa people vii

Ogra Chorcai 183–4, 192

Pakistan
river dispute 58
Palestinians 58
passion *see crime passionelle*
'The Peace Palace Heats Up' (Highet) 60
political judgement and negotiation 161, 179
Portugal
river disputes 54–6
post-modernism 8–9, 26
poststructuralist deconstruction 8, 26
power 9, 30, 192 *see also* international disputes
ideal communication 14–15
institutional and organized 197
judicial office 20
youth and authority 182–96
The Practical Negotiator (Zarman and Berman) 47
property
courts of Death 224
public and private spheres 7
without corporate groups 112–13
public humiliation 4

real-world contexts 181–2
religion 125
Islam on Mafia Island 203
ridicule 4
rights *see* civil and human rights movements

rituals
settlement of disputes 65–7
'The Role of Adjudication in International River Disputes' (Laylin and Bianchi) 50–2, 59–60
Rules and Processes (Comaroff and Roberts) 26
Rules of Evidence Act (1921) 86

self-help 4
sheria 217
Social Control in an African Society (Gulliver) vii, viii
social organization for disputes 3–4
social processes 1–2, 3–4
social relations ix
and moral values 21–2
society
Habermas on evolution of law 18–23
South Africa 44
Soviet Union
withholds dues from International Court of Justice 44
Spain
EC directives 55
river disputes 50–1, 54–6
spirit possession 239
state
and the public man 84–6
structural functionalism 24
Swahili people 204, 219–20
synchronic approach ix
Syria
Jordan Valley river dispute 57–8
systems 26

Tanzania *see* Mafia Island
Tayania 112
Theory of Communication Action (Habermas) 12
Thomastown 112–17
inhabitants versus George IV 117–22
making of the middle class 123–6, 131–2
old disputes shift power 126–30
Tradition and Transition in East Africa (Gulliver) viii
tribunals
Bank Rate 83, 86–7, 89–94, 101–3
Foster-Sutton 83, 86, 101–3
Turkana nomads vii

Uganda 67, 69 *see* Alur people
United Nations 43
   Law of the Sea 60
United States
   Colorado River dispute 52, 56–7
   separation from International
      Court of Justice 43–5

violence 4

witchcraft 4, 69
   Alur 139–40, 228, 230–5, 237–8
   and love 169, 175

Women Who Love Too Much
   (Norwood) 165
World Court *see* International Court
   of Justice
world-views 28
   mythical 19–20
   personal identity 20

Zambia 67
   court case example 77–9
   dispute settlement in Gwembe
      Valley 71–7, 79–80
   politics 75